SCHOOLHOUSE
BURNING

SCHOOLHOUSE
BURNING

Public Education and the Assault on American Democracy

DEREK W. BLACK

PUBLICAFFAIRS

NEW YORK

PublicAffairs
Hachette Book Group
1290 Avenue of the Americas, New York, NY 10104
www.publicaffairsbooks.com
@Public_Affairs

Printed in the United States of America
First Edition: September 2020

Published by PublicAffairs, an imprint of Perseus Books, LLC, a subsidiary of Hachette Book Group, Inc. The PublicAffairs name and logo is a trademark of the Hachette Book Group.

The Hachette Speakers Bureau provides a wide range of authors for speaking events. To find out more, go to www.hachettespeakersbureau.com or call (866) 376-6591.

The publisher is not responsible for websites (or their content) that are not owned by the publisher.

Library of Congress Cataloging-in-Publication Data
  Names: Black, Derek W., author.
Title: Schoolhouse burning: public education and the assault on American
  democracy / Derek W. Black.
Description: New York, NY: PublicAffairs, [2020] | Includes bibliographical
  references and index.
Identifiers: LCCN 2020011959 | ISBN 9781541788442 (hardcover) |
  ISBN 9781541774384 (ebook)
Subjects: LCSH: Public schools—United States. | Democracy and education—
  United States.
Classification: LCC LA217.2 .B574 2020 | DDC 371.010973—dc23
LC record available at https://lccn.loc.gov/2020011959
ISBNs: 978-1-5417-8844-2 (hardcover), 978-1-5417-7438-4 (ebook)
LSC-H
Printing 2, 2022

For the public school teachers of Clinton, Tennessee,
who made good on the promise of opportunity for all.

CONTENTS

PROLOGUE

M Y PATH TO THIS BOOK WAS AN UNLIKELY ONE. ALL TOLD, MY family accumulated more GEDs than college diplomas, which is to say we had a few of the former and none of the latter before me. The only thing pointing my way to college was the general, undefined idea that I should go. Knowing what I know now about education, I would not have bet on me making it.

My parents' marriage was so short that I don't have a single memory of them together. My mom's long hours as a waitress were just enough to make the rent when I was little. My father worked the night shift and lived an hour away for several years. My few comforts in life came from my grandparents, rides to school and elsewhere from my aunt.

Instability was familiar enough to be normal. I made my bed in so many different apartments, houses, and trailers that I never had a sense of belonging anywhere other than my grandparents' house. The cigar box filled with my mother's tips is my most vivid memory from childhood. The box moved with us from one place to another. She kept the silver. The pennies were mine.

I switched schools four times by the seventh grade. Losing friends and the anxiety of making new ones made each new school more

1

intimidating than the last. Low grades here and there coupled with a referral for speech therapy made my progress far from sure. I can still see myself sitting next to the window as my turn to read aloud in the second grade approached. Other students seemed to ease through their parts. But the fear inside me took hold as my turn neared. I think I managed the words correctly, but my only goal was to survive. A similar swirling of thoughts and emotions remains with me to this day when I wait to speak among a group of people.

Even less pointed my way toward the study of race and equality. I grew up in a staunchly religious, white, and conservative community. The three categories were so intertwined that I never thought to distinguish them. My family rarely jostled a counter-idea. Literature was the only possibility of a different perspective, though I wouldn't broach a rich booklist until I was in my twenties. For most of my life, I was a white student surrounded by white teachers, white students, and white ideas, including most of college.

So how was it that I made it to college, took up African American Studies as a major, excelled in law school, interned at the Office for Civil Rights at the US Department of Education, litigated school desegregation cases at the Lawyers' Committee for Civil Rights, became a law professor and founded the Education Rights Center at Howard University, worked on civil rights issues for President Obama's transition team, and eventually became one of the nation's leading experts on education law and policy, particularly as it pertains to disadvantaged students?

No doubt, my parents were hardworking, and my grandparents' overwhelming love, support, and stability doubled my relatively low chances at college. But much of everything else hinged on the opportunity that public education afforded me—sometimes when I did not even want it for myself. I can't count how many decisions teachers and administrators made to keep me on track and clear the path of opportunity. I can't count them because they made them without me or my parents knowing. Judged against today's calls for more transparency and autonomy, that sounds terrible. But schools can't run every detail by parents. We have to trust them to make some well-informed judgments themselves.

In theory, their judgment can make all the difference in the world for a kid. At the very least, it did for me.

But my schooling, like everyone else's, wasn't defined by singularly large decisions or tests. Ongoing relationships and experiences—ones strong enough to carry me through events that otherwise could have led to downward spirals—defined my education. For instance, I was lucky enough to have a tough but caring eighth-grade teacher who counseled me through the emotionally devastating grade I earned in his class. He helped me pick myself up and learn how to make some real effort. I was lucky enough to have a ninth-grade teacher excited about geometry and committed to us learning it. She let me and others spend our free time after lunch in her classroom until we figured it out. Later, in Algebra II, a seasoned teacher let me retake a test. I had scored a zero on it the first time because I was not sleeping enough at home and was making up for it every day in math class.

Then there were all the moments of generosity in between. Some of these teachers sent me into the hallway for the remainder of class because I couldn't keep my mouth shut. Even more made me write "I will not talk in class" a few hundred times an evening. But never once did those teachers send me to the office as a disobedient or disruptive kid in need of more serious punishment, let alone suspend me. Most often, they talked with me about my behavior, and I listened—well enough to course-correct for as long as you can expect of a young person.

I can't pinpoint why these teachers did not let me fail or see fit to seriously punish me. As a scholar, white privilege jumps to mind as a possibility. A black kid in my situation would have surely been more likely to slip through the cracks. Yet whiteness—at least not alone—cannot explain it. My school was around 90 percent white and a lot of white kids slipped through the cracks, too. Socioeconomics doesn't explain it, either. My family wasn't poor enough to be on public assistance, but we were overstretched enough to wonder where dinner would come from occasionally.

I see two plausible explanations: either the school system did its job or it took pity on me—maybe a bit of both. Teachers saw a kid with a little potential who could not manage to help himself, so they did. Someone at school made a final consequential decision, completely unbeknownst to me, during the spring of my sophomore year. The school handed out applications for AP English, which was set to start the following year. If we were interested, our parents were supposed to complete the application. But as soon as my teacher told us about the AP English workload, I knew I had no interest. I threw the form away and never gave it a second thought. So you can imagine my confusion next year when I discovered AP English on my course schedule. I immediately raised my hand high on the first day of class. "Ms. Calhoun, I'm not supposed to be in here." She didn't miss a beat. "Let me finish. We'll talk about that later," she said.

We never talked. I stayed in AP English for two years and on course in so many other ways with the guiding hands of my teachers. Because of that, I was able to occasionally find myself in literature. I saw results in math that suggested I was exceptional, not just in my school, but on a state level. However, my background and lack of personal ambition still gave me the chance to undermine myself. For instance, after earning an A in the first semester of calculus, I convinced a counselor that I needed to drop calculus and take something else more interesting. My calculus teacher was upset and gave me a stern lecture, but she did not really have the power to stop me, and I dropped. The truth, though, was that she saw through me. I was just being lazy. Fortunately, teachers like her prevailed more often than I did. Their helping hands balanced against my poor instincts and relatively limited outside supports added up to a respectable academic record. Somehow, I managed to finish not far behind the various valedictorians and salutatorians in my graduating class.

College presented a different set of challenges—with money and location being the primary obstacles. I commuted to campus from home and slept at friends' houses in between. Of course, the second challenge, finding my path, is one that all college students struggle to navigate. Like many young adults, I spent my first two years listlessly changing majors before finally landing on Philosophy. Then, rather than dropping majors,

I started adding them—Political Science and African American Studies. That last one changed my life. But the answer to why I chose African American Studies—a strange if not troubling choice to most who knew me—again lies in the public schools and a little bit of random luck.

I shared passing pleasantries with an African American Studies professor as I entered the classroom he was exiting three times a week. He was talkative and friendly. On a lark, I enrolled in his class the next semester. The depths the class eventually spoke to me were bound up in my earlier experience in public school. Public schooling had not only given me the chance for upward mobility; it had—as it should—thrust history and social experience on me. Though I didn't know it at the time, I went to some very special public schools.

My home address changed five more times between the seventh grade and high school graduation, but as luck would have it, I found a permanent academic home in the seventh-grade school in Clinton, Tennessee. Save desegregation scholars, few outside of Clinton know the town, but it holds a unique place in history. Clinton High School— which later served as the building for the junior high—was the first traditionally white high school in the South to enroll and graduate an African American student. The sleepy little town of thirty-five hundred was one of Thurgood Marshall's first stops after *Brown v. Board of Education*. His legal petition for Clinton was simple: let twelve black teenagers walk down a hill.

At the time, Clinton only offered its black students one option within the city limits: a little building serving students of all ages in one room. The one-room school rested just a few hundred yards behind the white high school. Black students who wanted a semblance of a high school education had to ride a bus to a different county, through scores of red lights and morning traffic to the black high school in downtown Knoxville. Even with today's improved roads and cars, the trip takes close to forty minutes. Back then, over an hour would have been normal.

Marshall's request to let the black teenagers walk off that hill was, as a practical matter, a very small one, and the federal court said yes, initially achieving integration with relatively little fanfare given the circumstances.

Clinton High School students and pastor walking downhill from the one-room black school.
Courtesy of Don Cravens/The Life Images Collection via Getty Images.

But when word spread, segregationists converged on Clinton and stirred unrest. Hoping to quell emotions, the pastor from the white First Baptist Church walked arm-in-arm with the kids to school. Two years later, someone bombed the high school. Rather than ripping the town apart, the bomb ironically brought it together. It was, after all, a traditionally and overwhelmingly white school that had been bombed. Both white and black students were victims of the atrocity. There were no winners.

I spent my junior high years in the same wing where the bomb had gone off. It was quite stirring to sit in a classroom and watch the reel-to-reel black-and-white movies of my town's desegregation story, particularly when we recognized many of the family names that popped up on the screen. I also surmised that Green McAdoo—the rustic building where I played basketball two or three times a week—was originally the one-room building for black kids and that Foley Hill, as we called it, bore the name of some of the black kids who had first walked off the hill during desegregation.

We lacked the mental and emotional skills to fully process what we saw—and to be honest, I don't recall anyone trying to help us. My teacher exited the room and left us to react to the film alone. I don't recall any subsequent lessons connecting the dots, either. But the film and later experiences made an impression. I roughly understood that my schools were desegregated, that some of my interracial friendships were possible because of someone else's courage, and that things that did not seem entirely right in the late 1980s and early 1990s might have a larger story behind them. For sure, I could see that racial lines still existed in more than one form.

The impressions were strong enough and the list of unanswered questions long enough that something in me needed to sort them out. Years later, African American Studies finally gave me the opportunity. Those classes helped me appreciate the role that public education, equality, and integration had played in my life. I reflected on the ways in which public education had failed other kids just as deserving as me. It helped me see just how lucky I was. I also began absorbing what we now call the benefits of diversity. I was suddenly in a totally foreign environment—at times, the only white student in the classroom and never in the racial majority. I confronted ideas and perspectives that forced my thinking to expand. The combined mental and emotional awakening lit a fire in me. I set my goal on building a more just world, even if I did not really know what that meant, with education being a key component.

My decisions from there were far more conscious. I chose the University of North Carolina School of Law specifically for its civil rights offerings. I used those classes to prepare me for a career as a civil rights attorney, which quickly enough led me to teach (and learn) at the Mecca—to the very place that had been instrumental in changing Clinton, Tennessee, my life, and ultimately the entire country: Howard University School of Law, where almost all the leading figures of the NAACP's legal team had studied or worked.

One cannot be at Howard long, regardless of race, without appreciating that you are standing on others' shoulders. Too many photos of people like Thurgood Marshall, Oliver Hill, Spottswood Robinson, Pauli Murray, and C. Clyde Ferguson Jr. hang on the walls. Too many testaments to Charles Hamilton Houston—from family heirlooms and a bust to the name of the building—adorn the halls. I never suffered from the naive illusion that I could fill any of their shoes, nor did I carry anything like their burden, but walking those halls alters one's worldview. As Charles Hamilton Houston famously wrote, and as the deans who followed regularly repeated at mass gatherings, "A lawyer's either a social engineer, or he's a parasite on society."

As far as I was concerned, the same thing went for law professors, which made my focus on education law natural. Yet the precise means of engineering anything other than a syllabus was less obvious. The Howard-NAACP team had covered almost the entirety of the legal landscape with their playbook and victories, so much so that by the mid-1970s, America was spending more time tearing down their legacy than expanding it.

For the modern civil rights advocate, that means playing defense, not offense. My goal as a scholar has always been to play offense, find ways to expand on the rights the NAACP helped establish and imagine new ones. Yet weighed against every good theory was cold, hard reality. The American legal system wasn't open to progressive civil rights theories anymore, which left me questioning the value of my work at times.

School funding litigation under state constitutions, however, was making tremendous advances early in my legal career. For a decade, I labored over school funding doctrines and how they might open new doors of opportunity, whether in terms of basic resources, integration, discipline, or teacher quality. The real breakthrough occurred when I stopped looking forward and gazed backward instead—almost by accident. What I found was a historical commitment to the constitutional right to education that, while lost for a long period, is almost impossible for the modern mind to believe. It stretches back to the earliest days of this nation and was reborn with even more vigor in the aftermath of the Civil War.

The goals the nation set during those times are humbling on so many different levels. However progressive we might think we are, our fore-fathers have us beat in spades when it comes to education. Think an adequate education for all is a modern idea? Think again. Think the NAACP dreamt up integrated schools in the 1950s? Think again. Think concerns with voter education and the corruption of the political process started with Trump? Think again. Think challenges in providing adequate school funding are a modern problem? Think again. And because these problems aren't new, the nation came up with solutions long ago that can still work today if we trust our roots.

Matched against the history we think we know, our forgotten history is so powerfully unsettling that it has the capacity to completely reorient the way we see our schools and democracy. If we can do that, who knows what is possible? It won't be just defending old victories.

I know now that the public education I received rested on decisions that people made for communities like mine well before I ever set foot on this earth. Those decisions, in many instances, were the result of pitched fights over how to better our schools and democracy as a whole. Most of those fights began in the 1800s and reverberated during times of cultural strife for the next two centuries. Public education is, in effect, the inheritance that we all share, and one that is crucially important for kids like me who never could have hoped for an inheritance in the literal sense. This book is about safeguarding and nurturing that inheritance for current and future generations.

What follows is my best effort to tell America's education story—and tell it in a way that is relevant to the challenges our kids face today: poverty, inequality, and a public education system under siege. I hope it resonates.

INTRODUCTION

TWO HUNDRED YEARS AGO OUR FOUNDING FATHERS GAVE US two gifts. Both were relatively unknown to the world at the time. The first was democracy—what they called a republican form of government. The second was public education. These gifts were inextricably intertwined.

A republican form of government would allow everyday people to govern themselves through elected representatives. Our founders knew what it was like to live and worship under a king. They wanted something radically different for themselves, their families, and the generations that would follow. Reality, of course, was slow to live up to their lofty ideas. They denied African Americans, women, and many poor whites the right to vote. But the full story of America is a long march to live up to its democratic ideas. Our founding ideas, though flawed in their initial implementation, were compelling enough to take root and bear fruit for generations to come. The contradiction between our democratic ideas and practical reality was also strong enough to spark a Civil War and then constitutional change. The post-war Constitution prohibited racial voting restrictions, and then later gender and wealth restrictions. Another century later, the nation doubled down on those ideas through the Voting Rights Act, again marching the country further toward its founding ideas, not away from them.

The story of public education goes hand in hand with democracy and voting. That story, however, is not as well told. In fact, some of the very best parts of the story have been lost to memory and never fully pieced together as part of the nation's democratic expansion. This book mines that history to help us better see who we are and have been—for better or worse. The lessons and values in that history also serve as an objective measuring stick for education today—something sorely missing from the conversation.

My first conclusion should worry you: The last decade aligns better with the darker periods of our history than the brighter ones. The trend is alarming not just for public education. It is alarming for democracy itself. But my second conclusion is that the power of the idea of public education remains strong enough to persevere. In fact, public education may be the one institution that helps rebind this nation's wounds, just as it has in the past, and moves us once again closer to our democratic aspirations.

From its first days, the nation's theory of government depended on educated citizens. The founders feared that democracy without education would devolve into mob rule, open doors to unscrupulous politicians, and encourage hucksters to take advantage of citizens even as they stood in line to vote. Our democracy might very well just fail. When asked at the close of our Constitutional Convention what sort of government the founding fathers had created, Benjamin Franklin reportedly said, "A republic, if you can keep it."

While our understanding of our democratic commitments primarily comes from the Constitution, the nation's commitment to public education predates the Constitution. Education was bound up in our nation's future from the start. In 1785, two years before the constitutional convention met, the Continental Congress was attending to the immediate business of the nation. The most pressing question was the future of the western territories—land that would later become the states of Ohio, Illinois, Indiana, Michigan, Wisconsin, and Minnesota.

The answer came in the form of one the most important sets of legislation ever passed—the Northwest Ordinances. In 1785, the Northwest Ordinance set the rules for how the nation would divide new lands into territories and towns that ultimately become states. Those same rules later governed the land that the United States had yet to acquire west of the Mississippi. In total, the Northwest Ordinance has shaped what would become thirty-one states.

Education was embedded into the very structure of these new lands. The Northwest Ordinance required that every town be divided into thirty-six lots. Four of those lots and one-third of each township's natural resources would be used to generate resources for public education. And the Northwest Ordinance chose a specific lot in every township on which to build a public school—the sixteenth lot.[1] Two years later, while delegates to the Constitutional Convention were meeting in Philadelphia, the Continental Congress passed the Northwest Ordinance of 1787. This update to the 1785 Ordinance moved beyond the mundane particulars of dividing up lots. It spoke in lofty terms, authoritatively announcing the guiding principles by which our political community would govern itself and grow. It provided that "religion, morality, and knowledge, being necessary to good government and the happiness of mankind, schools and the means of education shall forever be encouraged."[2]

Once the Constitution was in place, our first presidents implored the nation to expand public education as rapidly as possible. President George Washington, for instance, formally wrote to Congress, imploring that no "duty [is] more pressing on [the national] legislature" than "the common education of a portion of our youth from every quarter." The youth are "the future guardians of the liberties of the country" and, thus, the very "prospect of [a] permanent union" depends on their education.[3] John Adams argued that, as a matter of democratic theory, government had a responsibility to provide education to "every rank and class of people, down to the lowest and the poorest" and pay for it at "public expense."[4] He envisioned something so grand "that [it] never yet has been practised in any age or nation."[5] Thomas Jefferson was similarly

convinced that public education is "necessary to prepare citizens to participate effectively and intelligently in our open political system [and] to
preserve freedom and independence."[6] As president, he boldly proposed
committing the nation's financial treasure and future surpluses to education. Education was so important that he urged Congress, if necessary,
to amend the Constitution to allow for education's support.

With these leaders and ideas pushing it forward, the country made
enormous strides, distinguishing itself internationally. By the early 1800s,
the only country in the world with more educational access was Prussia, which had a century-long head start on America in nation building.[7]
Yet universal access to public education—much like the opportunity
for everyone to participate in self-government—was a concept honored
more in American ideas than reality for much of the nation's first century. The most glaring breach was slavery. Not only did the nation bind
slaves' bodies, it tried to bind their minds, making it a crime for slaves
to read and write. That breach also brought forth some of the nation's
most inspiring and redeeming moments—moments that the modern
mind struggles to fathom.

Shortly after the Civil War began, slaves fled for Union lines. Once
physically safe there, education was foremost on their minds. Make-
shift schools quickly swelled beyond anyone's expectation in places like
Fort Monroe, Virginia, and Port Royal, South Carolina. Underneath it
all was a preternatural longing. When a white missionary first arrived
at a freedmen's camp along the Mississippi River and announced that
she had come to teach, the elderly slave who greeted her at the water's
edge immediately responded that he already knew her purpose and that
"I'se been 'spectin you . . . for de last twenty years. I knowed you would
come, and now I rejoice."[8] When teaching actually began in these newly
secured locations, it was literally a sight to behold. In the Freedmen's
Camp in Vidalia, Louisiana, an observer told of a thousand slaves gath-
ering under a large magnolia tree to learn from a missionary teacher.
Elsewhere, slaves met anywhere they could for as long as they could to
learn, even deep into the night. An official report to Congress later rhe-

torically asked: "What other people on earth have ever shown, while in their ignorance, such a passion for education?"[9]

With swelling numbers and passion came strength. The chorus of freedmen asking for, and sometimes demanding, education reached a fever pitch in the coming years. Their expectation and articulation of what freedom meant literally redefined the nation's constitutional norms regarding citizenship. Education and voting were at the top of their list—and soon Congress's. As a condition for rejoining the Union after the war, Congress forced Southern states to rewrite their state constitutions and embed the right to education in them. Northern states soon followed suit. A constitutional guarantee of education became the new norm. No state would ever again enter the Union without guaranteeing education in its constitution.

Today, all fifty state constitutions protect the right to education. All fifty states, through constitutional language, place that right on a pedestal. They also attempt something quite curious: they try to insulate public education from partisan politics. As an inherent function of the state, they thought public education should operate under a different set of rules. One state constitutional convention delegate proclaimed in the late 1800s that "there are no political considerations connected with [education] in any part of the Commonwealth."[10] To keep it that way, that state constitutional convention included the state superintendent in the constitution and made it a position free "from all the contaminating influences of political manipulation and management." The person to fill the job, another delegate explained, should be someone "characterized by official purity."[11]

Over the past half century, these rights and protections have been so successful that one might conclude that the constitutional rights to education and voting, proceeding together, secured an irreversible triumph of values and rights. Our voting and educational systems still suffered imperfections, but individuals' rights to vote and education were no longer in serious dispute. The American experiment had succeeded in convincing the overwhelming majority of people that everyone ought to be able to vote and that the federal and state governments are responsible for providing a quality education to all.

In 2006, we saw Congress reauthorize the Voting Rights Act (first passed in 1965) with little, if any, controversy. The vote was overwhelming in the House of Representatives and unanimous in the Senate. We saw minority voter turnout exceed white voter turnout in many places. We saw state supreme courts enforcing the constitutional right to education in the North, South, East, and West. We saw the federal government consistently drawing our focus to racial, socioeconomic, and other achievement gaps. We even saw the nation elect its first African American president and some Southern school districts voluntarily integrating their schools long after federal courts had set them free. Our democratic ideas and constitutional rights had merged and seemed to be slowly but surely dragging reality into line.

My mistake was in thinking that democracy's triumphs were irreversible or settled. After reaching a number of cultural and constitutional milestones, states—aided and sometimes prodded by top federal officials—are now trying to take the gift of public education back. It should come as no surprise that they are doing so at the same time that some are restricting access to the ballot box. They are turning their backs on ideas and rights as old as the constitutions under which they operate. While threats to the ballot are immediately understood as threats to democracy, attacks on public education are not always fully appreciated as such. But rest assured, just as the gift of public education has helped build up our democracy, taking it back threatens to tear down our democracy.

Because public education has for so long served as the foundation of our democratic norms, it has also served as a battlefield for those who resist democracy or seek to bend it toward their own ends rather than the greater good. The extent to which public education has been available to the average citizen—particularly racial minorities and women—has closely tracked the expansion of democracy. The expansion, however, has rarely moved in a straight line. Progress has always been tempered by those who resist the political equality that public education promotes.

But the basic right to education and the legitimacy of the public education system have never been called into question. Today they are.

Politicians and advocacy groups couch today's education debates as
normal fights over legislative experimentation and efforts at fiscal equi-
librium, but so-called education reforms grow bolder each year and, in
the collective, represent a war on public education. States like Nevada
have passed legislation that authorizes the privatization of the entire
public education system. Others states, like Florida, Arizona, Indiana,
Ohio, and Michigan—just to name a few—have not yet gone that far
but have been growing their voucher and charter programs at staggering rates while public education funding falls. In fact, they have passed
legislation that takes money directly from traditional public schools and
transfers it to charter schools and voucher programs. Other states, like
Kansas and North Carolina, have exchanged the financial stability of
statewide systems of public schools for tax cuts for high-income earners
and corporations. The environment for public schools is so unfavorable
in some states that major cities are on their way to having more charter
schools than public schools. New Orleans, for instance, has already lost
all its public schools, operating nothing but charter schools now.[12] To
top it off, states have made the teaching profession so inhospitable and
underpaid that the pipeline of new teachers virtually dried up in 2015.
Local districts now struggle to put warm bodies in the classroom.

When advocates ring the alarm bell or claim that states are violating
students' constitutional right to public education, some state leaders have
proposed something even more unthinkable: constitutional amendments
that would shrink students' right to education and eliminate checks on
legislative abuses of public education. The Kansas legislature went so
far as to threaten its judiciary when it stood up for students, and two
members held the entire state's education budget hostage while they demanded a constitutional amendment to block judicial checks on education defunding. Less abrasive states have simply proceeded as though
students don't have any rights, ignoring courts and passing whatever
legislation they deem expedient. For the first time in our history, states
would shirk their education obligations and transition public education

from a constitutional right to a policy option. As such, public education would cease to be the foundational commitment of our state government.

Education "reformers," of course, do not state their agenda as an attack on public education or student rights. Their pitch is gentler. They say public schools already have enough resources; they just need to spend what they have more wisely. Or, the problem is not low teacher salaries but tenure and ineffective teaching. They say charter schools and vouchers offer the common man the chance to escape a flawed public education system and trade it for something else, for something better. Those who would deprive individuals of that choice are the ones who are anti-democratic and elitist, they say.

This line of argument rests on a radical idea—that public education does not hold a special place in our democracy, and government has no business providing it. Education, they say, is like any other commodity we might buy and should be customizable to meet the personal tastes of each individual, like the cell phone covers sold on the internet. But public education has never been a private commodity or a matter of individual choice. State government has provided it because it is a necessity of democracy—a necessity that the nation has never, at least openly, assumed could be left to the random chance of geography, income level, social networks, and the inevitable winners and losers that markets produce.

This line of argument hides the fundamental and enormous power imbalance between states and their citizens. That imbalance makes the trade that states are asking families to make far from fair. Many families have never seen their state fully commit to providing a quality education in their neighborhoods and have no reason to trust that the state ever will. So these families are not really choosing on an even playing field. They are not choosing between a decent public school and a charter or voucher. They are, instead, fleeing from what they perceive as a burning house. No one can begrudge families who feel they must leap from the windows and hope they land on their feet. It's no surprise that these families defend charter and voucher programs that would allow others to do the same.

Yet the interests of those pulling the political and financial levers behind the scenes to expand charters and vouchers do not align with disadvantaged communities. Their goal, unlike that of minority communities, is not to ensure that each and every child, regardless of wealth, race, or religion, receives an equal and adequate educational opportunity. The powerful interests behind the scenes want a much different system of government than the one our founders put in our state and federal constitutions. Undermining public education is a big part of making that happen. Education, they say, is "the lowest hanging fruit for policy change in the United States today."[13] In their minds, the scales of justice should tip away from mass democracy and the common good toward individualism and private property. That means less taxes, less government, less public education. While couched as more liberty, what they really mean is that government should let the chips fall where they may. It isn't government's job to ensure equal participation in democracy.

The amount of money they are pumping into political campaigns and lobbying efforts to "fundamentally transform" American education is unheard of—hundreds of millions of dollars from the Koch brothers' political network alone.[14] From governors' races and statewide referenda to school board races and local policies, they have made decreasing public education funding and increasing charters and vouchers their top issues. In 2018, for instance, the Koch brothers targeted Arizona as ground zero in the transformation of education, announcing plans for a statewide referendum to dump vast new sums of public money into private schools. They already had Arizona's governor, Doug Ducey, in their back pocket. Speaking of the privatization effort in Arizona, Ducey said, "I didn't run for governor to play small ball." In short, the real agenda of those pushing education budget cuts and alternatives to the public education system is not to improve the public education system or to create better educational opportunities outside of it but to fundamentally undermine or end, if possible, the public education system as we know it.

Their utterly dim view of public education is summed up in the pejorative phrase "government schools." A decade before she became Secretary of Education, Betsy DeVos's family championed the phrase "failing government schools" to undermine confidence in public schools and promote privatization. Now, as secretary, she calls public education a "dead end" and those who support it "flat-earthers."[15] The president who nominated her calls public education "inferior education" that "den[ies] young people the opportunity to join the ladder of American success."[16] Both Trump and DeVos ironically speak of private school vouchers—not equal and adequate public schools—as a "right."

The normalization of attacks on public education, however, did not begin with the Trump administration. Barack Obama's Secretary of Education, Arne Duncan, while surely more well intentioned, spurred enormous charter school growth during the recession and warned states that "put[ting] artificial caps on the growth of charter schools will jeopardize their applications" for federal funding.[17] Desperate for federal funding to ease the pain of plummeting tax revenues, states that had long limited charter schools quickly changed their laws. The rest is all but history. Duncan's support helped double the charter school population during his tenure and cement a way of thinking about education that is now proving hard to control or unwind. Duncan also helped fuel a war on public school teachers, requiring states to hire, fire, and retain teachers based on their students' standardized test scores. Regardless of his intent, it was his, not DeVos's, policies that first helped drive teacher morale to a historic low and dry up the pipeline of new teachers. With that solid foundation as a starting point, the Trump administration and wealthy donors' dream of a radically different system of government and public education is within reach.

Would the United States actually abandon public education? Simply posing the question as one worthy of serious consideration is frightening. The facts suggest it is warranted. In half of the states, school funding is in even worse condition than it was a decade ago—down more than 20 percent in some states.[18] Charter schools and voucher programs, in contrast, are growing rapidly. A nationwide shortage of qualified teachers is forcing untested experiments in teacher recruitment and computerized instruction on our kids. Half of the current certified teachers have seriously considered quitting in the past few years.[19]

Yet not all is doom and gloom. There is reason to be optimistic about the future of public education. Just as history offers a warning sign, it also tells us that we have been here before. There is truly nothing new under the sun. Many of the challenges confronting public education and democracy are variants of the ones we faced generations ago. Plantation and property owners resisted the cost of public education during Reconstruction. Segregationists considered dissolving public schools before they integrated in the 1960s and 1970s. Both times, public education suffered serious blows, but it survived as an idea and constitutional right. Survival ensured that later generations could call the nation back to its roots someday.

The assault on public education today is broader than that of the past. Past assaults were foremost about race, and although race remains part of today's story, the primary rallying cry is against public education itself. And by no longer explicitly vilifying minorities, ideologues are turning a much wider spectrum of citizens against public education and even including minorities in the movement. This shift and its broader implications are in some respects more dangerous. But as the backlashes to Reconstruction and the civil rights movement showed, public education is a hard idea to kill. Teacher protests across the nation, the recent failure of a few key legislative efforts to expand vouchers, and public polling show that average citizens still recognize the inherent value of public education. They may not have connected all the dots to recognize a war on public education, but they sense that something fishy is happening. It is hard to miss the fact that their schools do not have the resources they need and that their state legislators have their priorities out of whack.

The first signs of rising movement in support of public education came in 2016. Public school advocates beat back charter and voucher bills that previously seemed destined to succeed. In Massachusetts, the pro-charter governor and deep-pocket donors had the "wind at their backs" in a statewide referendum to expand charters.[20] They had $20 million in the bank and a majority of voters on board, but in the final weeks before the election, something shifted.[21] On election day, 62 percent of voters opposed charter expansion.

Protests against Betsy DeVos.
Courtesy of Drew Angerer/Getty Images.

More surprising was Texas—a state that prides itself on individualism, liberty, and conservative politics. Those factors, unsurprisingly, helped a bill to dramatically expand vouchers sail through the Senate and earn the full support of the governor. But then, regular people from around the state rallied against it and marched on Austin. Rural voices, in particular, wanted the state to look after its struggling public schools before it did anything for vouchers. Soon thereafter, the voucher bill suffered an embarrassing, lopsided defeat in the Texas House of Representatives.

The second sign that things had gone too far was the public response to Betsy DeVos as Secretary of Education. Her nomination immediately symbolized everything that parents and teachers had been angry about for a decade. The notion that she—"somebody who scorns public education, who never went to a public school, [whose] children never went to a public school"—would be Secretary of Education was too much for regular people, regardless of their political party, to stomach.[22] Furious constituents in swing states overwhelmed their senators with calls, emails, and faxes, demanding that they vote against DeVos. Things weren't much better in heavily conservative states. A South Carolina teacher who voted

Protestors in front of the Arizona State Capitol.
Courtesy of Ralph Fresco/Getty Images.

for Trump wanted to talk to her senator, Tim Scott, about his intention to vote yes on DeVos. When his office ignored her, she collected 4,500 signatures in a matter of days from other South Carolinians calling for a town-hall meeting. Neither Scott nor anyone else in Washington dared openly defend DeVos on her merits. In the end, it took raw, irrational political power—the tie-breaking vote of Vice President Pence—to secure her confirmation. DeVos got the job, but her nomination was more contentious than the country had ever seen with that cabinet position (one that most political figures and commentators ignore). Senator Jeff Merkley summed it up: "There is no one in America more unpopular than Betsy DeVos."[23]

The real uprising, however, had nothing to do with DeVos. In the spring of 2018, teachers across the nation waged a full-scale revolt, shutting down public schools and marching on state capitals in the reddest of red states. From West Virginia and Kentucky to Oklahoma and Arizona, teachers went on strike over the condition of public education. Stagnant and depressed teacher salaries were the initial focal point, but as the protests spread, it became clear that teachers were marching for far more than their own salaries. They were marching for school supplies, school services, class sizes, and more. They were marching for states to reverse the massive budget cuts of the past decade and stop funneling more resources into charters and vouchers. Families and students were right beside them, both in body and spirit. Deep in the heart of red country, three out of four voters said they saw quality gaps between schools and wanted states to close them.[24] Nationally, only 6 percent said teacher salaries are too high, and 73 percent said they would support their teachers if they went on strike.[25]

Yet these events and numbers are not enough to ensure public education gets back on sure footing. First of all, as this book was in its final stages and being prepared for printing, the coronavirus struck, and the nation began sheltering at home. We won't understand the full impact of the virus on the economy, education, or our democracy for years, but one thing was immediately obvious to me: education was on the verge of a new budget crisis without having fully recovered from the last one. One of the first things a few states did upon recognizing that the economy was about to take a hit was to cut their education budgets. Some states that had promised teacher raises and school funding increases during the first part of 2020 began cutting and pausing those increases. A few weeks later they began making far larger cuts. The instinct in most states, just like during the 2008 recession, has been to raid public education budgets rather than protect them.

Second, Betsy DeVos even hinted she might "try to use the widespread pandemic-driven shutdown to create a path to national school vouchers."[26] Even before the coronavirus, Betsy DeVos and others were undeterred in their plans. DeVos, for instance, downplayed the significance of the protests and said teachers should "keep adult disagreements and disputes in a separate place, and serve the students that are there to be served."[27] When challenged by a Trump voter and the Oklahoma Teacher of the Year at a private forum for teachers,[28] DeVos refused to validate teachers' concerns about public education's current woes and, instead, reiterated the mantra that school choice is the solution. DeVos and others have simply stuck to their playbooks and continued to secure important victories in state houses. They have shown they are ready to change any rules—even long-standing constitutional and democratic norms—to get their way. State leaders in places like Kentucky, Indiana, and Arizona have done things like orchestrate takeovers of what are supposed to be nonpartisan state boards of education, strip state superintendents of education of their statutory and constitutional powers, and propose constitutional amendments to achieve narrow policy objectives.

That DeVos and various state actors have the ability to stay the course belies a cold, hard reality. Those who would fight to save public education are playing catch-up with opponents who have no intention of playing fair. These opponents have secured major footholds for charter schools, and the list of voucher states is following suit. Those laws are not going away anytime soon. Public school funding remains woefully inadequate and unequal. The teacher pipeline, even if we acted immediately, could take a decade or more to reestablish. And it is only as the agenda to undermine public education edges ever closer to its biggest legislative triumphs—laws that make vouchers available to every student regardless of need, laws that place charters on equal or better footing than public schools, and laws that make teacher unions and teacher preparation programs obsolete—that public outrage has awakened. That outrage only provoked new strategies from opponents. It did not break their resolve. In other words, the nation is in the middle of a battle for the long-term viability of public education, not nearly to the point of assuring a conclusion.

So rather than take a deep breath of relief, we must acknowledge that the battle is much larger than the public policy debates of the past. Current policy debates are but the skirmishes in the war over the role that public education will play in our society for decades to come. This war raises much more fundamental questions than we have asked in a long time. These questions, like those that our founding fathers asked, go to the core of our democratic experiment.

What happens when education policy becomes a political football rather than the most basic obligation of government to its citizens? What becomes of American democracy if it abandons public education? Will it consign swaths of students to second-class citizenship? Can we still claim to be a democracy committed to the idea that all citizens have the right to equally participate if we do not maintain a robust public education system? Or are current trends steps toward our government becoming a shell of its former self, with democracy devolving into a competitive market among self-interested and disconnected individuals? More globally, just how fragile is our democracy?

The current political climate suggests these questions are not just food for thought, but questions that reveal how much is at stake. Far too many people are not equipped with the education they need to distinguish fact from fiction, good policy from bad, or even their own self-interest. Shockingly large percentages do not vote or understand the basic structure of government. A large chunk of society has lost faith in government's capacity to do anything good, so it lashes out against government. Those who know better are exploiting these knowledge and perception gaps and clamoring for restrictions on voting and public education. If education becomes the bystander in a political power struggle, democracy could lose the tool it needs to heal itself.

Yet these trends also come with an important silver lining. The dark clouds surrounding democracy may point toward public education as a bright spot. Since 2016, commentators and scholars have focused on what they call a populist uprising here and abroad.[29] They point out average citizens' growing love affair with autocratic rule and disdain for certain democratic norms and rights. Populist leaders insist that a sheer majority in their camp entitles them to set any agenda they wish. More bluntly, they insist that might makes right—even if history, constitutional norms, and the rule of law have always said otherwise.

Public education, unfortunately, got caught up in this populist revolt, and those on the far right—with designs set on changing democracy—took advantage. Yet the bipartisan awakening of support for education suggests that public education norms, although not irreversible like I once might have thought, are more durable than the last decade suggests. Yes, new political majorities took hold at the state level and were empowered to redefine public education. But political leaders mistook voters' desire for educational improvement as a desire for public education abandonment. They mistook the loudest voices as the voice of the people. The overwhelming widespread support for teachers and public education in response to legislative changes reveals that public education is one institution the populist revolt is not willing to tear down. If so, public education may very well be both the practical and ideological foundation upon which our democracy still continues to rest.

That silver lining alone, however, won't do. The assault on public education happened because of the general discontent with public education. That discontent will not go away by itself. And until it goes away, the attack will draw on a constituency that allows it to continue. The truth is that our public education system is broken in many respects, not because the concept of public education is flawed, but because we have yet to finish the task of living up to its purpose. The first step toward redemption is to take seriously the reasons why families have grown discontented. They range from the sense that schools are indoctrinating students to the sense that they are too focused on testing and simply not doing a good job of teaching students what they really need to know. It is not enough to respond that we owe fidelity to the public education system and its ideas. We know that families' fidelity will be to their own children first.

This disillusionment is partly cultural, but no matter what, it requires a school system that is more responsive to the fears and concerns of parents. This does not mean that schools cater their instruction and curriculum to every family, but it does require school leaders who can look parents in the eye, listen carefully, appreciate their concerns, and give honest answers. Parents have to believe those leaders will do everything in their power to ensure they are not crossing political boundaries they should steer clear of and they are not omitting instruction that students need. It is about building trust as much as changing reality. A decade of recriminations and politicizations requires a decade of mending fences.

One way to mend those fences is to relieve the pressure that our unflinching allegiance to standardized tests and curriculum creates. The best schools that I have been in are not ones that just do well on standardized tests. The best schools—the ones that really make a difference in children's lives rather than just replicating the advantages or disadvantages they bring with them from home—are those that focus on children's wellness and development—on what they eat, on their cultural awareness, on how they talk to one another, on how adults talk to them, on their roles as members of a community, on how they see themselves. Those things buy school leaders and teachers an enormous amount of purchase with families, even when we think school leaders might have gotten something wrong or a teacher should be focusing more on standard measures of academic success.

But our schools' problems are deeper than feelings and personal interactions. If this book makes anything clear, it will be that states have underfunded and abused their public schools. Welcoming administrators alone can pacify parents only for so long. Parents also need to know that the classrooms they put their children in will not be overcrowded or short on basic supplies. They need to know the teachers are qualified. Those things take money. The only way that schools will have that money is if states make the public education system their foremost financial priority. State constitutions demand as much, and voters agree. States cannot put tax cuts or anything else ahead of children.

Part of the failure in public education has been the confusion—or misinformation—over whether money affects student achievement. If it were ever in any serious empirical doubt, it no longer is. The collective weight of the research is as conclusive as it gets: money matters. As I was literally putting the finishing touches on the final draft of this introduction, four more new studies came out demonstrating the importance of school funding for student outcomes, particularly low-income students. For goodness' sake, the time has come to stop with what amounts to political rhetoric rather than a rational position—the notion that schools already have what they need and just need to be more efficient. No doubt, schools can and should find ways to spend their resources more wisely. We should not ignore the mismanagement that occurs in some schools. But the fact remains that about half of our schools are grossly underfunded, and no amount of efficiency can cure the problems these schools face. To suggest otherwise borders on perverse. It's like telling a child he can't have dinner today because he didn't save his leftovers yesterday. That's how most states' school funding policies effectively treat students in high-poverty schools.

Yet money alone cannot solve what has long been a root of education's ills—segregation. Racial and socioeconomic school segregation harm the entire public education system and society as a whole. Disadvantaged students suffer the most, but they are not the only ones. Separate and unequal public education perpetuates winners and losers. It incentivizes parents with privilege to take steps to protect their own interests. When enough do that, they compromise public education's ability to pursue the common good. And more practically, segregated schools deny privileged students the diverse learning opportunities they also need to succeed in higher education and employment, and as future citizens and leaders.

Our current political fractures and polarization are in no small part an outgrowth of our segregated and unequal school system. These fractures take a toll on us all. Yet the phenomenon works in reverse as well. Steps to reduce segregation and inequality will not only help address the various disadvantages that poor and minority students face; they will also improve public education and our democracy. Our public education system has bound us together and lifted us up before. We need it to do so again. Digging schools out of our self-imposed segregation hole may be the hardest thing we could do. Segregation has built up too much inequality and fear over the years. Privileged families too often see equality and integration as sacrificing their own children. Moving past that requires that we make integration part of a larger positive agenda in which we aim to make our public school system the envy of the world. Our forefathers banked on similar ideas when there was far more classism and racism than there is today.

Finally, we have to stop treating schools like businesses to be managed. The question with charters, vouchers, and any number of other education strategies is not simply whether some or most are economically efficient or produce higher test scores. The question is whether these policies reflect and further the democratic and constitutional values that we need public education to serve. If not, little else matters. This book offers a few clear-cut answers on these policies—which will roil people on one side of the debate. My other answers will roil their opponents because I ask whether we might alter bad policies in ways that further public education's mission.

Building an education system that serves the needs of democracy remains a long work in progress. While America has never fully lived up to its education promises, it is a mistake to think its shortcomings require or justify a new theory of education. Its shortcomings should remind us of what democratic education demands of the nation and just how hard living up to those demands can be. If those who care about public education concede the war over the fundamental concept of public education or make their war about something other than its fundamental values, they will wake up one day with nothing left to fight for. They may even wake up without a democracy.

CHAPTER 1

THE CURRENT CRISIS

T HE LAST DECADE STANDS OUT IN HISTORY AS A PARTICULARLY bad one for public education. Our fidelity to the constitutional rights to education and equal and adequate public schools for all seriously faltered after an important period of expansion in the 1990s and early 2000s. Some combination of factors is to blame. The rights previously established by state constitutions, courts, and laws provoked legislative resistance. Cultural norms changed. Social anxieties motivated irrational decisions. Some would even say sinister plots were hatched. You can decide for yourself. Regardless, the result was the same: major changes in how states and the federal government treat education. With the benefit of just a little historical perspective, those changes are alarming.

The first change was initially hard to see. But a decade later, a long-term global disinvestment in public education is hard to miss. Before the recession of 2008, the trend in public school funding remained generally positive. Students did not have everything they needed, but they typically had more than the prior generation. Then the recession hit. Nearly every state in the country made large cuts to public education. Annual cuts of more than $1,000 per student were routine—the equivalent of an assistant teacher in every classroom or a school's entire science and

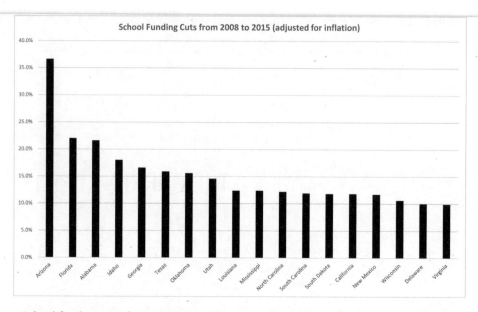

School funding cuts from 2008 to 2015.
Courtesy of the author.

foreign language departments combined.[1] In North Carolina and Florida, funding fell from over $10,000 per student to around $7,000 in just a few years.[2]

States did not take time to stop and seriously consider what they were doing, much less offer any good explanations to the rest of us. At best, they assumed schools could be more efficient. How much more efficient? They had no idea. Education, given its overall size, was simply the natural place to find savings. States took out their hatchets and started chopping. They never looked back.

The immediacy of the recession made it hard to second-guess them in real time. But in retrospect, many of the cuts were not about efficiency at all. Rather, the recession offered a convenient excuse for states to redefine their commitment to public education. This sad reality became clearer with each passing year. By 2012, state revenues rebounded to prerecession levels, and a few years later, the economy was in the midst of its longest winning streak in history. Yet during this period of rising wealth, states refused to give back what they took from education. In 2014, for instance, more than thirty states still funded education at a lower level than they did before the recession—some funded education 20 percent to 30 percent below prerecession levels.[3] Some states have since gradually increased education funding, but the general national trend of sustained and substantial underfunding of public schools persists.

The mismatch between state revenues and school funding levels was "unprecedented."[4] School budgets always bounced back relatively quickly after a recession in the past. This time, state coffers were getting fatter, but school budgets were not. In fact, many school budgets fell further behind. Costs for things like transportation, electricity, food, and teacher benefits rose with the times, whereas school budgets remained flat. The divergence begs the question of whether states intentionally gouged education—doing things that the courts, the public, and any reasonable politician would have never condoned under normal circumstances.

States did not have to stop funding education at adequate levels. They just stopped trying. A state might have defended only spending the resources it had available. This would have caused school funding to dip, but not plummet. Several states, however, decided to spend even less than what they had available. They took money out of public education and gave it away in tax cuts, shored up other government programs, or, as discussed below, expanded alternatives to public education. A mere eighteen states increased their efforts to fund education once the economy recovered. In short, state education budgets reflected goals and biases that had little to do with economic hard times.

The conscious decision to underfund education was obvious in North Carolina. North Carolina cut education funding by 15 percent while also giving out the largest state-level tax cuts in the nation's history (and giving them to the state's highest-income earners in what some called a systemic war on poor people). North Carolina then continued to starve education when its economy started to boom. In 2015, the economy was so strong that North Carolina had a half-billion-dollar surplus in spite of deep tax cuts. Yet North Carolina refused to use the surplus to repair the harm it had done to education in prior years.

The story in Kansas was similar. Governor Brownback sold the idea that $700 million in tax cuts would supercharge the state's economy. It didn't, and he called for enormous school funding cuts less than three years later.[5] Those cuts brought education spending 17 percent below prerecession levels.[6] Brownback also fought to keep those cuts in place when courts insisted that Kansas increase school funding. If you know a person by the friends he keeps, Brownback's goal for education was sinister. Brownback was the poster boy for Grover Norquist's agenda to shrink government to the size where you can "drown it in a bathtub"[7]—a plan that necessarily included public education.[8]

The real-world impacts of budget cuts of this magnitude had serious consequences for schools. The cuts were not just numbers on a spreadsheet. They affected schools' ability to staff classrooms and deliver services. They drove some districts to the brink of catastrophe. School funding shortfalls were so steep in Pennsylvania that they eventually morphed into tragic national headlines. Philadelphia schools, for instance, cut nursing services to two or three days a week. Students, however, still got sick five days a week. In 2014, a couple of sick students were not treated and died at home later in the day.[9] Whether a solid budget would have prevented the tragedies is impossible to say, but the funding crisis got so bad that national civil rights leaders descended on the state in protest, concluding that "Pennsylvania has become a national model of dysfunction in education."[10]

A year later Pennsylvania schools began the 2015 academic year without a state budget. They finished the school year in the same position. Wealthier school districts drew on "rainy day" reserve funds, increased local funding, and borrowed money. Poor districts could not. Some of those poorer districts asked teachers to work without pay. Others, like Erie, contemplated closing altogether—permanently.

These public school crises stood in stark contrast to how states were treating alternatives to public school. While states were reducing their financial commitment to public schools, they were pumping enormous new resources into charters and vouchers—and making the policy environment for these alternatives more favorable. Charter schools, unlike traditional public schools, did not struggle during the recession.[11] Their state and federal funding skyrocketed. Too often, financial shortfalls in public school districts were the direct result of pro–charter school policies. North Carolina, again, offers a clear picture of public schools and charters moving in opposite directions. Between the start of the recession and 2014, North Carolina more than doubled its charter school budget.[12] During that same period, it cut public school funding by more than $2,000 per pupil, falling from a state whose funding levels ranked twentieth in the nation prior to charter school expansion to one that ranked forty-sixth in 2012.

States fund charters through various mechanisms, but a recurring problem was the way states required local school districts to transfer funds to charters. In Pennsylvania—a state that already grossly underfunded high-poverty districts—state rules made a bad situation worse. The funding transfers intensified the financial struggles of districts like Chester as the charter school population increased. By 2012, the Chester Public School District owed charter schools $43 million—almost half of the entire budget for Chester's public schools.[13] Litigation later revealed that Pennsylvania's charter reimbursement system created perverse incentives for charters to take the most profitable students and leave the higher-cost students behind in the public schools. The result was a vicious cycle in which Chester's public schools sank further into a hole and nearly hit financial insolvency.

In Ohio, charter school incentives fueled so much growth so quickly that fraud and corruption took hold. The state itself later admitted the need for new controls. But it was like the Wild West until then. Ohio charter schools received substantial funding increases every year between 2008 and 2015. While public schools received increases in a few of those years, they were modest at best—in one instance just one-tenth the size of the charter school increase. In fact, public school increases were not really increases at all because the required funding transfers to charters eviscerated the increase. In 2013–14, Ohio school districts, on average, went $256 in the hole for every student who went to a charter. Some went deeper in the red. Nine districts sent charters between 20 percent and 65 percent more money than they received from the state—a hard reality to justify when Ohio was already sending charters other funding on the side. All told, charter schools received $7,189 per pupil in state funding. Public school districts received less than half that amount.

These stories from the above states, unfortunately, are not unique. They are just a few of the worst examples in a parade of horribles that stretches from California to New Jersey. Time and again, states expanded charters while hammering public schools. Up close, the economy and an ever-evolving landscape of education policy overshadowed the significance of what was occurring: a preference for public school alternatives.

In the past, the federal government might have raised objections to the disinvestment in public schools. But there, too, a major shift in thinking was taking hold. It started with President Obama's choice for Secretary of Education. The presumptive choice for the job was Linda Darling-Hammond. She headed up education policy for Obama's transition team and is one the nation's foremost education experts. When it looked like she might land the secretary's job, education reformers excoriated her as an old-school, pro-teacher type who would stymie reform. A leading school choice advocate and former Bush official called her the "worst case scenario."[14] Obama took the easy way out and tapped Arne Duncan instead—someone whose track record in Chicago involved substantially expanding charters.

Obama said his goal in picking Duncan was to end the ideological divides:

> For years, we have talked our education problems to death in Washington, but failed to act, stuck in the same tired debates that have stymied our progress and left schools and parents to fend for themselves. Democrat versus Republican; vouchers versus the status quo; more money versus more reform—all along failing to acknowledge that both sides have good ideas and good intentions.[15]

Yet rather than end ideological divides, Obama's choice ceded enormous ground in the larger war over education. Whether the president was duped or soft-pedaling the agenda he wanted does not matter much now. Either way, the department took a serious turn on charters and teachers under Duncan.

For the next several years, the federal government promoted and sometimes forced charter school expansion[16]—well beyond the baby steps prior administrations had taken.[17] The Obama administration basically condoned everything states were doing with school funding and made it a little worse. Federal funding for public schools remained flat while the federal budget for charter schools increased by nearly 20 percent between 2008 and 2013.[18] President Obama called for another 50 percent increase for charters on top of that in 2016 (though he didn't get it).[19] The real surprise, though, is how much Duncan managed to accomplish through administrative action. He used executive power—which was particularly strong during a time of economic and regulatory crisis—to ensure that states adopted pro-charter policies.

His biggest coup was the process he set up for doling out innovation funds during the recession. As part of the economic recovery legislation, Congress had set aside a substantial chunk of money for education innovation but didn't specify exactly what schools could spend it on. Duncan, however, told states that if they wanted access to the money, charter schools had to be part of the mix. States that "put artificial caps on the growth of charter schools," he said, "will jeopardize their [grant] applications."[20] States, looking for money anywhere they could find it during the recession, saw little choice but to lift their charter school caps and make the policy environment more inviting.[21] Many states got what they had once worked to prevent—rapid charter school growth.

The overall result of these state and federal actions was stark—nearly 40 percent growth in the number of charter schools[22] and 200 percent growth in their enrollment.[23] Charters secured solid footholds during this period that are difficult to dislodge. Attempts to reverse the trends are derided as attacks on the children in charters (even if the point is to phase out some charters without affecting current students). Attempts to just slow new charter growth are characterized as inequitable limits on familial autonomy, teacher union pandering, or, even worse, racial paternalism.

Charter schools, as much as public schools, now claim an inherent right to exist.

Similar narratives are fueling private school vouchers and tax credits, even though these alternatives cannot plausibly claim the mantle of "public education." The attempt to expand them represents the clearest agenda to reshape and shrink the state's role in public education—a goal that becomes more audacious and explicit each year. The traditional voucher rationale was to help disadvantaged students escape failing schools.[24] They deserved the same options as wealthy families, voucher advocates would say. That argument was hard to criticize if it really worked to create equity that was otherwise unavailable in the public school system.

Older voucher programs were structured to fit that narrative as best they could.[25] They included income eligibility caps and geographic restrictions that limited vouchers to particularly distressed communities.[26] In general, they were pet projects with relatively little effect on the overall education system. But after a long period of failing to gain serious policy traction, voucher supporters moved away from the stated objective of assisting disadvantaged students and communities.

Core voucher advocates' relationship with minorities had always been a strange one anyway. Vouchers originated as a tool to maintain school segregation during the 1960s. That history always made minorities an unlikely constituency to push voucher policy over the top. The real constituency was libertarians, religious conservatives at odds with public school values, and wealthy families who thought school taxes were too high and wanted a little something back to finance their private school choices. Faced with those realities, voucher advocates eventually came clean with their motives. New voucher laws fully reflect the change.

During the recession, states began eliminating restrictions on who could participate in the programs. Middle-income and wealthy families, regardless of where they lived or what public school their kids might otherwise attend, could finally participate.[27] This meant vouchers were not about education quality or closing gaps in opportunity anymore—if they ever were. They were about reframing the state's approach to education.

Rather than ensuring a robust system of public education for all or promoting common goals, states should promote individual autonomy and freedom—however the individual might define it. Stated another way, public education was the problem, not the solution. The public school system stood in students' way, whereas private schools could liberate them.

Florida initiated the shift. Its prerecession voucher program only applied to low-income students attending a "failing" public school. The program was short-lived. The Florida Supreme Court declared it unconstitutional because the state funded the vouchers with money that the state constitution specifically reserves for public schools. Florida then began experimenting with ways to get around the problem. It developed an alternative form of vouchers, what it called a "scholarship" program. In most respects, it operated just like a voucher, paying for tuition at private schools. But rather than funding the tuition directly out of the state coffers, Florida gave tax credits to businesses and individuals who donated to a state "scholarship" fund that the state then used to pay private tuition. The real farce, though, was that Florida reimbursed businesses and individuals for the full cost of their "donations." The scheme was so finely tuned that, until the federal government caught on, donors could make money by also claiming an additional charity deduction on their federal taxes. That doesn't sound like any donation I've ever made. It sounds like the state turned private companies and individuals into conduits for laundering state money around the constitution—and allowing a little profiteering on the side. It worked. Legal challenges fell flat. The only limit was how much the state was willing to spend on tax credits.

When Florida first created its neo-voucher system of tax credits and scholarships just before the recession, the state immediately pumped an impressive amount into private school tuition—$178 million in 2006 and $204 million the next year.[28] But after the recession, when it began expanding the program beyond just poor families and increasing the value of the neo-vouchers,[29] its investments skyrocketed, jumping a hundred million dollars every few years. By 2016, Florida had more than quadrupled its investment in private school education to $759 million.[30] Current estimates predict that Florida is on the verge

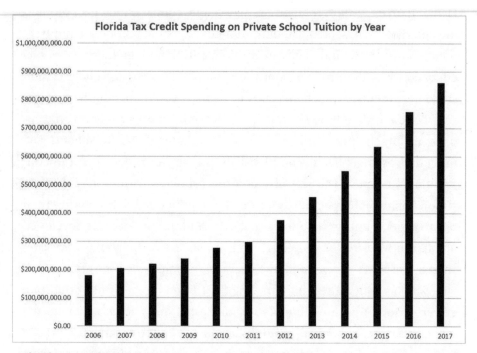

Florida tax credit spending on private school tuition, by year.
Courtesy of the author.

of spending $1 billion a year. Yet even that was not enough to satisfy the current generation of choice advocates. When Ron DeSantis was elected governor, they went back for more.

Florida's tax credit system may have solved the constitutional problem, but it created a practical one. The tax credits relied on middlemen, which meant a practical limit and inefficiency to the program. With DeVos cheering him on, DeSantis tweaked and revived the old voucher system in 2019, renaming it the Family Empowerment Scholarship. For all intents and purposes, it was the same type of voucher program the state Supreme Court previously struck down. No middleman. Just state revenues into private coffers, coming right out of the state's "operational formula for traditional public schools."[31] To the extent the voucher program had changed, it was in a bad way: the new one was not reserved for the state's poorest students. It was open to families making triple the federal poverty level: $77,250 for a family of four.[32]

Other states followed Florida's lead in redefining what was possible with vouchers. They drastically increased funding and raised income eligibility caps, sometimes effectively eliminating them altogether.[33] Some states never even bothered with tax credits. They just went straight for the public education dollars. With each year that passed, voucher legislation looked like a privatization arms race. New states vied to outdo the record-setting program others had passed the year before, wowing the school choice crowd with bolder payouts for broader cross sections of students.

Indiana started the race. In 2013, Indiana's school funding was on a bad run, down a total of 12 percent in real-dollar terms since 2008 (even though the economy had rebounded).[34] It chose that moment to enact the most expansive voucher program in the nation's history.[35] Over the next four years, voucher enrollment grew by roughly 600 percent and state funding for vouchers by more than 700 percent.[36] Two years later, Nevada blew that model out of the water, making a voucher theoretically available to every single public school student in the state. More dazzling was the handsome dollar amount the state was willing to spend on those vouchers. Nevada authorized the transfer of close to every state public school dollar to private school tuition. For each special education student, the state would transfer 100 percent of state per-pupil funding from the school district to a private account. Presumably, in an attempt to keep up the ruse that it was not favoring private over public education, vouchers for non–special education students were 90 percent of the public school allotment.[37]

The program had the potential to eliminate public education as we know it in certain parts of the state. It all hinged on how many students took the state up on its offer. If enough students signed up, public schools would have found it nearly impossible to operate at some point. In the end, only the state constitution stopped the threat. Nevada's Supreme Court declared the measure unconstitutional because it violated the state constitution's rules for public education funding.

Regardless, Nevada's legislature had shown what was politically possible, and others tried to do the same in places like Arizona, South Carolina, Tennessee, and Florida. Florida's new voucher program, for instance, is worth 95 percent of state education funding per pupil. At levels like that, the line distinguishing the state's role in public and private education—or favoring public education rather than private education—grows razor-thin. DeSantis's and DeVos's justification for pursuing this parity was an absurd redefinition of public education: "Look, if it's public dollars, it's public education."[38]

The last major sign of change in public education doesn't require a calculator or interpretation. During the recession, the teaching profession was turned upside down, and that was the explicit point. Teachers were labeled as the bad guys or girls, sometimes even called the "enemy." Such a narrative could justify everything else described above regarding money, public schools, and privatization. Think we spend too much on schools? It's because teachers are overcompensated and have too many benefits. Think students aren't learning enough? It's because of ineffective teachers. Think we need more experimentation? Get rid of unions. Think public education does not respond to your child's needs? Well, vouchers and charters can break the monopoly that caters to teachers rather than students. In almost every aspect of their professional life—salary, classrooms, expectations, and public persona—teachers were on the defensive. Commentators, including the front page of *Time* magazine, dubbed it a "War on Teachers."

Teachers have never been accorded high salaries or the professional status they deserve, but they have long held a special place in the public's heart. That special place did not always show up in their bank accounts, but it was reflected in tenure, respect, and reasonable expectations—whether it was in public policy or face-to-face interactions. Teachers, after all, spend enormous amounts of time with our children. The least we owed them was our goodwill. Knowing as much, the public at large and public education families, in particular, freely afforded it. Even if a few teachers were ineffective or difficult, teachers on the whole were not the ones to target with vitriol. If there was an enemy of public education, it was not teachers. During the recession, that all changed.

Conservatives who believed the unions had too much political power teamed with education reformers who thought the teaching profession

needed an overhaul. Government leaders looking to shrink public investments were eager to listen. The recession provided a perfect opportunity
and justification for scaling back teachers' salaries, rights, and political
influence. Why let a good crisis go to waste? What had previously looked
politically impossible suddenly looked feasible. With reform, anti-union,
and fiscally conservative groups working together, they might just fundamentally change states' relationship with teachers.

It worked. Across the nation, states made major changes to teachers' collective bargaining agreements, salary structures, overall benefits,
and teaching expectations without giving teachers anything in return.[39]
One of the first salvos was in Wisconsin, where Governor Scott Walker
made it his mission to break teacher unions (which would later open
the door to his school privatization reforms). In 2011, the state passed
new legislation to restrict, if not eliminate, public employees' collective
bargaining rights and slash their benefits. The real target of the law,
however, was teachers. The proof was in the pudding. Walker exempted
police, firefighters, and state troopers from the collective bargaining
changes, leaving teachers as the primary group to see its rights change.
Teacher compensation took a direct hit too, "decreasing by 8.2 percent
in inflation-adjusted terms."[40] Within four years, it fell even more—a
whopping $10,843 from teachers' paychecks and benefits disappeared.

Why the sudden attack, and in Wisconsin of all places? The Koch
brothers. As one democratic politician remarked, "The Koch brothers
are the poster children of the effort by multinational corporate America to try to redefine the rights and values of American citizens."[41] The
Koch brothers' own advocacy organization, Americans for Prosperity,
proclaimed that it was "going to bring fiscal sanity back to this great nation."[42] If that was the goal, Wisconsin education was on the trail to the
Holy Grail. Education is the largest state program by a long stretch in
all states, but Wisconsin was a state where the teaching profession was
particularly strong. If the Koch brothers could win there, they could
win anywhere. So they chose Wisconsin as the opening battleground to
reimagine and shrink the size of government through a war on public
education.

It also helped that Scott Walker looked to play the role. He was brash and eager to make a name for himself, maybe even propel himself to national office. He was happy to run with their playbook and make teachers the foil. Early in his administration, Walker and the Koch brothers got almost everything they wanted. They broke teacher unions, cut public education funding, adopted a statewide voucher program, and instituted a cap-free charter school system that local districts couldn't block.[43]

Their success stoked a new national discourse around teachers that spread. Some of the commentary was downright shocking. For example, reflecting on his experience fighting teachers and his qualification to fight terrorism as president, Walker said he would "do everything in [his] power to ensure that the threat from radical Islamic terrorists does not wash up on American soil. . . . If I can take on 100,000 [teacher] protesters, I can do the same across the world."[44] Although comparing teachers with terrorists is nonsensical, the fact that he would mention them in the same train of thought speaks volumes to how Walker saw teachers—or wanted others to see them—as villains. Governor Chris Christie took a similarly combative stance. He said teachers' unions deserved a "punch in the face" and were the "single most destructive force in public education."[45] They just don't care about children, he claimed.

With the normalization of that type of rhetoric, the opportunity to go after more than just collective bargaining was ripe. The other prize was teacher tenure. In the media, state legislatures, and even the courts, the war on teachers focused on tenure. By 2014, eighteen states had eliminated or restricted teacher tenure.[46] Rather than a benefit to attract talent to an underpaid profession or protect academic freedom, tenure became the boogeyman that protects countless scores of lazy and ineffective teachers. It was tenure, not low salaries, segregation, poor teaching conditions, or overtesting that held students back, they said. If states would just eliminate tenure, schools could sort the good teachers from the bad—and get rid of the latter.

The anti-teacher movement was so aggressive that it turned its policy argument into legal theory. In states where legislatures did not fully turn against teachers, the movement found individual plaintiffs to sue the state. Most famously, plaintiffs in California filed *Vergara v. State*, arguing that teacher tenure and seniority rights were unconstitutional. Tenure and seniority were supposedly the cause of inadequate education in high-poverty urban environments and, thus, violated students' fundamental right to education under the state constitution. The *Vergara* plaintiffs managed to convince the trial court that they were right. The California appellate courts eventually reversed the decision, noting that other far more important factors drive teaching and educational inequality, but by then, it was too late. The trial court decision was shaping a national narrative and encouraging copycat cases elsewhere.

Also fueling the agenda was the idea that new teacher evaluation systems could help us better manage teachers and improve instruction. In the past, there was only so much a state or principal could do to micromanage a teacher, to insist that he or she work harder or better. But new measurement tools might change that. Good measurement tools would eliminate a major stumbling block: how to fairly evaluate and compare teachers. They might even offer a justification for changing teachers' rights.

New statistical models could supposedly harness the power of all the tests that teachers had been administering for years. Teachers could be rated based on how their students performed on standardized tests. Those ratings would be an objective tool for determining how much to pay teachers and whether to terminate, transfer, or retain them. This idea took hold more than any other. Almost every state adopted a new evaluation system in one form or another during the recession.

The evaluation systems had an obvious surface appeal: identify the students demonstrating the most learning in each subject and figure out who taught them the material. Those would be the most effective teachers. The real world, unfortunately, is far more complicated. Isolating one teacher's effect on a student's scores from the effects of all the other teachers a student had that year (and in prior years) is nearly impossible. Isolating the effects of teaching from those important factors that exist outside school—poverty, family crisis, parental engagement—is just as hard.

Even if the models could deal with those things, the other obvious problems were huge gaps in the tests themselves: not all subjects are tested every year, and some—like social studies and foreign language—might not be tested at all. How could one even begin to statistically evaluate those teachers? States were so audacious that they implemented the evaluation systems anyway. It was fair enough, Florida thought, to rate social studies teachers based on how their students performed in other teachers' classes!

The flaws there and elsewhere showed up quickly. Individual teachers' ratings often varied wildly from one year to the next. Some teachers were labeled highly effective one year but ineffective the next—a hard conclusion to swallow unless you think good teachers turn into bad ones in a single year. A person recognized as "teacher of the year" under the old system in Houston was actually labeled as ineffective by the new statistical model. Equally inexplicable, teachers could, in a single year, fluctuate from effective to ineffective—and vice versa—depending on which exam they administered to their students.[47]

Details don't matter in war, though. They did not matter to the Secretary of Education, either. It was Arne Duncan, not Betsy DeVos, who fueled the fire. Duncan, for instance, praised the California trial court decision that struck down teacher tenure, saying it provided the nation with the "right lessons."[48] And he, as much as anyone, was responsible for the monumental shift toward statistical evaluations in nearly every state in the country, making new evaluation systems a condition for receiving federal grants and, later, waivers from No Child Left Behind sanctions. Not only did states have to adopt evaluation systems, they had to use them to make decisions about hiring, firing, and retaining individual teachers. Teachers' jobs would literally be on the line based on the ratings the statistical models spat out.

As these teacher attacks intersected with long-term cuts in education funding, things went from bad to worse and eventually decimated the teaching profession. Between 2009 and 2012, schools lost 300,000 teaching positions.[49] In the first year, one out of three school districts made plans to cut teachers in core subjects, not just electives. The following year, two out of three schools planned cuts.[50] Too often, the very teachers schools needed most—bright and committed teachers—were the ones who left. Droves of teachers fled the profession altogether, never to come back. The next generation of future teachers also saw what was happening and began looking for different careers before they even finished their degrees or entered the classroom. Nationally, the number of people pursuing education degrees fell by 30 percent.[51] The number of students pursuing and completing education degrees in California fell by 55 percent.[52]

At first, no one seemed to notice, but when states finally tried to hire a few teachers in 2014 and 2015, they had an all-out shortage on their hands and no levers to make it go away. The long-term damage had already been done. Every year since then, districts have struggled to hire even the most minimally qualified people. Some districts resorted to desperate measures just to get a warm body in the classroom. Kansas was mocked (or mourned) when it bought space on billboard signs begging for applications, seemingly regardless of qualifications. Soon enough, states from Texas to New York were doing the same thing. Had the teaching profession really become the equivalent of the trucking industry?

When qualified applicants did not come calling, districts had no choice but to cancel courses, increase class sizes, assign teaching overloads,[53] and hire substitute teachers to fill full-time positions.[54] States had no choice but to waive certification,[55] overlook college degree requirements, and let college interns teach full-time.[56] The shortage added insult to injury for the neediest students, driving teacher quality further down and class sizes further up in districts that struggle, even in the best of times, to hire and retain highly qualified teachers.[57]

Surely, I thought, things couldn't get much worse. Then 2016 happened. The Trump administration arrived, appointed Betsy DeVos, and proposed a radical new federal budget that suggested the public education crisis should be the new normal and intensify. The Trump administration made it clear that it wanted states to shift away from public education permanently and for the federal government to facilitate it. The vast expansion of vouchers, tax credits, and charter schools during the recession had not been enough. The recession-era policy changes may have seriously hobbled public education, but it had not mortally wounded it. Charters and vouchers needed to draw even with, if not eclipse, public education. So rather than leverage federal funds to en- sure equity in public schools, Trump sought to leverage federal funds to get states to spend their own money on school choice. The goal was to "provid[e] school choice to every American child living in poverty."[58] This, he said, would "fix" the nation's "broken education system."[59]

Since then, Trump's budgets have taken particular aim at a host of programs that serve needy students in public schools. Trump's very first federal budget proposal called for a total of $4 billion in cuts to literacy for students with disabilities and limited English proficiency, class-size reduction initiatives, and after-school and summer programs. Those funds would instead be spent on the school choice agenda. And any new money that might be added to programs serving low-income students in public schools would come with two major caveats. First, to get access to additional money for poor students, districts would have to agree that every penny would go toward school choice. Second, districts would have to completely revamp the way they assign students and fund schools. More precisely, districts would have to let parents choose their own schools. Those schools could even be private. All state, local, and federal money—not just new additional federal money—would have to follow students to their new schools. In other words, Trump proposed the possibility of every single federal and state education dollar flowing somewhere other than the traditional public school. If that ever hap- pened, all bets were off as to public education's future.

While Congress has yet to sign off on those radical changes, Betsy DeVos has achieved others through administrative action. She has shrunk the Department of Education from within and eliminated students' reg- ulatory protections. She has also used every bit of her political capital and power to push states to adopt and expand their charter, voucher, and tax credit programs. On that score, she has been particularly successful.

Maybe the administration's most notable victory, however, was through the tax code. Though rarely understood in the popular discourse,

Trump's signature achievement—tax reform—included two hits on public education. The first allowed families to transform their college savings accounts by using them to pay private elementary and secondary school tuition tax-free. The real beneficiaries of the change are those already in or planning to go to private schools and wealthy enough to pay for it. The second hit was to cap the amount of state and local taxes that an individual can claim as a credit on their federal tax return. That may sound bland, but the lion's share of state and local taxes go where they have always gone—public education. Eating into that deduction disincentivizes (or penalizes) states that heavily invest in public education. In short, Trump's tax bill expanded tax exemptions for private school education and narrowed them for public schools.

States' first steps after the financial reality of the pandemic set in suggest that they are ready to repeat all these same mistakes again. Gouge education and look for silver bullet alternatives. The Trump administration is, likewise, urging them on and looking for ways to divert coronavirus aid money from public schools to private schools.

Lawmakers, lobbyists, and commentators will tell you that charters, vouchers, school funding, and teachers are questions of education policy. They will tell you they want to improve educational opportunity. If you aren't sure about that, you will get sucked into policy papers about things like the effectiveness and cost of charters versus public schools, vouchers versus public schools, markets versus monopolies, and organized labor versus incentivized and competitive labor. If you are not already an education expert, your mind might very well go numb as you sort through the statistical calculations and terms of art. At the very least, you will be unsure of where the evidence actually stands—and even more so if you recognize that private choice lobbyists and advocates financed many of the studies.

The point of this book is to help you see that entertaining those policy questions is partly to blame for the current mess. Sounds like a strange point from a man who has made his career in education policy. It might even sound like something to say if you do not like the answers to the policy questions. So, to be clear, I have studied the facts closely and believe the strong weight of the evidence indicates we have made big policy mistakes. But I won't rehash any of that here because today's policy debates skew our frame of reference, trick us into looking at the wrong measures of education's value and purpose, and distract us from fundamental questions about the role of public education in our democracy. The important question is whether the rise of charter, voucher, and anti-teacher movements involves something more than just an education debate. Is the firm etching of these movements into state law a sign that government (or at least those running it) does not believe in public education anymore, that government is giving up on it? If so, do these changes pose a threat to our democracy?

Our recent education debates have been occurring in a historical vacuum—long on numbers and short on historical context. The debates are caught up in the here and now of politics, individual desires, and corporate interests. Education decision-making—and thus policy—has always been part of a much larger historical and constitutional framework. That framework has long defined who we are as a nation, what type of democracy we want, and how far we have to go. That history and constitutional framework represent the hopes and dreams of a nation where all men and women might be equal citizens and participants in this thing we call democracy, or, in the precise words of our Constitution, "a republican form of government." While the nation has never quite realized those hopes, it has, in the best of times, looked to its core ideas and commitments to propel the nation to a closer approximation. In the worst of times, it has looked away and fallen victim to the times. It has shamed itself.

Education has always been at the center of those ideas and commitments. At our founding, in our most significant constitutional moments, and during our most serious political challenges, the commitment to public education—to the right to education—has served as the ideological and practical anchor for democracy. My telling of this history is to remind us of our fundamental guideposts and offer a fair lens through which to assess today's education discussions. You can judge for yourself whether we are moving toward our highest ideas or away. But to do that, you must start at the beginning.

CHAPTER 2

A NATION FOUNDED ON EDUCATION

If a nation expects to be ignorant and free . . .
it expects what never was and never will be.

THOMAS JEFFERSON[1]

TALK OF THE RIGHT TO EDUCATION GENERALLY BEGINS AND ends with the text of the Constitution. The word "education" cannot, *implied* to the surprise of many, be found in the Constitution, so they conclude that education holds no special place in our constitutional structure. This isolated fact dominates the thinking of those who should know better. The list of scholars, judges, and politicians who say the federal government has no role in public education is a long one. Even worse, some thought leaders are now saying that the concept of public education—whether run by state or federal government—is a farce. They ignore an incredibly rich education history.

TJ Our founding fathers were deeply concerned with common people's access to public education. That concern has stuck with our nation ever since. At the nation's two most pivotal periods—Independence and the

51

Civil War—the nation embedded education in our constitutional democracy. This simple claim about the role of education in our constitutional democracy upsets a lot of people. If you repeat the history you are about to read, they may even tell you it is not true. That's because they won't like the conclusions you'll draw, not because your facts are wrong. Don't be dismayed.

The power of history is often best measured by the emotions it elicits and how much it forces people to rethink what they thought they knew. Accepting that the conventional wisdom is incorrect or incomplete is not easy, not something the mind is eager to do. We grow accustomed to the conventional wisdom. We absorb the conventional wisdom until it becomes our own. We build values and rules around it. And the more we repeat the conventional wisdom, the further the truth gets buried. Yes, we might still occasionally find shreds of truth, but we minimize, discredit, or ignore them—not because we want to delude ourselves, but because we do not recognize the truth for what it is.

I have been studying and writing about education rights for two decades. I have litigated school cases, written dozens of research articles, given even more lectures and interviews, and testified as an expert. I did not, however, clearly see the full scope of our education history until recently. I knew the desegregation story very well. But I knew overall education history in bits and pieces—some parts extremely well and the rest just well enough to follow the overall story. Never once had I put the pieces of the public education origin story together for myself. The origin story remained something akin to a puzzle with important pieces missing. Then an up-and-coming Reconstruction-era historian alerted me to how easy the internet has made it to access original archival documents, and I began to dig into the history for myself. I was completely blown away by what I found.

Three years of research and a lifetime of background knowledge slowly led me to a single conclusion: the ideological, legal, and constitutional roots of our public education system stretch to the very founding of our nation. I did not reach this conclusion lightly. *How could such an important point have been lost on others?* I asked myself. Maybe I was misinterpreting something. But as the facts mounted, my skepticism faded and I followed the facts where they led. In retrospect, I can appreciate why the conventional wisdom is so sticky with education. Its narrative is painted so well that we never ask the right questions. And without the right questions, we look for information in the wrong places or miss its importance even when it stares us in the face.

The best jumping-off point for dislodging conventional wisdom is those important historical facts that are beyond dispute. Those facts, standing alone, beg for an explanation, and even the skeptic may begin to ask questions that should raise the possibility that there is something more to education's origin story.

The undisputed and easiest facts to verify are these: All fifty state constitutions include an education clause or other language that requires the state to provide public education. Most of these clauses were first enacted or substantially amended in the immediate aftermath of the Civil War. By law, Congress explicitly conditioned Virginia's, Mississippi's, and Texas's readmission to the Union based on the education rights and obligations they had just put into their constitutions. And while some states previously made no education commitments in their constitutions, after the Civil War, no state would ever again enter the Union without an education clause in its constitution. The single one to try it, New Mexico, saw its initial petition for statehood rejected. The commonalities in these state constitutions pose a straightforward question: Are these commonalities coincidental, independent accidents of history or the result of some larger constitutional principle?

The second set of undisputed facts are these: Save the original colonies that predated the Constitution, states' public education systems have all been funded and expanded by federal land grants. The federal land grant system started in the late 1700s, just a few years after national independence. To this day, states still hold these lands and natural resources, which, by federal dictate, can only be used for public education. In short, that land resides in a centuries-old legal lockbox. Why did the federal government dictate how states would use this land and under what constitutional authority or theory?

These facts put the conventional wisdom on the defensive. The historical proximity of states' education clauses, the nearly uniform approach to their substance, and the original federal role in financing the schools they produced don't look like random coincidences. Once we begin to look for an explanation of these facts—to believe we actually need an explanation—the history of education makes it hard to accept the notion that fifty different states have acted independently (many for more than two centuries) and somehow ended up in roughly the same place in terms of their constitutions and plans for delivering education. It is far easier to accept the idea that, notwithstanding the various differences in the development of education across the states, our national commitment to public education stretches to our formal founding and has guided the nation ever since. Now to that story.

PUBLIC EDUCATION WAS EMBEDDED IN THE IDEAL IMAGE OF THE nation our founders sought to create. Before the United States had a constitution, our founders believed the nation needed a public education system. The United States was an experiment in democracy unlike anything the world had ever seen, turning away from government dominated by elites and hoping that the common man could rule himself. They believed that if this experiment had any chance of standing the test of time, the nation needed to ensure everyday citizens had access to learning opportunities that prepared them for self-government. As James Madison, our fourth president and "father of our Constitution," remarked: "a popular Government, without popular information, or the means of acquiring it, is but a Prologue to a Farce or a Tragedy."[2] But the nation's education agenda was clearest in the writings and work of two of our other most prominent founding fathers—John Adams and Thomas Jefferson.

Adams served as the nation's first vice president and second president. Well before that, he and Thomas Jefferson, the nation's first secretary of state and third president, worked closely to secure America's independence. Both were delegates in the Continental Congress that declared independence from Britain, and both served on the committee assigned to write the formal Declaration of Independence. Jefferson was the principal author of the Declaration and Adams one of its fiercest advocates.

They, as much as any others, built and laid the ideological foundations of the nation. Public education was part of that ideological foundation. Well before they were elected president, even before their work on the Declaration of Independence, Jefferson and Adams explained the role that education would have to play in our democracy. Their initial thinking expanded over time and influenced education policy both before and well after they had left the presidency. In short, their perfectly articulated thinking captures the national education imperative and ultimately the legal agenda to pursue it.

Adams detailed his thoughts first. As early as 1765, he began making the case for public education and tying it to independence—a decade prior to the Declaration of Independence. In a moment of prerevolutionary bluster, Adams wrote, "A native of America who cannot read and write is as rare . . . as a comet or an earthquake."[3] While a gross factual overstatement, his underlying message was that America was distinct from the European monarchies. He continued: "All candid foreigners who have passed thro' this country, and conversed freely with all sorts of people here, will allow, that they have never seen so much knowledge and civility among the common people in any part of the world." But if America was to have liberty and self-government, he urged, the country could not rest on its laurels. It had to provide for the education of its youth. American education was both a predicate to self-government and a justification for independence itself. His plans for education in this respect were plans for American independence.

A nation that placed political power in the hands of the people made it in everyone's interests, even the interests of the elites, to support public education. Adams wrote: "The preservation of the means of knowledge among the lowest ranks, is of more importance to the public than all the property of all the rich men in the country. It is even of more consequence to the rich themselves, and to their posterity."[4] The lowest ranks, as much as the highest, would set the course of public policy. In other words, the stability of government, protection of private property, and all the other rights that Americans valued would rest on the education of the common man.

This thinking, which Jefferson shared, was a natural extension of the radical idea of America itself. America was to be a bold new society of self-made men. A man, so the myth goes, could chart his own economic destiny in America, limited only by his personal merit and effort. And all would have an equal say in public policy, from the richest to the poorest. Public education had to match the boldness of these democratic aspirations. For that reason, Adams envisioned an education system so grand that it is "unknown to any other people ancient or modern."[5]

The trouble in those early days was that the country still had a long way to go to deliver that education. Criticizing that gap, Noah Webster, the author of the iconic dictionary, wrote that our underdeveloped education system was a "glaring contradiction in a country where 'every citizen who is worth a few shillings' can vote." Wanting far more for the nation's children, he chided the national and state constitutions as professing republican values but retaining "monarchial" tendencies toward education.[6] The challenge, he was pointing out, was not to declare independence but to actually educate citizens to exercise independence. The nation's formal political independence, of course, came first. Once it did, the education imperative followed even more intensely.

Benjamin Rush captured the shift perfectly. Rush was an influential figure in the Revolutionary period. He signed the Declaration of Independence and his peers considered him the equal of George Washington and Benjamin Franklin. Rush wrote that "education has acquired a new complexion by the independence of our country. The form of government we have assumed, has created a new class of duties to every American. It becomes us, therefore, to examine our former habits upon this subject and . . . to adapt our modes of teaching to the peculiar form of our government."[7] Making a similar point, Jefferson questioned the legitimacy of a government that did not care for the education of its people.

Jefferson, in the text of the Declaration of Independence, reasoned that the legitimacy of government rests on individual autonomy and consent: "Governments are instituted" to "secure" the right to "Life, Liberty and the pursuit of Happiness." But those governments only "deriv[e] their just powers from the consent of the governed." Writing elsewhere, Jefferson explained that education makes consent possible. To meaningfully consent to the exercise of governmental power, the common man must be able to fully appreciate his own interests, resist the political agenda of those who would exploit him, and preserve his own liberty. His ability to do those things depends on education. Absent education, a man simply lives under the unjust thumb of others.

One of the first steps in dealing with this quandary of self-government was to shift education responsibility from the individual to government. This was no small task. Education had been almost entirely a private and religious affair to that point. But insofar as education was a natural extension of republican government, public education was a duty that government owed its citizens—at least if republican government was going to live up to its name. Adams was particularly forceful on this point, writing that education "ought to be the care of the public" and "maintained at the public expense."[8] In carrying out this duty, "no expense . . . would be too extravagant."[9] By public, Adams meant government, both national and state.[10] Jefferson agreed, later explaining in an address to Congress that government is the only body fit for the job of educating all citizens.[11]

Shortly after the Declaration of Independence, Jefferson and Adams began the practical work of building public education in their home states. Jefferson, in a state with far less experience with public education and its fiscal demands, struggled against the odds, while Adams accomplished remarkable firsts in a state predisposed to support them. But their work's importance goes well beyond what it did or did not achieve for the people of Virginia and Massachusetts. The broader importance lies in the ideas they planted and the real-world examples they provided. Those ideas and examples eventually grew and spread at both the state and federal level. State constitutional clauses on education, land division to support and protect education, and centralized systems of education would take years and, in some instances, decades to fully develop. But their origin traces back to Jefferson's and Adams's initial frameworks.

If Adams offered the first inspirational vision for public education, Jefferson offered the first comprehensive plan. Jefferson proposed a bill to establish an education system in Virginia before the Revolutionary War was even over, which is telling. In the middle of war, Jefferson saw education as so central to the idea of American democracy and independence that he worked consistently on "A Bill for the More General Diffusion of Knowledge." In 1776, the bill began its way through committee in the Virginia General Assembly.[12] In 1779, just a few days after the third anniversary of the Declaration of Independence, the bill formally came before the full General Assembly. In terms much like those used in the Declaration of Independence, the bill's preamble explained its motivation:

> Certain forms of government are better calculated than others to protect individuals in the free exercise of their natural rights . . . , yet experience hath shewn, that even under the best forms, those entrusted with power have, in time, and by slow operations, perverted it into tyranny. . . . The most effectual means of preventing this would be, to illuminate, as far as practicable, the minds of the people at large, and more especially to give them knowledge of those facts.[13]

Rather than allow education to depend on "wealth, birth or other accidental condition or circumstance," the bill proclaimed the path toward democratic equality required that children be "educated at the common expence of all."[14]

The bill went on to specify a number of details, including the election of public officials, their responsibility to build schools, the subjects to be taught, the appointment of school leaders, the compensation of teachers, the raising of education revenue, and even the materials to be used in building grammar schools. In a letter to Adams, Jefferson summarized his plan this way:

This [bill] proposed to divide every county into wards of five or six miles square, like your townships; to establish in each ward a free school for reading, writing and common arithmetic; to provide for the annual selection of the best subjects from these schools, who might receive, at the public expense, a higher degree of education at a district school; and from these district schools to select a certain number of the most promising subjects, to be completed at an university, where all the useful sciences should be taught. Worth and genius would thus have been sought out from every condition of life, and completely prepared by education for defeating the competition and birth for public trusts.[15]

[handwritten margin note: attempt to eliminate opportunity barriers caused by class]

Much to Jefferson's dismay, however, the bill never saw its way to legislative victory.

Many today look on the bill's failure as a wholesale rejection of public schools, but they ignore context. Writing to George Washington, Jefferson explained that the cost and means of creating a vast system of state-supported schools, at that particular time, scared the General Assembly—understandably so. The cost of the war was already staggering, no end was in sight, and Jefferson's bill called for new taxes. This new burden, during and in the immediate aftermath of war, was one that the state believed it could not yet carry.[16] Jefferson, in fact, later indicated that he fully appreciated the state's hesitance. He did not begrudge the result nor let it dampen his spirit for education. To the contrary, he was encouraged: "I never saw [a bill] received with more enthusiasm than that was . . . by the House of Delegates, who ordered it printed. And it seemed afterwards, that nothing but the extreme distress of our resources prevented its being carried into execution, even during the war."[17] *[handwritten margin note: why wasn't it revived after war debts?]*

John Adams's work in Massachusetts moved forward under a different set of circumstances. Massachusetts's economy and demographics were far different and the foundations of education older than in Virginia. Timing was also important. Adams's most significant education work came after the French had joined the war in support of America and victory appeared more likely. These differences allowed John Adams, in 1780, to achieve one of the most significant accomplishments in educational history: he wrote the Massachusetts Constitution and placed education at the center of the state's understanding of government.

MGSS is #1 best public ed state today

The Massachusetts Constitution of 1780 is the oldest working constitution in the world. Yet its significance goes beyond its age. It included two crucial innovations. First, it separated the powers of government into three different branches—the executive, the legislature, and the judiciary. The broader wisdom of this innovation was confirmed later when the US Constitution copied it. The second innovation was its education clause. The Massachusetts Constitution declared that "wisdom and knowledge . . . diffused generally among the body of the people [are] necessary for the preservation of their rights and liberties. . . . [Thus,] it shall be the duty of legislatures and magistrates, in all future periods of this commonwealth, to cherish the . . . public schools."

These two fundamental concepts—that education is the citizenry's best guarantee of their other rights and that the collective political body has a duty to provide it—became a model for state and national activity. Massachusetts's impact on other states' education systems is well documented. Too often missed is its influence at the federal level. Jefferson's work is similarly understood as a local state affair. But Jefferson's and Adams's deep impact on federal education policy can be seen just a few years later if one stops to connect the dots.

In the mid- and late 1780s, Congress was focused on westward expansion. It needed to wrest away the colonies' claims to the western territories and establish a coherent plan for developing those lands. Systematically developing the territories would offer Congress the opportunity to define the nation not just in words, but in practice. Congress could create new ideal states and governments, free of the weight of the status quo and historical biases in the colonies that often divided them. That agenda would culminate in the Northwest Ordinances of 1785 and 1787.

As an accident of circumstance, neither Adams nor Jefferson had a front row seat to these monumental legislative steps in the nation's development, which explains why their influence on them is obscured. Adams and Jefferson were serving abroad as the nation's foreign ministers to Britain and France. They both, however, still held their passion for the nation's domestic education plans. In 1786, Adams wrote of the task that lay ahead for the country: "Before any great things are accomplished, a memorable change must be made in the system of Education and knowledge must become so general as to raise the lower ranks of Society nearer to the higher." He reiterated that the "Education of a Nation . . . must become the National Care and expence."[18]

Jefferson also called for the United States to make a national commitment to public education. He wrote to George Washington to make his feelings known. From his post in France in 1786, Jefferson implored George Washington: "Establish the law for educating the common people. This it is the business of the state to effect and on a general plan."[19] Jefferson also wrote to his constitutional law professor at William and Mary in 1786:

> The most important bill in our whole code is that for the diffusion
> of knowledge among the people. No other sure foundation can be
> devised for the preservation of freedom, and happiness. . . . Preach,
> my dear Sir, a crusade against ignorance; establish and improve the
> law for educating the common people. Let our countrymen know
> that the people alone can protect us against these evils [that "kings,
> nobles, and priests" invariably visit on the people], and that the tax
> which will be paid for this purpose is not more than the thousandth
> part of what will be paid to kings, priests, and nobles who will rise
> up among us if we leave the people in ignorance.[20]

In the context of a fledging nation struggling to find its balance, Jefferson was clearly articulating education as a central component of meeting democracy's challenges.

The timing of these letters was auspicious for other reasons. Adams and Jefferson were writing while the Northwest Ordinances and the US Constitution were under active consideration. And Jefferson continued to agitate even after those documents were formalized. Just a few months after the Constitutional Convention hammered out its final draft, Jefferson wrote to James Madison, the principal drafter of the Constitution. Jefferson remained as adamant about the nation's education agenda as he had ever been, repeating his fundamental belief that: "Above all things, . . . the education of the common people [must] be attended to; convinced that on this good sense we may rely with the most security for the preservation of a due degree of liberty."[21]

Jefferson's concerns were well founded in important respects. His experience in Virginia had revealed that the states and the nation had a long way to go in establishing the type of education system he and Adams envisioned. And this is to say nothing of places like the western territories, which remained a scattering of settlements in the wilderness (though Native Americans, of course, had their own there). But in another respect, Adams and Jefferson had already won the ideological battle for education. This victory can be found in the text and structure of the Northwest Ordinances of 1785 and 1787.

The Ordinances placed public education at the literal center of the nation's plan for geographic expansion and statehood in the territories. The 1785 Ordinance specified how every square inch of the territories would be divided into counties and towns. Every new town had to set aside one-ninth of its land and one-third of its natural resources for the financial support of public education. And every town had to reserve one of its lots for the operation of a public school. Congress even specified the precise lot for the construction of schools. In towns divided up into thirty-six equally sized squares, four lots touched the exact center of town. One of them was lot 16—the one on which towns were to build schools.

The Northwest Ordinance of 1787 reiterated and expanded on these details and how territories could become states. But the final provisions of the Ordinance took a different, less technical tone. Written in a constitutional tone, the final provisions declared the various rights of citizens and the goals their states must pursue. Many of these constitution-like ideas would, a few years later, become part of the US Constitution itself.

For instance, the Ordinance included the familiar rights to freedom of religion, "trial by jury," and bail. It likewise included prohibitions against "cruel and unusual punishment" and deprivations of "liberty or property." Alongside those rights, it declared that as a necessity of "good government and the happiness of mankind, schools and the means of education shall forever be encouraged."

The Ordinance's lofty language and provision of land alone were not enough to cause a nationwide system of education to spring forth. Land in an undeveloped frontier was not that valuable. It sadly never generated enough resources to support a system of schools in places where no formal government, no tax base, and no system of doing things existed. What the territories really needed was money. The United States did not have any money, so it gave what it had—land. But it was the nation's willingness to give what it had, to demand very specific commitments in return, and to articulate education as the foundation of government, not the short-term efficacy of the plan, that makes the Northwest Ordinances so important.

In those same aspects, we can also see straight lines moving forward and back in time—back to Jefferson's and Adams's education ideas and work, forward to Congress's demands for affirmative education guarantees following the Civil War, and onward to a time when every state in the nation would guarantee education through its constitution. It borders on implausible to tell a story of education that disconnects these events and ideas.

The Northwest Ordinance's provisions were the natural corollaries of Jefferson's and Madison's work in their home states. Just as Jefferson's Virginia bill called for six-mile square townships with a central block reserved for the schools, a decade later so, too, did the Northwest Ordinance carve townships into squares and situate education at their center. Just as Adams's 1780 Massachusetts Constitution declared education "diffused generally among the body of the people [to be] necessary for the preservation of their rights and liberties," so, too, did the Northwest Ordinance declare education to be "necessary to good government and the happiness of mankind." And the Northwest Ordinance's declaration that "schools and the means of education shall forever be encouraged" was but a simplified restatement of Massachusetts's constitutional command to its legislature that "in all future periods of this commonwealth, to cherish the . . . public schools."

If those textual connections weren't enough, Jefferson's and Adams's hands were all over the dealmaking that led to the Northwest Ordinances. John Adams was part of the US team that negotiated the treaty that ended the Revolutionary War and relinquished Great Britain's claims to the Northwest Territory. Jefferson then authored the plan for the individual states to cede their claims in the Northwest Territory to the United States. That plan became the Northwest Ordinance of 1784, which, as its name suggests, was the first version of the more important and detailed Northwest Ordinances of 1785 and 1787. Viewed from start to finish, then, Jefferson's and Adams's early theories of education in American democracy succeeded in becoming part of the legal plan the nation adopted for itself.

SKEPTICS OF THE RIGHT TO EDUCATION MIGHT STILL SAY: "So what?" Nice story, but the Ordinances, after all, were only statutes and superseded by the Constitution in any event. The Ordinances, and education's role in them, however, cannot be so easily dismissed. The Northwest Ordinance of 1787 is one of the most significant legal documents in our nation's history and the current United States Code treats it as such. Every bound volume of the United States Legal Code begins with a section called Front Matter. The Front Matter includes the nation's four "organic laws" in chronological order. Three of them should be obvious to most: the 1776 Declaration of Independence, the 1777 Articles of Confederation (our first fatally flawed attempt at a constitution), and, of course, the US Constitution. The final member of the organic law quartet—the Northwest Ordinance of 1787—sets nestled between the Articles of Confederation and the Constitution.

It rests alongside these three other pivotal documents because of its direct connection to our constitutional structure. While the Declaration of Independence and Articles of Confederation often provide historical context for interpreting our Constitution, the Northwest Ordinances are intertwined with the Constitution's actual adoption. In many important ways, the history and effect of the Constitution and the Ordinances are inseparable. First, the documents were passed by many of the same people. Several delegates to the Constitutional Convention simultaneously served in the Continental Congress that passed the Ordinances. In fact, the Continental Congress could not manage a quorum for most of the summer of 1787 because too many delegates were at the Constitutional Convention in Philadelphia. But when it came to the Northwest Ordinance, the Continental Congress saw its work as equally important. In midsummer, the Secretary of Congress sent a letter to some of the constitutional convention delegates telling them that it was "absolutely necessary for the great purpose of the union" that they return to Congress.[22] In response, delegates from North Carolina and Georgia quickly set out for New York (where Congress met at the time). Within days of their arrival in New York, Congress passed the Northwest Ordinance and—in remarkable fashion—with a unanimous vote. Shocking

Second, the Northwest Ordinance's substance is a constitutional charter of sorts. Practically speaking, it established the foundational structure for the nation to grow and organize itself for the next two centuries. Precise rules for dividing up land, developing the nation's vast territories, and detailing the path that these territories would follow to become states are not the work of everyday legislation. They are the work of a national charter. Those rules and their effects remain in place to this day. The Northwest Ordinances and their principles have dictated the admission of more than thirty states to the union—basically all the states except the original colonies. As one scholar put it, "The Northwest Ordinances were the colonial Americans' institutional thumbprint on the American continent all the way from the Ohio River to the Pacific."[23] More concretely, the Ordinances were the first detailed legal articulation of the norms and rights around which we would build the nation. Many of those legal norms and rights were directly transferred into the Constitution shortly thereafter.

Third, the final deal struck in the Northwest Ordinances was intertwined with the deal struck in the Constitution. In the decade following independence, states held all the power and resources. They effectively remained sovereign nations operating under a joint contract called the Articles of Confederation. The Articles even characterized the states' relationship as "a firm league of friendship with each other." Any national action required a supermajority agreement among the states, meaning that individual states held tremendous power to veto national policy. As sovereigns, the states also asserted independent claims to the western territories, claims that conflicted with one another. New York, Connecticut, and Virginia, for instance, all claimed the land that eventually became Ohio. Settling these disputes, ceding those lands to a national government, and devising even-handed rules and principles for later incorporating those territories as states were key to unifying the existing states into a nation rather than just a league of friends. Together, the Northwest Ordinances and a new constitution represented the grand design to achieve that end.

FROM THIS PERSPECTIVE, THE NORTHWEST ORDINANCE'S EDUCATION agenda cannot be separated from our constitutional structure and vision. And it was under this constitutional structure and vision that George Washington, John Adams, Thomas Jefferson, and James Madison took office and served as presidents of the United States. To no surprise, all would assert education's utmost importance and call for its expansion. For instance, in his farewell address to the nation, written as an open letter republished throughout the country, President Washington refocused the nation on the unique challenge of our democracy. He offered this maxim: "Promote then as an object of primary importance, Institutions for the general diffusion of knowledge. In proportion as the structure of a government gives force to public opinion, it is essential that public opinion should be enlightened." In other words, the more power that is given to people, the more education is demanded for the people.

Again, in his final Annual Message to Congress three months before leaving office, Washington pressed Congress to make good and build on its education commitments:

> The assimilation of the principles, opinions, and manners of our country-men by the common education of a portion of our youth from every quarter well deserves attention. The more homogenous our citizens can be made in these particulars the greater will be our prospect of permanent Union; and a primary object of . . . a national institution should be the education of our youth in the science of government. In a republic what species of knowledge can be equally important and what duty more pressing on its legislature than to patronize a plan for communicating it to those who are to be the future guardians of the liberties of the country?[24]

President Jefferson made similar but even bolder claims and requests. In his 1806 address to Congress, he called for future taxes and excess trust funds to be spent on education and explained precisely why: "Education is here placed among the articles of public care [because] . . . a public institution can alone supply those sciences which, though rarely called for, are yet necessary to complete the circle, all the parts of which contribute to the improvement of the country, and some of them to its preservation." President Jefferson offered one more crucial request—a request that directly contradicts those who today claim that the federal government lacks a legitimate role in public education. Jefferson said that education was so important to the nation that Congress should, if necessary, amend the Constitution to allow for education's support. The request itself is remarkable. Jefferson was no fan of consolidating power in the federal government—quite the opposite. This request reveals his conviction that Congress should play an important role in education no matter what. That Congress continued to support education without such an amendment likewise demonstrates members' thoughts on the permissible and appropriate federal role in education.

James Madison's presidency lacked any dramatic pleas for education. The time for offering foundational ideas and vision may have passed by the time he took office in 1809. The task then was not to articulate democratic education ideas but to address practical issues like improving the financing, delivery, and access plans for education. Those practical issues were more local in nature and the work of resolving them getting underway in the states—circumstances generally beneath presidential involvement. But when Madison left office, he dove into the more practical challenges confronting public education, devoting a substantial portion of his post-presidency work to education.[25]

Madison's 1830 letter discussing Virginia's schools reveals just how closely he followed the details of public education expansion. He began the letter with the same urgency that Washington and Jefferson had offered in their addresses to Congress, writing that a "satisfactory plan for primary schools is certainly a vital desideratum in our Republic." Then Madison moved to details, lamenting that such an education plan is "found to be a difficult one everywhere" and urging Virginia to look to other states' plans for solutions. Madison also clearly understood regional differences in educational opportunity and took them seriously. He even hinted that those regional differences said something about our democracy, writing about Southern states' "serious difficulty" in providing education and reasoning that the lack of "density in the free parts [of those states was] the main cause of the little success of the experiment now on foot with us."

Madison's 1822 correspondence with Kentucky's lieutenant governor is similarly telling—first, that the lieutenant governor would write to Madison seeking advice on the subject and, second, for the substance of Madison's response. In the 1820s, Kentucky's common fund for schools struggled due to failures in the bond market. These challenges presumably played a role in the lieutenant governor reaching out to Madison. Regardless, Madison's response offers a glimpse of how Jefferson's and Adams's theories and work on education had come full circle into reality.

Kentucky reached statehood during the early years of nation building. It was the second new state following the passage of the Northwest

Ordinance of 1787 (although it was not part of the Northwest Territory itself). Madison emphasized the important strides Kentucky had made in living up to democracy's promise. He wrote:

> The liberal appropriations made by the Legislature of Kentucky for a general system of Education cannot be too much applauded. . . . Knowledge will forever govern ignorance: And a people who mean to be their own Governors, must arm themselves with the power which knowledge gives.
>
> . . . I was myself among the foremost advocates for submitting to the Will of the [people in the region] the question and the time of its becoming a separate member of the American family. Its rapid growth & signal prosperity in this character have afforded me much pleasure; which is not a little enhanced by the enlightened patriotism which is now providing for the State a Plan of Education embracing every class of Citizens, and every grade & department of Knowledge.[26]

The final founding father to become president, James Monroe, stands out primarily for his uneventful tenure when it came to education, but the two presidents who followed him—John Quincy Adams and Andrew Jackson—oversaw the establishment of additional important milestones. John Quincy Adams's presidency revisited the Northwest Ordinance, the foundational document his father and Thomas Jefferson helped shape. Recognizing the need to create more public schools, an 1826 amendment to the Northwest Ordinance required that new townships reserve more land for schools. Andrew Jackson's presidency followed that with what may have been the most significant event since the original Ordinances. In 1836, the nation made an enormous new financial investment in public education. Tariffs, the collection of war debts, and sale of federal lands generated an "unprecedented surplus" that amounted to "the largest asset" in the country's history up to that point.[27] Congress distributed those assets to the states. Ohio's governor referred to the transfer as "the inheritance of the people, originally gained by the toil, and suffering, and blood of their revolutionary fathers,"[28] and the revolution's children invested in public education just as their forefathers would have wanted. With cold, hard cash in hand, states directly funded education. Twenty-two of twenty-six states spent substantial portions of the "people's inheritance" on public education. Eight states spent every penny of their inheritance on public education.[29]

The federal story of education did not end there; it shifted to more practical questions. Those questions were necessary for fully completing the task of building the education systems the founders had envisioned—and maybe even for correcting some of their errors. There was simply too much to do, too little time, and too few guidelines to get it right the first time. After the founders passed, contentious debates arose over whether to centralize, secularize, and professionalize public education. Even fiercer debates arose over statewide taxes to support education. The founders had never imagined many of these debates.

Reflecting on this period, education historians have traditionally evaluated the founders and their principal legislative framework—the Northwest Ordinances—based on their short-term effectiveness in sustaining a system of public schools. That assessment is empirical, much like the assessment one might offer today of legislation like the No Child Left Behind Act or Every Student Succeeds Act. The Ordinances don't fare well on that score. Lawyers, on the other hand, understand the Ordinances primarily as a land deal that spelled out how it should be used, transferred, and converted. Both groups miss the forest for the trees.

The immediate success—or lack thereof—of the founders' rhetoric and the Northwest Ordinances is beside the point. The Ordinances earned a place next to the Declaration of Independence and Constitution because they represent the hopes and aspirations of what the nation was trying to become. Even if the nation fell far short, and for far too long, the founders were articulating education aspirations that, once put to paper, would call the nation back to its roots generations later, as the subsequent chapters will reveal. Consider for just one moment how radical these early ideas were.

The founders articulated education goals not with any certainty that they would spring into reality simply by writing them down, but in hope that we might one day live up to them. Lest one doubt the crucial importance of remaking the world through long-term vision rather than just short-term deeds, Abraham Lincoln's reflections offer an important lesson on the dynamic. Prior to becoming president, he would say, "Let us readopt the Declaration of Independence, and with it the practices and policy which harmonize with it." He understood that foundational documents may ask more of us than we can reasonably bear in the moment we write them, but if their ideas are just, they will endure and propel future generations toward a better reality than the drafters first imagined. The nation's earliest legal commitments, he said, were "meant to set up a standard for free society . . . ; constantly looked to, constantly labored for, and even though never perfectly attained, constantly approximated, and thereby constantly spreading and deepening its influence."[30] The articulation of the nation's self-evident truths of life, liberty, and property, for instance, were an attempt to

> reach[] forward and seiz[e] upon the farthest posterity. [The founders] erected a beacon to guide their children and their children's children, and the countless myriads who should inhabit the earth in other ages. Wise statesmen as they were, . . . they established these great self-evident truths, that when in the distant future some man, some faction, some interest, should set up the doctrine that none but rich men, or none but white men, were entitled to life, liberty and pursuit of happiness, their posterity might look up again to the Declaration of Independence and take courage to renew the battle which their fathers began—so that truth, and justice, and mercy . . . might not be extinguished from the land; so that no man would hereafter dare to limit and circumscribe the great principles on which the temple of liberty was being built.[31]

The Northwest Ordinances are not so different. They can only be fully understood through their reach, not their real-world grasp.

Through their reach, we can see them for what they were—the nation's first attempt to set a North Star for public education. Before the US Constitution would mandate a "republican form of government" in the states, and before Congress would demand public education as an aspect of that government following the Civil War, the Northwest Ordinances mandated republican government and provided for education's role in it. In doing so, the Ordinances placed public education on a plane distinct from any other government function. Geographically, education was to be at the physical center of all future development. Financially, education would be inviolably supported by the nation's public resources. Governmentally, education would be a central function that states and localities must carry out. Symbolically, public education would be the foundation of "good government and the happiness of mankind."

CHAPTER 3

EDUCATION AS FREEDOM

War broke the chains of slavery, but only education would make former slaves—and the nation—free.[1]

OUR FOUNDING IDEAS AND FATHERS SUFFERED FROM INTERNAL contradictions. One need look no further than the institution of slavery and its denial of all the rights and aspirations of the American idea to an entire race. Many elites who propped up that institution cared little for anyone's rights—white or black—other than their own. But finally, in 1867 and 1868, in the shadows of the Civil War, Congress attempted to build a new and lasting democracy. That meant reframing the Constitution and the Union. Those years, not the years surrounding the nation's founding, were the most pivotal for the right to education. In 1867, Congress rededicated the nation to its education goals, taking concrete steps to cure past failures that had helped cause the Civil War itself. Congress helped fund and build schools throughout the South, created a federal Department of Education, and forced Confederate states to rewrite their constitutions to guarantee the creation and maintenance of statewide systems of public education open to all. In fact, Congress conditioned Confederate states' readmission to the Union on them rewriting their constitutions and providing for education.

That story, as it unfolded in Congress and state constitutional conventions, cannot, however, be fully appreciated apart from the lived experience of the newly freed slaves. The Civil War exposed the deep contradictions between the nation's original democratic aspirations and everyday reality. And freedom for those who had never tasted it revealed education's deep meaning for humanity, citizenship, and democracy. It was education—public, free, and open to all—that lay at the center of individual freedom and resolving the nation's internal contradictions. It was education that could finally give the nation a chance to make good on its aspirations and build a real democracy that offered the possibility of full freedom for all its people.

African Americans understood this better than anyone. Before the war ended or the nation outlawed slavery and guaranteed equal citizenship, African Americans' first steps beyond the reach of their masters marked their understanding of democracy and liberty. Their first steps demonstrated a human yearning that could have never otherwise been understood—a yearning far more telling than the philosophical theorizing of the nation's founders. Their first steps told the rest of the country what citizenship and the social contract must be in our constitutional system. Their firsts were toward education. Their unrelenting desires, commitment, and demands for education helped define the federal and state plans to reconstruct the nation into a republican form of government that finally approximated the one first envisioned a century earlier.

America's recommitment to the right to education is, in large part, the story of the freedmen, beginning with slaves' first interactions with the Union army at the outset of the war. As the Union took and secured strongholds along the East Coast and then the Mississippi River, African Americans made their way to Union lines. African Americans were foremost seeking freedom and shelter. But once behind Union lines, they made it clear that education was their first priority upon reaching freedom.

Runaway slaves seeking freedom at the gate of Fort Monroe.
Courtesy of the Library of Congress.

Freedom and education had long been intertwined for slaves. Slave owners not only controlled their bodies; they sought to control and limit their minds, using mental slavery to reinforce physical slavery. Slaves believed that education could do the inverse, too, freeing their minds and then their bodies. Fort Monroe in Virginia provided the first glimpse of this conviction. When war broke out in April 1861, Fort Monroe was one of the few Southern locations that the North managed to hold. Trusting that freedom was just behind the fort's walls, a few slaves fled their plantations for the fort. General Benjamin Butler, the fort's commander, welcomed them, declaring them "contraband" of war. But rather than holding them as property, General Butler gave them freedom behind the fort's walls. When news spread, thousands of other slaves followed in their footsteps. As they poured into the fort, officers were struck by their widespread desire "to know how to read."[2] This impression and the surprising wonder it evoked reverberates throughout the countless stories of officers and missionaries across the South as they first encountered the freedmen.

On the other side of the Confederacy, along the banks of the Mississippi River, Mrs. Porter, a missionary teacher, followed Union troops to a freedmen's camp at Holly Springs, two and a half miles south of Memphis. When she first arrived, "an old negro came out to meet her." His "head had been whitened by the frosts of ninety winters, and [he] was almost blind, supporting himself by his staff." He reached out his hand and offered an ethereal introduction: "Well, you have come at last, I'se been 'spectin you, lookin for you, for de last twenty years. I knowed you would come, and now I rejoice." Mrs. Porter politely responded, I have "come to teach you." He wasn't surprised. He simply said, "Yes, yes, I know it, and I thank de Lord."[3]

When teaching actually began in newly secured locations, masses of slaves flocked to open spaces where someone might offer them the opportunity to read and write or build on what they already knew. Hundreds of slaves, sometimes a thousand, would gather for long periods under a large tree, in a forest clearing, or an abandoned church to learn from a missionary teacher. They carried that same passion with them throughout their daily lives, including deep into the night. The army chaplain in Corinth, Mississippi, remarked, "You will find [the freedmen] every hour of daylight at their books. We cannot enter a cabin or tent, but that we see from one to three with books." Even as late as half past nine, the chaplain found a boy reading by the light of burning pine chips.[4]

Recounting those earliest contacts with freedmen in Mississippi, James Yeatman told of his visit to President's Island in the Mississippi River. He came upon a new school with about 250 students. Most were between five and twenty years old, but he noticed "one old woman, aged eighty-five, who was intent on her books." He asked her if she wasn't "too old to learn." She said she wasn't, explaining that "she must learn now or not at all, as she had but little time left, and she must make the most of it." But wouldn't it still do her little good at that stage in life, he asked. Again she disabused him of his assumptions, explaining the point was that she would be able to "read the bible and teach the young."[5] Another woman in Maryland, eighty years old, said: "I am determined to make the effort to learn to read my Bible before I die, and if I fail I will die on the way." The historian Walter Fleming captured the zeitgeist best: "The whole [black] race wanted to go to school; none were too old, few too young."[6]

Of all the things freedmen might have done or chosen in those early days—retribution, relocation, aimless roaming, loafing in plain sight or private—the most common choice was to seek education. Harriet Beecher Stowe, who wrote one of the most popular and controversial books of the pre-war period, *Uncle Tom's Cabin*, remarked that the freedmen "rushed not to the grog-shop but to the schoolroom—they cried for the spelling-book as bread, and pleaded for the teachers as a necessity of life."[7]

The freedmen's choice was more than a plain fact to be recounted; it was an uncanny act of humanity. William C. Garnett, a recent Harvard graduate who spent three years among the freedmen, captured the ethos of the deep desire. Reporting from Savannah, Georgia, on April 28, 1865, he wrote that the "Freedmen here betook themselves to education" with "speed and energy. . . . It was their first act on coming to the surface, a kind of instinctive head-shaking, and clearing of the eyes, after emerging from the waters."[8]

Seen this way, education was more than just learning. Education was liberty—"as much a natural right as the right to breath [*sic*] the air"[9]—and emblematic of the citizenship to which the freedmen would later aspire. Christopher Span, a scholar of the period, explained that "becoming literate proved as much a psychological victory for many freedpeople as it was an intellectual one. Illiteracy was a vestige of slavery, a reminder of the blatant denial of one's rights to self-advancement; it served as a badge of inferiority and societal impotence. To become literate challenged this status."[10] Hilary Green, another scholar, similarly wrote of those early days that African Americans saw the "schoolhouse as the fundamental vehicle for distancing themselves from their slave past" and "essential to the transition to freedom."[11] Span boils it down to one blunt notion: "They were in school to learn how to be something other than a slave."[12] This made the "struggle for education . . . an expression of freedom."[13]

Adults wanted that freedom for their children in particular. From a freedmen's camp on the banks of the Ohio River, just inside the safety of the North, a visitor wrote that the parents were then fully "awake to the possibility of their children becoming 'something.'"[14] Once awake, they wanted it all the more. For instance, in Louisiana, when a shift in federal policy threatened to undermine the freedmen's newly opened schools, petitions representing 10,000 blacks poured into the military superintendent's office. He wrote: "It was affecting to examine [the petitions] and note the names and marks (x) of such a long list of parents, ignorant themselves, but begging that their child might be educated, promising that from beneath their present burdens, and out of their extreme poverty, they would pay for it."[15]

As time wore on, parents did not simply ask for education or thank those who offered it; they claimed it as a human right. In February 1864, while the war was still raging, a Union officer overseeing the freedmen's labor in New Orleans recounted a story fit for a Hollywood script. Testifying before the Freedmen's Inquiry Commission, the officer said that a freedman came to him and "demanded his children at my hands." He wanted his kids brought from the plantation where they were working. The officer was not inclined to act. The plan was to maintain the economic stability of the region, not upend it. This meant African Americans would continue to work the land, and that meant staying put. Taken aback by the demand, the officer questioned the father as to why he was so adamant about getting his children. Matter-of-factly, the father responded: "I want to send them to school." The officer still was not impressed and tried to persuade the father to drop it, saying the children "were in a good home with their former owner" and it was best to leave them there. At that point, the father lost his patience and deference. Speaking to a white man, an officer no less, the father rebuked him: "I am in your service; I wear military clothes; I have been in three battles; I was in the assault at Port Hudson: I want those children; they are my flesh and blood."[16] This father's story was not the only one. Freedmen in North Carolina similarly protested and "wanted to know what wright [an official] has to take our boy Children from us and from the School and Send them New Bern to work . . . without they parent Consint."[17] A people so long oppressed, so long forced to avert their eyes, so long suffering, and so long without expectation of anything for themselves or their children now stood erect to claim their rights as parents and what they believed to be the human rights of their children: education.

The gravity of these first interactions—the fact that freedmen knew exactly what they wanted after having been held in the dark for their entire lives—is hard to fully capture with the written word. Firsthand witnesses said you simply had to be there to experience it. Booker T. Washington, one of the two preeminent African American leaders of the late nineteenth century, wrote that "few people who were not right in the midst of the scenes can form any exact idea of the intense desire which the people of my race showed for education."[18] A Union general similarly recalled that "the earnest and touching anxiety of these freed people to learn cannot but make a profound impression upon the mind of any one who has had the opportunity to observe it."[19]

Booker T. Washington was born a slave in Franklin County, Virginia, in the late 1850s—the exact time and place he wasn't sure. As a slave, life's comforts were foreign to him. He tells, for instance, of sleeping alongside his brother and sister on a "bundle of filthy rags laid upon the dirt floor."[20] His only experience with learning was to go "as far as the schoolhouse door with one of my young mistresses to carry her books." But "the picture of several dozen boys and girls in a schoolroom engaged in study made a deep impression on me, and I had the feeling that to get into a schoolhouse and study in this way would be about the same as getting into paradise."[21] He resolved that if he was going to do anything in life, it would be to learn to read.

When emancipation came, he persuaded his mother to get him a spelling book. He planned to teach himself to read. They were so poor that he wasn't sure "how or where she got it," but she did. His mother, illiterate herself, tried her best to help and encourage him. When a school finally opened nearby, he experienced "one of the keenest disappointments" of his life. He couldn't go because his family needed him to work during the day. He later settled for night school, which meant extremely long days, as his workday did not end until nine in the evening.

A "CONTRABAND" SCHOOL.

Mary S. Peake teaching runaway slaves at Fort Monroe.
Courtesy of Project Gutenberg.

Military leaders sought to match the freedmen's yearnings with their own concerted efforts to provide schools as quickly as possible. On September 17, 1861—less than half a year into the war and more than three from its end—Union forces established a school at Fort Monroe, Virginia, with the assistance of a few Northern missionaries. The records of the school are relatively sparse and the geography of the fort necessarily limited the number of freedmen it could serve. Fort Monroe, however, laid the groundwork for something larger farther south.

A few weeks after establishing the Fort Monroe school, the Union prevailed in the Battle of Port Royal in the South Carolina Sea Islands. The Sea Islands offered the perfect location for an ambitious experiment in rewriting the nation's racial narrative. Port Royal lay fifty miles south of Charleston and Fort Sumter, the site of the first shots of the war in defense of slavery. In the heart of the Confederacy, yet geographically shielded, Port Royal offered a vast natural refuge—potentially a utopia. Here, the Union could give freedmen their own land to work and the opportunity to develop a fully functioning social system outside the influ-

Laura Towne and students assembled in front of the newly constructed Penn School. *Courtesy of Corbis Historical/Getty Images.*

ence of white oppression. The freedmen proved more than capable. In fact, self-sufficiency in the Sea Islands fueled later calls for reparations in the form of "forty acres and a mule."

Too often lost in the Sea Island story, however, is the emergence of a rough system of schools. With Port Royal secure, Flag-Officer Samuel Du Pont and Brigadier General Thomas W. Sherman wrote letters to Northern benevolent societies in February 1862, asking them to send teachers. The societies were waiting on the request. Within days, they held public meetings in three different cities: Boston, New York, and Philadelphia. A few weeks later, fifty-two teachers and missionaries set sail from New York.[22] More followed shortly thereafter. By summer, eighty-six teachers and supporting staff were in Port Royal.

The first formal school was on St. Helena Island, run out of the "Brick Church" that slaves had initially built for whites a few years earlier. When the Union soldiers took the island, they gave the church to African Americans, who put it to immediate use as a school. The number of students quickly swelled and outgrew the church's space, so another plot of nearby land was purchased for the construction of a three-room schoolhouse. They named it the Penn School—the first structure in the South specifically built for the education of former slaves.[23]

In the months following the Penn School's establishment, other schools sprung up along the Eastern Seaboard. By the end of 1862, almost two thousand children attended school on Port Royal, Saint Helena, and Ladies' Islands alone. Those numbers continued to grow, with thirty-five different schools operating on the islands the next year.[24] Three hundred miles north, schools spread in North Carolina's coastal region, too, opening in New Bern, Morehead City, Roanoke Island, and Beaufort.[25] One of the missionaries noted the immense significance: "After the lapse of the one hundred and forty-four years since the settlement [of Beaufort, North Carolina], the Freemen are building the first public school-house ever erected here." The same could have been said in countless different communities; Major General Wager Swayne said in Mississippi, "To open a school has been to have it filled."[26]

With each passing month, the schooling effort grew larger, more audacious, and more formal. The effort even reached the desk of President Abraham Lincoln. In 1863, President Lincoln penned a letter to General Nathaniel Banks. Banks had taken control of the Mississippi River and the state of Louisiana. Lincoln commended Banks for his important success before broaching the purpose of the letter: how Louisiana might "adopt some practical system by which the two races could gradually live themselves out of their old relation to each other, and both come out better prepared for the new." Lincoln struck a delicate and respectful tone, saying that "while I very well know what I would be glad for Louisiana to do, it is quite a different thing for me to assume direction of the matter." It is for the people of Louisiana, Lincoln explained, to hold a constitutional convention and form a new government. While deferential as to what that government might look like, Lincoln was notably direct on one point: "Education for young blacks should be included in the plan."[27]

An education dispute in New Bern, North Carolina, the year before surely influenced Lincoln's thinking on education. According to New Bern's education superintendent, the state's military governor said that the state's prohibition on African American literacy remained in force, even if the Union had taken the region. The superintendent took this to mean he must close the New Bern school, and he did. But he also reached out to Massachusetts' US senator, Charles Sumner. Sumner was a leading national advocate for African American education.

Incensed by the news, Sumner went straight to the White House and confronted Lincoln. Lincoln acted as though the matter were beneath him—an uncharacteristic response for Lincoln, who was normally generous to a fault with his time. This time, however, Lincoln snapped: "Do you take me for a school-committee-man?" Sumner matched Lincoln's irritation with shaming indignation: "Not at all. I take you for President of the United States; and I come with a case of wrong, in attending to which your predecessor, George Washington, if alive, might add to his renown." Lincoln backed down but wouldn't undermine his military governor without all the facts. Instead, he carefully ended the conversation without any precise promise of next steps.

Convinced the principle at stake was too important to let go, Sumner raised the New Bern matter in the Senate on June 2, 1862. The story also made it to the House of Representatives, which, on that same day, passed a resolution pressing the president to explain whether the military governor "interfered to prevent the education of children, white or black, . . . and if so, by what authority if any."[28] Merely asking this question belied a deeper sense of the importance of education and where the nation might go in the coming years. At that moment, no law or constitution guaranteed education in North Carolina. No federal statute did, either. But on behalf of people who saw themselves as free and hoped to be citizens, Congress asked those charged with impeding education to explain themselves. It's hard to imagine that any explanation could have been satisfactory.

Whatever the truth of the North Carolina fiasco, Lincoln's letter to General Banks in Louisiana the next year made it clear that access to education was of the utmost importance. Acting on Lincoln's letter, General Banks issued a military directive, formally titled General Order 23. Banks's order replaced Louisiana's governmental system with one that divided the state's "parishes into police and school districts" and required "the establishment of a sufficient number of schools, one at least for each of the police and school districts, for the instruction of colored children under twelve years of age, which . . . will be placed under the direction of the superintendent of public education."[29] With the President's blessing and the stroke of the pen, Banks instituted a new world order in Louisiana and laid public education as its foundation.

In his second directive, General Order 38, Banks moved beyond general principles and spelled out a detailed education system. The directive established a board of education and its immediate duties: to acquire land, build schools, hire teachers, compel attendance, buy books, and regulate the course of study. The most aggressive measure, by far, was a tax. Banks provided: "for the full accomplishment of these purposes and the performance of the duties enjoined upon them, the Board shall have full power and authority to assess and level a school tax upon real and personal property . . . in each and every before-mentioned school district."[30]

Mundane to the modern eye, a school tax was a radical idea at the time. Even Northern states had struggled to financially support their schools, with many of the problems revolving around tax controversies. For the first half of the 1800s, states with education histories as storied as those of Massachusetts and New York fought and waivered over the politics of statewide school taxes, going without one for decades. With no tax base, the reach of Northern education systems was necessarily limited. Until the 1800s, most of rural Pennsylvania, for instance, had no schools at all. And regardless of the state, high school remained a luxury that only the wealthiest and most populous Northern cities could afford.

In the South, the challenge was steeper. The North fully supported the idea of public education; the only fight was over the details. But in the South, political elites opposed both education and taxes. Elites who held the vast majority of Southern wealth had no interest in paying taxes. They maintained, funded, and ruled their own mini-societies on plantations. The idea of funding services for other planters or communities was counterintuitive, particularly if it was for the education of poor whites and slaves. These were the very people elites needed to keep politically disempowered.

In other states, grassroots organization, commitments, and sacrifices of tens and hundreds of thousands of African Americans substituted for

Slaves flocking to see President Lincoln after the fall of Richmond.
Courtesy of Wikimedia Commons.

general military directives. As soon as they found themselves no longer slaves, they forced schools into existence with or without taxes—almost out of thin air. One of the most dramatic and detailed accounts came literally as the smoke cleared from the fall of the Confederate capital: Richmond, Virginia. As the Union arrived, learning and yearning that had once been hidden from sight immediately came into full view and grew organically.

On April 2, 1865, Confederate president Jefferson Davis and his cabinet fled Richmond, leaving a war-ravaged city burning behind. The next day local authorities surrendered Richmond to the Union. President Lincoln and his son Tad were waiting nearby and began their way up the James River by ship, entering Richmond on April 4. Former slaves recognized President Lincoln as he set foot on the river bank. Word of his presence ran like an "electric" current through the city. "As far as the eye could see the streets were alive with negroes and poor whites rushing in [the ship's] direction, and the crowd increased so fast," the ship's admiral said, "that I had to surround the President with sailors with fixed bayonets to keep them off. . . . They all wanted to shake hands with Mr. Lincoln or his coat tail or even to kneel down and kiss his boots!"[31]

Lincoln toured Richmond for four days, hoping that a nearby Robert E. Lee would surrender soon. Lincoln left Richmond a day too early. The day after Lincoln left, Lee surrendered to General Grant at the Appomattox Courthouse, ninety miles west of Richmond. But local events in Richmond were just as important for the freedmen. They immediately changed the reality of daily life there. In meetinghouses across the city, the freedmen plotted their very first mass act of freedom—to build some semblance of an education system.

The precise date is unclear, but within just a few days of Richmond's fall, freedmen met with Northern missionaries in the First African Church of Richmond to discuss the scope of what they might attempt and need. The freedmen's interest level would dictate the necessary space and teachers. So the first thing they needed to know was how many people wanted education. They decided to call for a sign-up day to get a better measure and, on April 14, an outsized crowd arrived to "give in their names as scholars."[32] Four days later, school officially opened in the First African Church. One thousand seventy-five students attended—a startling number for a city with around 12,000 adult and young slaves,[33] many of whom still lived under the violent influence of their former masters.

The teachers who came to Richmond and elsewhere were, on multiple levels, shocked by what they encountered. First was the adversity that freedmen were willing to face to go to school. Freedmen came, again and again, under the threat and scorn of their former masters. Some made good on their threats, turning families out of their homes and resorting to violence. Those freedmen who didn't face duress still had to sacrifice time and money, forgoing much-needed work hours and giving up scarce resources for school supplies and fees. With no immediate revenue sources to support education, freedmen in many locations paid whatever tuition they could afford. Monthly tuition ranged from fifty cents to a dollar and a half—the equivalent of 10 percent of an agricultural worker's wages.[34] And many families did not even have access to regular wages.

These families struggled for basic subsistence and education at the same time. The stories teachers told of their students are heart-wrenching.

When one asked her student why he was not writing on his slate, he responded: "Sold [my] pencil for a piece of bread."[35] Another student, when queried about his absences, explained that he "walks four miles to school [and] stays at home three days in the week to lend his shoes to his sister, so that she also may learn."[36] With no legal obligation to be there, students and families like these pressed on against the weight of a life just months removed from slavery. Education was the light at the end of the tunnel.

Federal reports reveal that the freedmen spent over one million dollars on their own education through 1870, with roughly 30,000 students paying tuition.[37] Adults also regularly contributed in-kind services and group-based donations. In some states, the freedmen covered 10 percent or more of the cost of education statewide. And in some towns and cities, they covered the entire cost. This is not even counting the independent schools that freedmen operated themselves, sometimes out of need and other times out of pride. As early as 1863, the Freedmen's Inquiry Commission noted that "one of the first acts of the negroes when they found themselves free was to establish schools at their own expense."[38] By 1867, freedmen were funding, in whole or part, over six hundred schools of their own. They ran additional education services at six hundred churches called "Sabbath schools."[39]

These enormous sacrifices and commitments reflected a desire to make up for years, if not decades, of lost time. James W. C. Pennington, a former slave, eloquently explained that slavery's "irreparable" injury was to "ro[b] me of my education. . . . It cost me two years hard labor, after I fled, to unshackle my mind; it was three years before I had purged my language of slavery's idioms; it was four years before I had thrown off the crouching aspect of slavery; and now the evil that besets me is a great lack of that general information."[40]

When education was finally open to them, many freedmen devoted every spare moment to learning. Richmond teachers recounted stories of freedmen about town with their reading primers stuffed in their pockets so that when the opportunity came they could find a place to sit and read. Those with heavy workloads during the day waited till the evening, reading deep into the night even though another long day of work awaited them in the morning. One witness before the Joint Congressional Committee on Reconstruction testified that freedmen "have scarcely a leisure moment that you cannot see them with a book in their hand learning to read."[41]

The other surprise to teachers was the number of freedmen who could already read and write—some quite well. They discovered that slaves had long met under the shadow of night to teach one another. Unbeknownst to the rest of the world, they passed "secret knowledge" among friends and family for generations. Many slave families in Richmond, for instance, kept a book hidden in their homes. Two weeks after the fall of Richmond, one teacher remarked that "nearly every colored family . . . has one or more members who can read." Slave literacy was a holdover from times before Nat Turner's Rebellion, when some masters had allowed slaves to read. Following the rebellion, states made reading and writing illegal for slaves, but the law "could not plant ignorance where letters were [already] fixed." Those mothers and fathers who had tasted the forbidden "fruit . . . [also] gave to their dear ones what they so much prized themselves."[42]

This secret learning was bound up in the very idea of freedom—and defiance of slavery—across the South. Black learning posed a practical and ideological threat to the institution of slavery. Slave masters saw it as the tool through which some slaves might effectuate their own freedom. Frederick Douglass's master put it in the most brutal terms when he found out that his wife was teaching Douglass to read. Forbidding her from continuing Douglass's instruction, he said that a slave

> should know nothing but to obey his master—to do as he is told to do. Learning would spoil the best nigger in the world. Now . . . if you teach that nigger . . . how to read, there would be no keeping him. It would forever unfit him to be a slave. He would at once become unmanageable, and of no value to his master. As to himself, it could do him no good, but a great deal of harm. It would make him discontented and unhappy.[43]

Reflecting this sentiment, Southern states went to extreme lengths to prevent African Americans from learning. The South Carolina legislature, for instance, did not just prohibit African Americans from reading and writing—the perceived cause of slave rebellions—South Carolina prohibited "mental instruction" altogether and made it unlawful for slaves to assemble or meet in contexts that might be construed as efforts at mental instruction.[44] Louisiana went further, prohibiting anyone, whites included, from writing or publishing materials that might incite slave insubordination. Simply bringing such materials into Louisiana, even if written and published elsewhere, was a crime.[45]

For slaves, education became part forbidden fruit, part defiance, and part faith in what education might bring. At the very least, the "written word . . . revealed a world beyond bondage," a world in which they "could imagine themselves free to think and behave as they chose."[46] Even if unable to free their bodies, the ability to read and write freed the slave's mind, placing it beyond the brutal control that slave masters asserted at so many different levels. And in that respect, learning—whatever ideas it did or did not offer—was also a conscious act of defiance, an assertion of freedom, even if only in secret. Of course, some slaves sought reading and writing to secure actual freedom, plan insurrection, share information about the path to freedom, and even forge their own written passes to freedom.[47] After being banned from reading, Frederick Douglass, for instance, said that he immediately "understood the pathway from slavery to freedom" lay in education; he "set out with high hope, and a fixed purpose, at whatever cost of trouble, to learn how to read."[48]

While the lengths to which African Americans had gone to learn to read and write during slavery made perfect sense, the details still boggle the mind. Whereas in Richmond the secret learning happened primarily within the family, a literate black woman in Savannah operated an actual school for about twenty-five students. She held regular classes inside an ordinary-looking building. She hid the school in plain sight, directing students to sneak in and out through the front door at various times of the day.[49] No one suspected a thing. In more rural areas, slaves relied on the natural terrain to hide their learning. One young man said he had learned to read and write in the depths of a cave. Another common route was to literally go underground. In Mississippi, "pit schools" were the norm in certain areas. Slaves would find or dig out holes in the ground and then cover them with bushes and vines.[50] Frederick Douglass, after being found out at home, did not have a teacher or hidden place to learn, so he continued his learning in the streets. He convinced the young white boys he encountered when running errands to teach him, using his master's bread to barter for literacy, offering hungry kids bread in exchange for the "more valuable bread of knowledge."[51]

This secret learning, combined with the intense desire among those who had none, provided the foundation for rising literacy levels that defied conventional wisdom and would otherwise be hard to believe. By 1864, a Norfolk school, for instance, enrolled 1,400 pupils, nearly a thousand of whom could spell and read. A few hundred could also do math calculations.[52] Numbers like these were not unusual across the South. Including children and adults, missionaries in the Gulf Coast area indicated that they taught more than 40,000 African Americans to read and write during the war's last year and a half.[53] After the war, those numbers multiplied again. Through the end of 1865, over 90,000 freedmen were attending 740 schools staffed by 1,314 teachers.[54] By 1870, 150,000 students were enrolled under the direction of 3,300 teachers.[55] And daily attendance in some Southern cities exceeded even that of the North. Daily attendance in Memphis was 72 percent. In Alabama and Virginia, it was 79 percent and 82 percent, respectively. By comparison, daily attendance in New York was 43 percent. Apparently, only in public education's birthplace, Boston, was attendance substantially higher than these hotbeds of Southern education.

Unfortunately, there was also a dark side to these remarkable stories. Numerous schools were burned, teachers physically attacked, and freedmen made to suffer the consequences. Often lost in the telling of those stories, however, is the more important lesson of how ineffective the violence was. The moral courage propelling both teachers and students was indefatigable. For the freedmen and their family, education, once seized, was "an impulse onward never to be lost."[56] For the teachers, it was a calling. Those there to witness it remarked, "The tenacity and high-souled courage of teachers were admirable. It was more than heroism. There seemed a divine inspiration over the whole work," as though "a creative power had said 'let there be light.'"[57] Together, the "steady system of effort [to expand education] cannot be resisted," explained one Union official to a white Southern planter. "They would find it harder fighting the alphabet and spelling-book than they did Grant and Sherman."[58] The planter conceded the point in silence.

Yet to reduce education to only a moral or humanistic yearning would be to ignore the obvious political stakes. The freedman wanted to be more than just free; he wanted to be a citizen. Committing to and acquiring education was, in effect, to assume the role of a citizen, to justify equal status, and ultimately to demand self-government and self-determination. Over the course of their lives, slaves had experienced and "seen power and influence among white people always coupled with learning."[59] They wanted that same power and influence for themselves. As an education leader in North Carolina remarked in 1866, the "school-house would be the first proof of their independence."[60] Inside those esteemed walls, former slaves could "prepare . . . for full citizenship" and hope to exercise it soon.[61]

This meant that reading, writing, and arithmetic were not just about recapturing that part of humanity that had been stolen; education was about being ready for the evolving political future that lay ahead. That future, the freedmen hoped, would be one in which they could control their own lives on a daily basis—politically, economically, and practically. An illiterate man could not understand the labor contract he would now be asked to sign. For that, the illiterate freedman relied primarily on the Freedmen's Bureau. But even if he understood the contract, he likely couldn't calculate whether he had been underpaid for his goods and services. Even with Union officers nearby to theoretically enforce the rules, freedmen "still suffer[ed] from frauds, easily practice[d] upon remaining ignorance, especially in the payment of their wages."[62] And maybe most important, an illiterate people could not demand their rights from distant politicians, much less hold them accountable. "Freedpeople were anxious for education precisely because [they understood] its direct relationship to power within the society."[63]

The stories told at the Freedmen's Inquiry Commission in 1863 made the point as clearly as any since. The Commission was interested as to whether the freedmen could live alone—apart from whites—and govern themselves. Could the Port Royal experiment be replicated on a larger scale and without the federal government to prop it up? Harry McMillan, a slave of forty years in Beaufort, South Carolina, appeared before the Commission to testify. McMillan was extremely industrious in his own right, later buying a sixty-five-acre plot of land and employing twenty-one workers.

McMillan anchored African Americans' political future to education. The freedmen could do most everything on their own, but for the time being, he startlingly confessed, they would need whites to administer the law. He meant no slight to blacks, explaining that "black people have a good deal of sense but they do not know the law," nor how to interpret it. But in a future that included education, McMillan was sure they could manage their own affairs:

> With the children coming up[,] white men will not be needed. They are learning to read and write—some are learning lawyers, some are learning doctor, and some learn minister; and reading books and newspaper they can understand the law; but the old generation cannot understand it. It makes no difference how sensible they are, they are blind and it wants white men for the present to direct them. After five years they will take care of themselves, this generation cannot do it.[64]

At a camp in North Carolina, another freedman remarked that education was also about self-defense: "I don't know much, but one thing I do know: I want edication, and we, as a people, want edication. We must learn to keep books and do our own business, for already the white man is marking and thinking how cheap he can hire us, and how easily he can cheat us out of our pay."[65]

From the mouths of men just removed from slavery, literacy, self-determination, citizenship, and the law were all part of a single inter-connected whole. And even before fully securing education and rights for all, freedmen leveraged education to affect the whole. Freedmen and Northern transplants who were advanced in their studies filled the communities' leading advocacy roles. These men were the race's representatives and leaders precisely because they could read and write. The undereducated freedmen understood that they needed "men who could put their concerns into writing."[66]

Before the war's end, the freedmen had already put the most literate among them to work writing appeals to federal, state, and other authorities. The appeals unsurprisingly involved claims for education, civil, and human rights. The very act of writing (and delivering) such letters was a show of force, and well-written letters offered the possibility of progressive change. Elijah Marrs, for instance, was so bold as to write a letter to Secretary of War Edward Stanton and complain about the conditions and wages being paid to soldiers and freedmen as they returned to plantations for work. Not only did he complain, he lodged artful rhetoric that could persuade: "If you call this freedom, what do you call slavery?"[67] Marrs and others continued in this type of written advocacy for years to come.

The foremost among them also organized what they called the Colored People's Conventions. These conventions met to hammer out the freedmen's vision for the future and their expectations as to how government should treat them. Freedmen's collective action, transposed into writing, had a powerful effect. At the very least, it helped change how the rest of the world saw them. An 1866 federal report indicated that "their right to a higher status is already being conceded, even at the south. Not a few there are asserting for them an equal capacity; more are advocating continued instruction, and civil rights are being yielded to these freedmen which two years ago would have been scoffed at as the morbid fancies only of the fanatic."[68]

THESE POLITICAL REALITIES, COMBINED WITH THE FREEDMEN'S own sense of their place in the world, marked the path the nation was soon to take on a broader scale. Congress, if it was to heal and reunite the nation, needed to both elevate the freedmen and rebuild the nation's democratic foundations. Southern states had clearly failed their people—black and white—even if to obviously different degrees. Southern government was anything but republican in form. Southern slave owners meant it that way. They understood the link between education, democracy, and political power and sought to block all three.

Southern elites did not just object to taxes for education or fear slave rebellions; they objected to the symbolic message public education would send. Their entire political system had been built on the notion that skin color, not education, made one fit for citizenship and power. If they conceded that education was important, the normative lines separating poor, uneducated whites from slaves would thin. So, too, would elites' stranglehold on power. Poor whites' lack of education had long fed a convenient, vicious cycle in which elites dominated government and kept taxes low.

The result was the absence of any real functioning public education system in most of the South. Whereas several Northern states had adopted formalized structures to support public education and begun centralizing education, Southern schooling was random. As one commentator lamented, "All effort to go beyond a patchwork quilt of public, quasi-public, religious, and pauper schools on the elementary levels failed until Reconstruction."[69] The effect on both basic literacy and democracy was stark. Illiteracy among Southern whites was four times that of whites in the North. The spillover into political power was inevitable.

If the South was to have the democracy the nation's Constitution first promised in 1787, it would begin with an education system. A system so vital could not depend on the varied organic efforts of freedmen and missionaries. Such a system would have to be formal and vested in law. That is the story of the next chapter.

CHAPTER 4

RECONSTRUCTION

*A National Recommitment
to Education and Democracy*

THE EDUCATION EFFORTS THAT OCCURRED DURING AND IMME-
diately after the war were inspiring, but an education system that
outlived war would take formal and irreversible action at the highest levels of government. Fortunately, Congress retained the founding fathers'
instincts about education and the common sense earned from the recent
experience of civil war. Congress knew that if Reconstruction was going
to work and a real democracy was to take hold in the South, Congress
needed to rapidly expand public education to all, not just the freedmen.
Senator Charles Sumner was the strongest voice on this issue.

In 1867 on the floor of the Senate, Sumner offered his take on the
link between democracy's failure and the nonexistent education system
in the South:

> In a republic Education is indispensable. A republic without edu-
> cation is like the creature of imagination, a human being without
> a soul, living and moving blindly, with no just sense of the present
> or the future. It is a monster. Such have been the rebel States. . . .
> But such they must be no longer. It is not too much to say that had

these states been more enlightened they would have never rebelled. The Barbarism of Slavery would have shrunk into insignificance, without sufficient force to break forth in blood. . . . [But a] population that could not read and write naturally failed to comprehend and appreciate a republican government.[1]

Senator Morton, from Indiana, followed Sumner with a reality check on the practical challenge ahead and what it demanded of Congress. Many of those most in need of education, Morton argued, were too poor to secure it for themselves. Education "must be provided for by the State or they will remain uneducated; and until they are educated the political power remains almost entirely in the hands of the present rebel-educated class." This, he said, was too dangerous to risk. "Republican government may go on for a while with half the voters unable to read or write, but it cannot long continue."[2]

Rhetorical arguments and good faith attestations regarding education, however, would not be enough. The founders' lofty praise and general encouragement of public education had achieved all that it could. Just repeating the sentiment would do little at this point. The truth was that the United States was no longer just a democratic experiment; it was an experiment that had failed in crucial respects. Too much deference to states had proved too divisive, too disastrous. The South had substituted aristocratic rule for republican government. Ignorance for education. National peace had devolved into civil war.

Three-quarters of a century after its founding and a civil war later, the nation stiffened its resolve and took a decidedly different approach to ensuring education. If education was, in fact, the foundation of our democracy, the nation was in serious need of immediate, nonnegotiable action. The nation did just that. Between 1865 and 1868, the nation embarked on the most aggressive education project before or since, rapidly turning the education world upside down. Where Congress had previously been hands-off, it became hands-on. Where states had previously done almost nothing to support education, they amended their constitutions to immediately require it. It was in this magic period that public education became not just a national aspiration, not just a fundamental value, but a constitutional requirement.

The first formal steps lay with Congress. Before the war was over and before the Fourteenth Amendment's guarantee of equal citizenship was even close to becoming part of the Constitution, Congress began the practical work of building an education system throughout the South. That work was carried out through the Bureau of Refugees, Freedmen and Abandoned Lands, more popularly referred to simply as the Freedmen's Bureau. Congress established the Freedmen's Bureau as a unit of the War Department just before the war's end.

The legislation creating the Bureau stated its job as being "the supervision and management of all abandoned lands, and the control of all subjects relating to refugees and freedmen from rebel states."[3] Its primary function, however, was the well-being of the freedmen—hence the shorthand name. The legislation made the Bureau responsible for "provisions, clothing, and fuel, as [may be] needful for the immediate and temporary shelter and supply of destitute and suffering refugees and freedmen and their wives and children."[4] The Bureau quickly moved from basic subsistence work to transitioning the freedmen toward lasting freedom and citizenship, accomplished foremost by education.

Once appointed to head the Freedmen's Bureau, General Oliver Howard rooted the Bureau's work in education. He and various officials working under his direction fully understood what was at stake. Early in his tenure, Howard wrote that "education underlies every hope of success for the freedman." Echoing what the freedmen themselves had been saying, Howard further elaborated that "through education . . . the fearful prejudice and hostility against blacks can be overcome. They themselves will be able to demand and receive both privileges and rights that we now have difficulty to guarantee."[5] The Freedmen's Bureau superintendent in North Carolina was more blunt. The freedmen, he implored, needed education as a tool of self-defense to resist the "tyranny under which they have been ground" and which they would no longer suffer if they had it. The solution to our "delicate social dilemma," he reasoned, was not to just let education happen where it may, but to "send out teachers . . . in the track of every conquering army. Let them swarm over the savannahs of the South."[6]

Reflecting on his work leading the Bureau, General Howard wrote: "From the first [I] devoted more attention to [the education of the freedmen] than to any other branch of [my] work."[7] And with each year, he expanded that work and education's infrastructure. If money is any sign of commitment, Howard's seriousness was clear. More than two-thirds of the Bureau's total budget was spent on education during most years.[8] But the Bureau's education work went far beyond spending money.

The Bureau facilitated education at a granular level. It secured, leased, and helped build facilities for schools. It coordinated with Northern missionaries, as well as local African Americans, to staff those buildings with teachers. It devised strategies to finance these efforts, initially through the sale and rental of tens of thousands of acres of abandoned and confiscated property and later through funding from Congress. The Bureau's education efforts were so ambitious and complex that education required its own specialized leadership within the Bureau. John W. Alvord initially filled that role as inspector of schools and finances. After two years, General Howard elevated Alvord to general superintendent of education in 1867. Below Alvord were the various state superintendents. According to their reports, the Freedmen's Bureau assisted black communities in establishing and maintaining 4,000 schools, hiring over 9,000 teachers, and educating over 200,000 black students over the course of its eight years of operation.[9]

The point, however, was never for the Bureau to be its own freestanding education agency, operating in perpetuity. Nor was it to overshadow the work of state and local officials and volunteers. General Howard addressed the concern in an official circular, writing that the Bureau had come to work with and assist "benevolent and religious organizations and State authorities in the maintenances of good schools (for refugees and freedmen), until a system of free schools can be supported by the re-organized local governments."[10] The goal of the Bureau was "to systemize and facilitate" those private and public efforts, not to supplant them.

As those schools grew and systems began to take shape, tough political questions arose. How would federal support and control transition into state support and control? More fundamentally, could the South be trusted with freedmen's and poor whites' education? Whatever the answers to those questions, one thing was clear: Having opened the schoolhouse door and all that it promised in terms of citizenship and democracy, Congress dared not close it. The freedmen, among others, would not tolerate it. The education system taking root in the South was not just the work of the federal government or Northern missionaries; it was also the freedmen's work. They, more than anyone, fully appreciated that transitioning to a permanent education system was crucial to their future place in the world. They also knew there was little reason to trust in that future. Left to their own devices, many whites would work to stamp out or restrict public education. Short of that, they might just discriminate against blacks.

African Americans organized to make their voices heard and resist those possibilities. In 1865 in Arkansas, for instance, they formed the Freedman's School Society. They raised enough funds to support free schools in Little Rock for the remainder of the year. After that, African Americans' education desires turned, for all intents and purposes, into political platforms premised on legal rights.

Having financially stabilized the schools on their own, African Americans in Arkansas convened their own state convention to demand that the state afford them all the rights they deserved:

> Clothe us with the power of self-protection, by giving us our equality before the law and the right of suffrage, so we may become bona fide citizens of the State. . . . That we are the substra, the foundation on which the future power and wealth of the State of Arkansas must be built . . . [,] we respectfully ask the Legislature to provide for the education of our children.[11]

Emphasizing that the economic system of the state also depended on their labor, the implication was clear: provide a system of education for our children or else. Christopher Span, a scholar of the period, characterized it as a "nonnegotiable manifesto."[12]

African Americans made equally poignant demands of state, local, and federal leaders elsewhere. Most notable were those regarding upcoming constitutional conventions. In Alabama, African American leaders organized and primed delegates to the constitutional convention to deliver on two precise goals: prohibit racial discrimination in the nomination of delegates to the convention and establish "a thorough system of common schools throughout the State, and indeed the Union, for the well-being of such ensures to the advantages of all."[13]

Similarly, in South Carolina, African Americans gathered at the "Colored People's Convention of the State of South Carolina" just half a year after the war had ended. Once the convention had assembled itself and agreed on rules, it made education its very first formal move, unanimously adopting an education resolution. The resolution was framed as a remedy for past wrongs and a guarantee against future ones:

> *Whereas*, "Knowledge is power," and an educated and intelligent people can neither be held in, nor reduced to slavery[,] . . . we will insist upon the establishment of good schools for the thorough education of our children throughout the State . . . [and] solemnly urge the parents and guardians of the young and rising generation, by the sad recollection of our *forced* ignorance and degradation in the past, and by the bright and inspiring hopes of the future, to see to it that every child of proper age, is kept in regular attendance.[14]

As South Carolina's Convention drew to an end, the members penned a letter to Congress as well. The letter opened by thanking "our late President, Abraham Lincoln," the Union army, and the Freedmen's Bureau for all that they had done. It then turned toward a few requests. The first two pertained to continued military protection and the services of the Bureau. The next one looked to the future and began: "We ask that the three great agents of civilized society—the school, the pulpit, the press—be as secure in South Carolina as in Massachusetts or Vermont."[15] Alongside those pillars, they asked for the practical tool of self-government: "equal suffrage."

AGAINST THIS BACKDROP OF FREEDMEN ADVOCACY AND THE Bureau's data and insights, Congress took a second major step to guarantee education. Once the war was over and the North firmly in control of the South's political future, Congress was in a position to secure education not only for the freedmen but for all. And in 1867, Congress began reflecting the thinking of General Howard, General Alvord, and the freedmen. Congress knew democracy could not rebuild itself without public education, so it used its legislative power to make it a reality.

The first move was short-lived but of enormous symbolic significance: Congress created a federal Department of Education to work alongside the Freedmen's Bureau and continue the federal education agenda once the Bureau inevitably wound down. Moving education outside the Freedmen's Bureau also signaled that the project to expand public education was not just for the freedmen. It was for all. It was about continuing the promise and vision first laid out by Washington, Adams, Jefferson, and others. The legislative preamble made that connection clear, reiterating the founders' sentiments, acknowledging the nation's educational and democratic failures, and aiming for a recommitment of purpose:

> Whereas republican institutions can find permanent safety only upon the basis of the universal intelligence of the people; and whereas the great disasters which have afflicted the nation and desolated one-half of its territory are traceable, in a great degree, to the absence of common schools and general education among the people of the lately rebellious States[,] . . . the Joint Committee on Reconstruction [is] instructed to inquire into the expediency of establishing in this capital a national bureau of education, whose

duty it shall be to enforce education, without regard to race or color, upon the population of all such States as shall fall below a standard to be established by Congress, and to inquire whether such a bureau should not be made an essential and permanent part of any system of reconstruction.[16]

The possibility of a wide-reaching federal Department of Education, however, made some in Congress squeamish. They claimed it was a new and radical innovation. Those cries were largely drowned out. New Hampshire Representative Mace Moulton, for instance, responded that the Department would do no more than honor the nation's founding ideas and the lives that were given in their service. Those ideas and lives demanded that Congress act to further public education:

> The two great pillars of our American Republic, upon which it rests, are universal liberty and universal education. We have established universal liberty through a bloody conflict, through four years of carnage and war, and Congress by the passages of the civil rights bill has provided the machinery by which universal liberty can be enforced and guarantied [sic]. . . . One of these pillars, then, rests upon a solid foundation. The other pillar is universal education.[17]

So long as that second pillar was on unsure footing, so, too, would the nation. "In this republican Government," Moulton added, "the perpetuity of our institutions depends on the intelligence of the people, and without that intelligence we can have no guarantee of the continuance of our republican form of government."[18] A Department of Education— through "which the various conflicting systems in the different States can be harmonized, by which there can be uniformity, by which all mischievous errors that have crept in may be pointed out and eradicated"— is the "crying necessity of this nation to-day."[19]

Moulton pointed to his own home state of Illinois as proof that the Northwest Ordinance's land grant system was insufficient to support a modern system of public education. By the mid-nineteenth century,

Illinois's schools had fallen into "chaos." There was no real "education system at all" and "the immense amount of land which had been given by this Government to the State of Illinois for educational purposes was substantially dissipated."[20] At that point, Illinois took matters into its own hands, finally centralizing education under state leadership and responsibility.

The federal government, Moulton reasoned, needed to take analogous steps to systemize education where states could not or would not. "Every child of this land is, by natural right, entitled to an education at the hands of somebody, and that this ought not be left to the caprice of individuals or of States."[21] It was ultimately Congress's responsibility, he argued, to ensure that "every child in the land should receive a sufficient education to qualify him to discharge all the duties that may devolve upon him as an American citizen."[22]

In the end, Congress created the Department by a wide margin. The rationale supporting it was hard to deny, particularly given the current historical context. For those concerned about the possibility of the federal government taking over education, the vote to create the Department was made all the easier by the fact that its formal powers were limited in scope. The legislation structured the Department primarily as an investigation and advisory agency that would collect "statistics and facts as shall show the condition and progress of education in the several states." It would then share that information with Congress and state officers so that they could act upon the data as they saw fit.

On the other hand, this was an incredibly important first step in systematically growing the nation's system of schools. Congress clearly envisioned a great purpose for the Department, providing that the Department's goal was to "aid the people of the United States in the establishment and maintenance of efficient school systems, and otherwise promote the cause of education throughout the country."[23] Toward that end, the Department was to make annual reports to Congress and include recommendations on how best to expand education access. Yet the agency's lack of independent power proved to be a problem. It could not compel states to do anything and lacked the resources to do much itself. For the moment, it would simply assist and enlighten states and Congress.

Rather than cure the limitations in subsequent years, Congress shrank the Department.[24] It would be wrong, however, to interpret the Department's failure as a sign that Congress's nascent education agenda had failed or stalled. Congress just shifted tactics. The long-term significance of the Department was the fact that there was motivation to create it. Its creation reflected a rekindling of the nation's founding ideas about education, as well as a painful recognition that public education would not flourish on its own without government leadership. But just a few months after creating the Department, Congress moved on to even grander plans, imposing education conditions on Southern states seeking readmission to the Union. The readmission process afforded Congress far more leverage over states than any department ever would. Congress had the possibility of doing something "constitutional," not just legislative.

THE CIVIL WAR FORMALLY ENDED ON APRIL 9, 1865. THE THIRteenth Amendment to the US Constitution was ratified on December 6, 1865, abolishing slavery. The following year, Congress passed the Civil Rights Act of 1866, prohibiting discrimination in various aspects of life and extending citizenship to African Americans (though doing so raised questions about its constitutional authority). Congress did not get down to the legal and constitutional details of how it would reunify the states and rebuild our democracy until 1867. By then, ten Confederate states in the Deep South were still waiting to rejoin the Union (the border states had never really left and had formally reentered in summary fashion).

The legislative terms of their readmission came in the form of the Reconstruction Acts of 1867 and 1868. The Reconstruction Act of 1867 spelled out four distinct conditions for readmission. First, the states had to "for[m] a constitution of government in conformity with the Constitution of the United States in all respects." Second, "the elective franchise shall be enjoyed by all such persons as have the qualifications herein stated." Third, states must submit those constitutions to Congress, which will determine whether they are consistent with the US Constitution. Finally, states must adopt the Fourteenth Amendment (which, among other things, prohibited states from denying anyone equal protection under the law or depriving individuals of life, liberty, or property without due process). These terms of readmission were unequivocal. As the preamble to the Reconstruction Act bluntly stated, "Peace and good order should be enforced in said States until loyal and republican State governments can be legally established."[25]

The condition that elicited the most national and long-term attention was requiring states to ratify the Fourteenth Amendment. Congress was facing an enormous problem with the Fourteenth Amendment. In 1867, the Amendment was still eleven votes short of the number necessary for final ratification and inclusion in the US Constitution. Some Northern states had voted against the Amendment and the only way to get it across the constitutional finish line was with positive votes from all the Confederate states. Congress solved the problem by tying readmission to the ratification of the Fourteenth Amendment. The radical nature of this requirement—a requirement that some argued made the Fourteenth Amendment itself an illegitimate addition to the Constitution—obviously generated tremendous controversy.

The other conditions flew under the radar, to some extent, but were no less important. An education hook was carefully embedded in them. The requirement that new state constitutions conform to the "Constitution of the United States in all respects" was a requirement that they establish republican forms of government. To the casual observer, the requirement of a republican form of government might sound pro forma. The US Constitution already had a clause in it requiring that each state maintain a republican form of government, so Congress might have simply been reiterating constitutional verbiage. But in historical context, it was the ideological concept for demanding public education. Since the nation's founding, a republican form of government had been linked to education. Explicitly invoking the concept called attention to the fact that Southern states had so clearly failed to meet it for years. The implications for education—and voting—were unmistakable. Congress was now calling Southern states to task for their failures and using the power of readmission as the tool to fix the problem.

The real question was whether the requirement of a republican form of government was sufficient to accomplish the goal or whether Congress should go one step further and make education an additional explicit condition of readmission. On the one hand, Congress had made its view clear that public education was a central component of a republican form of government. Debates on the Reconstruction Act, the Department of Education, and the extensive education work it was supporting through the Freedmen's Bureau all confirmed Congress's view. On the other hand, laying out education as a term of readmission, just as Congress had with voting, had its merits. But the challenge with education, as opposed to voting, was in the details. The Northwest Ordinance had shown that it is one thing to make a general commitment to education. It is an entirely different thing to resolve all the issues involved in implementing public education.

Senator Charles Sumner of Massachusetts sided with leaving nothing to doubt. Sumner moved to make education an explicit condition of Confederate states' readmission. His proposed amendment to the Reconstruction Act would require states "to establish and sustain a system of public schools open to all, without distinction of race or color."[26] Sumner believed that this condition was as important as any other Congress could impose. Sumner said he could forgo all his other amendments (aimed at ensuring the stability of the reconstituted Southern governments) for the promise of public education. He argued that if the Senate did nothing else, it should guarantee education in the Confederate states. Only education could cure the underlying causes of the Civil War and ward off future tensions.[27] Sumner detailed the high illiteracy rates in the South, which stood in stark contrast to the North. "A population that could not read and write," he reasoned, "naturally failed to comprehend and appreciate a republican government."[28] This left the slaveholding elites free to march common whites into a war that did nothing in the service of their own interests. This elitist domination, he pointed out, had deep roots in the South and was averse to public education.

Sumner made it clear, however, that imposing education as a condition on readmission was not about "vengeance" on the South. As he spoke, the South remained under military rule, meaning no civil—much less democratic—government was in place. Some in Congress would have been content to keep it that way for a while longer. But Sumner argued that ensuring education in the South was for its own "good with which is intertwined the good of all." A system of public education would serve as "a new safeguard for the future" and "would not impose any new burden." To the contrary, substituting "schoolmasters," books, and "schoolhouses" in the place of "soldiers," "bayonets," and military "headquarters" would allow peace to replace military rule.[29] Such a transition would represent "a new triumph for civilization."

Sumner was not alone. Several other senators trumpeted his points and added their own distinct ones. Senator Morton simplified the issue into one of basic political reality. "When you add to the uneducated whites the uneducated negroes you have a full half of the whole voting population unable to read and write; and we cannot expect the men who own the property to voluntarily tax themselves to provide education for the others." Unless the state provides public education at public expense, the masses will remain illiterate and "the political power will remain almost entirely in the hands of the present rebel-educated classes." If the North wanted to break that power dynamic, it had to act decisively in education. "Republican government may go on for a while with half the voters unable to read or write, but it cannot long continue. . . . Now, sir, at this last, this most important hour in this great work of reconstruction, let us provide for the education of these people."[30] In other words, Congress was just wasting its time with Reconstruction if it was not serious about guaranteeing public education. Illiteracy was too disabling and vested property interests too strong to expect change without it.

Senator Cole hammered what is, in effect, the thesis of this and the previous chapter: the nation's track record of providing for education stretched from the founding through the most recent legislative session.

To step into the breach once more is no radical thing. The radical thing is to walk away. Cole explained that Congress began providing "liberal grants of the public lands to the States for purposes of education" in the 1700s. The folly was not with Congress, but with Southern states that did not put those lands to their intended use. "Those communities which were lately in rebellion . . . diverted [their school land grants and resources] to other uses." This "evil" alone now justified corrective action and Congress knew it. That's why it "establish[ed] a Department of Education" a year earlier in 1866—to study what had gone wrong with those grants and devise a new plan for education expansion. This is to say nothing of the fact that Southern states had criminalized the education of African Americans. Against this backdrop, conditioning Southern states' readmission on education was a plain and logical extension of everything that had preceded that moment.

Yet it wouldn't be the Senate without a vigorous debate. True to form, several senators contested Sumner's amendment, but the precise basis for their objections is telling. They did not object to expanding education or question its role in a republican form of government. They questioned the fairness of conditioning readmission in general, regardless of the specific condition. Senator Hendricks, for instance, emphasized that he had supported "universal education" in the past, but he was voting against the amendment because it was wrong to condition Southern states' readmission. He was, however, careful to leave open the possibility of voting against the readmission of a Southern state that failed to put education in its constitution. In other words, it was a matter of ordering for him. He thought Congress could not legitimately dictate in advance what states must put in their constitutions. They were, after all, the states' constitutions. Congress should, instead, wait until states submitted their constitutions. At that point, Congress could decide whether a state's constitution was republican in form.[31] Another senator argued that even if Congress could impose conditions, springing new ones on Southern states at the last moment would be an act of "bad faith." Congress had already laid out its conditions to Southern states and the South was relying on them.

The only substantive concerns with Sumner's amendment were in regard to its racial implications, not education. Senator Frelinghuysen raised the mildest complaint on this score, arguing that Sumner's requirement that schools be open to all without "distinction to race or color" served no purpose. Congress already prohibited discrimination through the Civil Rights Act of 1866 and the Fourteenth Amendment would constitutionalize the principle. Another race prohibition would be redundant. This argument assumed that the new state constitutions would provide for education. So the problem with Sumner's amendment was not that it required education, but that it went one step further to mandate anti-discrimination.

Whether Frelinghuysen's real objection was redundancy or he was executing a calculated strategy to doom Sumner's amendment is hard to discern. Either way, those who joined Frelinghuysen were direct about their racial concerns. Senator Williams drove home his core opposition to Sumner's amendment with a simple question. Williams pressed Sumner to admit that states would be forced to "appropriate enough money out of [their] treasury to support a system of common schools" and then asked: "Does this proposition mean that . . . there shall not be such a thing as a school for white children and a school for black children, but that each and every school shall be open to children of both races?" Sumner flatly replied: "If I should have my way . . . it would be that the schools, precisely like the ballot-box or the rail cars, should be open to all."[32] Shortly thereafter, the amendment went to a vote and failed by a vote of 20 to 20.[33]

Considering the broader racial context, though, this tie vote speaks volumes to the strength of support for public education. The support for education was nearly enough to carry the day for a more radical principle—integrated education. One group of Southern-sympathizing senators objected to conditions no matter what they might be. Another group, surely not limited to Senator Williams, objected to racial equality in schools. Sumner's own hometown of Boston had even maintained segregated schools through 1855. But imposing education as a necessary part of a republican form of government drew no challenges in the

Senate. And at least one senator, who would have broken the tie, voted against the Sumner amendment as a matter of process, reserving the right to later reject state constitutions that came before Congress without an education provision. In short, with issues of race and the general politics of readmission weighing Sumner's amendment down, it still managed a tie vote because of education's importance to a republican form of government. It was that uncontested notion of education as a pillar of republican government that helped shape how Southern states handled their constitutional conventions. Those who handled it poorly would not easily make it back into the Union.

In the end, the Reconstruction Act forwent the explicit guarantee Sumner wanted, but the fact that states would still have to submit their constitutions to Congress for final approval meant that Congress's general expectations regarding republican forms of government remained crucially important.[34] And no one doubted Congress's expectations regarding education in a republican form of government.[35] Congress had made that expectation abundantly clear not only with this debate but with the creation of the Department of Education and the work of the Freedmen's Bureau.

The final and clearest indication of Congress's expectations came in 1870 when it admitted the last Confederate states to the Union. As the state constitutions rolled in for congressional approval, Congress began to fear problems with its own plan. All the state constitutions through 1868 had done exactly what Congress expected—extend the vote to African Americans and provide for education—but some states seemed ready to exploit gaps in the Reconstruction Act and revert to earlier practices in defiance of it. Georgia was the most troubling.

Shortly after Georgia passed its new constitution, ratified the Fourteenth Amendment, and gained readmission to the Union, Democrats met in Atlanta in "the largest political mass meeting ever held in Georgia,"[36] pushing an anti-Reconstruction agenda and slate of candidates. The fervor of that meeting quickly made itself felt in the General Assembly. Democrats handily defeated Republicans in the next election and took majority control of the state house. They then sought to further consolidate their power by expelling black legislators from the Assembly. They audaciously claimed the Reconstruction Act allowed it, as the Act had only required that African Americans be allowed to vote, not hold office.

If a readmitted state would be so bold, what might those other states that were slow to seek readmission do once they got it? Virginia, for instance, had yet to ratify an acceptable constitution and was already showing troubling signs of recalcitrance. With this reality before Congress and the Fourteenth Amendment's ratification behind it, Congress took the step Sumner had called for a year earlier: Congress imposed education as an explicit condition of readmission for the last three Confederate states to reenter the Union—Virginia, Texas, and Mississippi. In the legislation readmitting those states, Congress explicitly provided that the constitutions of these final three states "shall never be so amended or changed as to deprive any citizen or class of citizens of the United States of the school rights and privileges secured by the constitution of said State[s]."[37]

The final legislation dropped the direct reference to racially integrated schools found in Sumner's earlier proposal, but this new legislation was broader, protecting the rights of all citizens to education. This broader protection made perfect sense. It represented the principle that education is a basic right of citizenship in a republican form of government, not just an instrumental tool to remedy past racial transgressions. Yet, at the same time, the final legislation reflected a keen awareness of how circumstances on the ground might change, like they had in Georgia. Guarding against that threat, the legislation sought to lock in the education rights in those constitutions in perpetuity. The states could expand education rights, but they could not retract them. Those rights were, in effect, the baseline of what it took for those states to call themselves republican forms of government and reenter the Union.

CHAPTER 5

A CONSTITUTIONAL CHORUS
FOR THE RIGHT TO EDUCATION

THE HALLS OF CONGRESS TELL ONLY HALF THE STORY OF securing the right to education during Reconstruction. Those individuals who participated in state constitutional conventions across the South proved equally committed to ensuring education's status as a constitutional duty of the state. They fully understood the meaning of Senator Charles Sumner's speech: constitutionalizing education would not only serve the North's interests but the South's ability to operate governments for and by the people. In the span of just two years, the Southern states that provided the final votes to ratify the Fourteenth Amendment transformed themselves from a region in which education was not guaranteed anywhere to one in which it was guaranteed everywhere (even if only in a legal sense).

The state constitutional conventions began meeting immediately after Congress passed the Reconstruction Act of 1867.[1] Delegates were crystal clear on their task of creating a republican form of government.[2] They were equally clear in their conviction that a public education system was the top priority in meeting at this challenge.

The conventions had countless different issues, small and large, to address as they threw off the shackles of the old way of doing things—everything from the structure of the judicial, legislative, and executive branches (along with their exact powers), to elections, state debts, taxation, and regulation. Education always received its own distinct attention, with most conventions establishing a committee to give education exclusive focus.

South Carolina's well-documented constitutional convention provides a poignant example of Reconstruction's robust ideological debate. On the first day, Delegate Craig announced that he had come to the convention "to frame a new constitution, or to make such changes in the old one as were necessary to secure a Republican form of Government."[3] This refrain did not let up until the convention was complete. In one six-day stretch, delegates referenced a "republican form of government" more than fifty times.[4] Invoked so often, the references might be dismissed as rhetorical flourish or linguistic filler. Surely, they were at times. But just as often, the references were an ideological lodestar through which policy ideas had to pass, particularly those affecting voting and education.

The convention's Education Committee got to work quickly and proposed a robust, detailed, and mandatory system of public education.[5] A constitutional preamble followed by twelve distinct sections specified everything from school funding and taxes to compulsory education and teacher training. A close reading of the preamble and the main section that followed South Carolina's constitutional provision for education also reveals a common thread stretching through recent debates in Congress and all the way back to the nation's founding.

The preamble reads as though it were lifted straight out of the Massachusetts Constitution—the nation's first to include an education clause in 1780. Both constitutions declare that a "diffusion" of "knowledge . . . among the body of the people . . . [is necessary] for the preservation of their rights and liberties," and both made it "the duty of legislatures and magistrates, in all future periods of this commonwealth, to cherish the interests of literature and the sciences, and all seminaries of them; especially the . . . public schools." The only substantive divergence between

South Carolina and Massachusetts was South Carolina's attempt to improve upon Massachusetts's original idea. South Carolina proposed that
the schools be "open to all the children and youths of the State, without
regard to race or color." This language unmistakably came from Sumner's
proposed amendment a year earlier in Congress.

Below the surface of these broad shared principles, however, South
Carolina detailed far more aspects of the education system than Massachusetts and did not blindly follow Yankee ideas—as one delegate put
it—in any event.[6] South Carolina's delegates staunchly debated those
details and often fought for principles and protections even more radical
than those found in the Massachusetts Constitution. This progressive
local sentiment showed in issues ranging from how best to raise money
for education to whether the constitution should compel school attendance and mandate racially equal access.

The question of school funding, one of the most complex in terms
of practical implementation, came up early in the convention. The delegates intended to do more than just commit aspirations to parchment,
more than the founding generation's decision to just encourage good
faith efforts. So, rather than just put education into the constitution,
South Carolina's delegates specified a plan that would force an education system into existence. Doing this required money, far more money
than the prior government had required. The delegates did not shirk
from the cost of government and a vastly expanded education system.
The chairman of the Finance Committee said it was simply a cost the
state had to plan for: "We who make the Constitution are deeply interested in advancing [the cause of financing it], for upon this rests our
hope of perpetuating the Government we ordain. To realize the greatest
practical benefit from the new Government we create, we must adopt
such measures as will sustain such Government. . . . We are not legis-
lating for today."[7]

Yet there were those who feared the state, no matter how well laid
its plans, couldn't afford an education system. The state was only a few
years removed from a war that had claimed tens of thousands of lives
and devastated the economy. Confederate currency was cancelled and

much of the state's infrastructure was in shambles. Large parts of the state capital had been destroyed, and a fire had burned central Columbia to the ground. On top of that, General Sherman's forces destroyed whatever was left of military value in the capital—warehouses, manufacturing, and railroad depots. In this context, some convention delegates thought the state needed more time to regain its financial footing before taking on significant new costs. They did not oppose a constitutional obligation to create education, but they favored language giving the legislature time to complete the task. These voices, however, represented a small minority. The overwhelming sentiment wanted an education system immediately. To see it done, the convention enacted extraordinary financing measures.

Whereas Northern states had resisted and waffled on statewide taxes for education for half a century, South Carolina's delegates addressed education taxes head-on with the intent of settling any uncertainties. Delegates feared that leaving education taxes and funding to legislative discretion could result in insufficient or delayed school funds—something the delegates would not tolerate. They wanted "a system of free schools at as early a day as possible" and mandated that the state act immediately on taxes. The constitution required the General Assembly to "levy at each regular session after the adoption of this Constitution an annual tax on all taxable property throughout the State for the support of public schools."[8] But the convention went one step further. Delegates thought that the property tax might falter because "the property holders are few in number, and their property is not remunerative."[9] So they adopted an insurance policy of sorts: a poll tax.

Today poll taxes are seen as a tool of racial and socioeconomic oppression. In 1867 and 1868, a poll tax was meant to be liberating, reserved solely for the support of public education. They were quite sure that a poll tax would raise the necessary resources for schools. And lest one doubt some ulterior motive was afoot, the poll tax provision included a caveat: "no person shall ever be deprived of the right of suffrage for the non-payment of the said [poll] tax."[10] The delegates wanted to guarantee as many resources as possible for schools as quickly as possible, but they did not want to deprive poor people of the right to vote.

Ironically, the most contentious debate was over something that doesn't raise an eyebrow today: compulsory education. This mundane aspect of modern education sparked intense debate on two grounds. The first was on principle. Some delegates charged that compulsory education was "anti-republican." Parents had the right and liberty, they said, to decide for themselves whether their kids should labor or learn. It was not a bad argument. A similar argument made its way to the US Supreme Court half a century later, but the Court validated the decision that South Carolina and several other states had made: It is fully within the state's power, if not its solemn duty, to see that all kids are educated.[11]

Delegate Ransier chided those who would make children's education optional, arguing that "the success of republicanism depends [on] the progress which our people are destined to make. If parents are disposed to clog this progress by neglecting the education of their children, for one, I will not aid and abet them."[12] The delegates expanded on this idea, explaining that republican government and individual liberty are reinforcing principles, not enemies. The attempt to pit them against one another is nonsensical. One delegate said that he was "willing to accept the widest, highest, and most expansive definition of freedom, but I am not disposed to accept the term as synonymous with unbridled licence. Men, living in a savage, uncivilized state are perfectly free. . . . But the first thing, when a man goes into society, is to concede certain individual rights necessary for the protection and preservation of society."[13] In other words, individuals who want a republican government dedicated to freedom cannot have their cake and eat it, too. Republican government has to restrain individuals in certain respects so as to expand liberty for all.

When Delegate Ransier rose to speak again, he captured his peers' imagination. They allowed him to deliver one of the convention's longest commentaries. Hitting his stride, Ransier captured a century's worth of thinking about education in a republican government but added the immediate real-world context that rebutted any notion that the matter was theoretical. Speaking in the ashes of a society that had left education to chance, Ransier defended compulsory education, arguing

> that it is the sacred, solemn, and imperative duty of the State to vouchsafe to all its citizens all their rights, and all their privileges, [but] I also maintain that it is just as much its bounden duty to check and restrain the abuse of those rights and privileges, that the government has the prerogative to assume to act as the regulator, and monitor, as well as the faithful defender and preserver of liberty. No one will deny that individual rights should and ought to be subservient to the great interests of the common weal and prosperity. "No one has a right to do as he pleases, unless he pleases to do right.". . .

> In the present relationships of our mixed population in the United States, this law of compulsion is called for as a defence of our liberties. We have in our country more than a million children between the ages of five and sixteen who can neither read nor write! Do you ask what we are going to do with them? That is not the question. The question is, what are they going to do with us? Think of their future power at the ballot-box!

> I appeal to gentlemen of the Convention to know whether they desire to see a state of anarchy, or a state of confusion in South Carolina in the future. I desire to know whether they wish to see an independent people, engaged in industrious pursuits, living happy and contented. The child that remains in ignorance until grown up will never learn the first duty that ought to be learned by every man, which is to love his country and to love his State. If a man is so ignorant as to know nothing of political economy of his State or country, he can never be a good citizen. . . . If you give a man the privilege of remaining in ignorance, it is anti-republicanism to punish him. You must compel them to learn. Do that and you will have peace in the future. If you neglect to do this, you must expect confusion, vice, and everything of the sort.[14]

Hon. J. J. Wright, judge of the
Supreme Court of South Carolina.
Courtesy of Wikimedia Commons.

Ransier's commentary drew but one response. Interestingly, it was
from Jonathan Jasper Wright, a Northern-born African American lawyer
who came to South Carolina at the end of the Civil War to organize and
teach in freedmen's schools. Later, General Howard appointed Wright
to head the Freedmen's Bureau in Beaufort. Two years after the constitutional convention, Wright became the first African American to serve
on the state supreme court. Wright's standing, particularly on the subject of schools, could not have been much higher.

Wright pointed out that some children would need to cover long
distances to attend schools. In rural areas, where public schools might
not be available at all for some time, complying with a compulsory attendance requirement would be all but impossible for many families.
Wright offered a lawyerly solution to the problem: direct the legislature
to provide for compulsory attendance but give it the discretion to adjust
the law across time. The fervor supporting immediate, unqualified education, however, wouldn't stomach Wright's measured approach. The
convention pressed forward.

If there was to be a stumbling block for education, it would be that
the schools that students were compelled to attend would be open to all,

regardless of race or class. In other words, compulsory schooling could mean integrated schooling, a thing far more unsettling to some. Delegates feared the prospect of integrated schools might bring the whole education system down. Many white families would, no doubt, protest sending their kids to school with blacks. Wealthy families might also object to mixing with lower classes. These protests could grow into something larger than individual families' belief that their children did not need education. Disaffected white families could easily coalesce around racial animosity and boycott schools, regardless of what they thought of education itself. Then the state would have a serious problem on its hands. It would have to actually enforce compulsory education against recalcitrant families or conveniently ignore them. Enforcement, if it was even possible, could be counterproductive. But turning a blind eye would deprive swaths of students of the education that they and the revival of democratic society desperately needed.

Against this backdrop and just three years after the fall of the Confederacy, integrated education stood as an issue that could have split the convention and doomed the passage of the education clause. Rising above the times, the convention delegates responded with a level of idealism and equality so radical that it puts modern society to shame. John Chestnut,[15] an African American delegate who had also served as a delegate to the Colored People's Convention of South Carolina in 1865, saw equal education as a first-order principle that could not be sacrificed to practical concerns:

Republicanism has given us freedom, equal rights, and equal laws. Republicanism must also give us education and wisdom. It seems that the great difficulty in this section is in the fact that difficulty may arise between the two races, in the same school, or that the whites will not send their children to the same schools with the colored children. What of that? Has not this Convention a right to establish a free school system for the benefit of the poorer classes? Undoubtedly. Then if there be a hostile disposition among the whites, an unwillingness to send their children to school, the fault is their own, not ours.[16]

His point echoed through the voices that followed him. For instance, Delegate Robert Elliott, who later served as a member of the US House of Representatives and as South Carolina's attorney general, argued that "it is republicanism to reward virtue. It is republicanism to educate the people, without discrimination."[17] The breadth and depth of the principles the convention adopted would reverberate beyond the immediate moment. The state's entire future hung in the balance. "The question," Elliot said, "is not white or black united or divided, but whether children shall be sent to school or kept at home. If they are compelled to be educated, there will be no danger of the Union, or a second secession of South Carolina from the Union."[18]

Sensing that this perspective was about to carry the day, Charles P. Leslie, a white delegate who later served as a state senator, implored the Convention to come to its senses. "Right upon the heel of [our other successes], and at a time when everything is going on sensibly, so that it is believed no power in the State can by any possibility defeat the adoption of our Constitution, comes a proposition that must be odious to a large class of people in the State."[19] South Carolina, he argued, needed a constitution that would pass and secure black people's rights and privileges, not "a Constitution that is in all respects just exactly what we would have it. . . . There are a great many provisions that I myself would be glad to insert in that Constitution, but I will never be guilty of doing an act when my own good sense condemns that act."[20] It was time to compromise in the realm of what was possible. "If you do not happen to get all you want; if you do not want to insert a provision which will endanger the result of the vote on the Constitution when it goes before the people, then for heaven's sake have sense enough to leave it out."

This provision, he was quite sure, would do no good, even if it somehow managed to become part of the constitution:

> Every time you undertake to force a people to do what you know they do not want to do, it can never be carried out. . . . Who is going to execute this law if made? . . . Our friend . . . undertakes to tell us the loyal men are going to do it. Who are they? Are they the black

people in the State? You cannot force them any more than you can the whites. There is no use making a law unless you can enforce it; but if you undertake to go on with this wild business, I warn you of the consequences.[21]

But when the final votes were tallied, none of these concerns, not even the racial ones, managed a serious constituency. The votes for compulsory education were in the bag. The convention did not even vote on compulsory education separately, just including it in the vote for the overall education provisions. The more controversial requirement that education be provided without any racial distinctions was put to its own vote. Eighty percent of the delegates supported the prohibition on discrimination.[22] The annual poll tax to support public education passed with similar ease. Interestingly, African Americans supported the poll tax by a larger margin than whites.[23]

Also important to note is what went entirely unchallenged over the course of the convention: education as a necessity. No one dared challenge the idea. No one dared stand in the way of the state taking on its republican duty to educate its citizens. Not a single voice rose to offer a substantive objection to the state's duty—to articulate the notion, for instance, that it was for families, not the state, to educate children. The most that could be mustered in opposition to the education provisions was the notion that the state might need more time to raise resources and that pressing on matters of race might undermine the larger goal of education for all.

When the convention was called to a close, the president of the convention called their work a rebirth of republicanism with education at its center.

Here we have made every needful arrangement for the free education of our people, so that if future legislators shall carry out in good faith the provisions which we have ordained on this vital subject, in a few years the stain of ignorance which now pollutes our history will be forever obliterated, and the happy period will have arrived when no son or daughter of South Carolina will be unable to read and write. Thus have we broadly sown the seeds of public education, and thus shall we, in no distant time, reap the rich harvest of public virtue. Crime and ignorance are inseparable companions. We have stricken a heavy blow at both, and may look for the natural and inevitable result in the elevation of all our people to a social, political and religious eminence, to which, under the former Constitution and laws of the State, they had never attained.[24]

South Carolina's Constitutional Convention, while more emphatic and detailed on education than others, was not unique. Similar debates, rationales, and objections were offered across the South.[25] Issues as weighty as race and meager state finances were not enough to dissuade those states from enacting education clauses, either.[26] If anything, states strengthened their education clauses rather than concede to these concerns.[27] On the question of funding, which was a widespread concern, several state constitutions designated specific sources of funding for

African American delegates at the Virginia Constitutional Convention of 1868. *Courtesy of the Library of Congress.*

education, ensuring both that the funding would be available and that it would exclusively support education. Alabama, for instance, required that all proceeds from state lands "be inviolably appropriated to educational purposes" and that one-fifth of the state's general annual revenues "be devoted exclusively to the maintenance of public schools."[28] Like South Carolina, other states also imposed poll taxes for education.[29]

As often as not, these education clauses sailed through the conventions with relatively little debate.[30] To the extent states differed from South Carolina's sentiment, it was on race. Delegates in some states lodged racist appeals against education.[31] In North Carolina, for instance, a delegate remarked that "we cannot view, without serious apprehension, the admission to all the highest rights and privileges of citizenship of a race, consisting almost entirely of those recently emerged from slavery and unfitted by previous education and habits."[32] This sort of comment may have been tempered in South Carolina because African Americans held a majority in the convention delegation. Yet even in these more racially hostile environments, delegates in these other states did not question the centrality of education to republican government. At most, they contested racial equity in education, as they understood that offering education would have ripple effects throughout public life, most notably the real chance of equal citizenship and democratic power.

Nonetheless, state after state enacted education clauses mandating that the state provide public education.[33] These education clauses represented nothing short of a constitutional revolution. While some Southern states had mentioned education in their pre–Civil War constitutions, they had not affirmatively obligated the state to establish a statewide system of schools. Tennessee's and Kentucky's pre-war constitutions were the strongest, but still short of that affirmative duty.

Kentucky was the first new state to enter the Union after Congress passed the Northwest Ordinance and its formal commitments to education. While not technically subject to the Northwest Ordinance (because it was carved from an existing tract of land), Kentucky adopted the Ordinance's language into its constitution, indicating that the state should "encourage" education.[34] This language was, again, part of that unbroken line between the nation's founding ideas, the Northwest Ordinance, and states' action in support of education. But Kentucky's constitutional language suffered from the same flaw as the Northwest Ordinance: it didn't mandate an education system. Tennessee's constitutional provision was even weaker. It established a fund for schools, but did nothing to require the state to create schools, much less a system of them.

By 1868, everything had changed. Nine out of the ten states readmitted through the Reconstruction Act included a new affirmative education clause in their state constitution.[35] Almost all of them used the phrase "system" of schools, making statewide and consistent access to public education clear. Several went even further, including modifiers that required a "thorough" or "uniform" system of schools.[36] They were building on Ohio's constitution, which had required a "thorough and efficient" school system in 1851. In Ohio, the purpose of the language was "to see a system of schools as perfect as could be devised, and to see it improve so as to keep pace with the most rapid progress of the most rapid element of our social or political constitution."[37] Southern states readily adopted this phraseology and variations on it, presumably with the same purpose.

A couple of states, however, invoked their own unique language. Alabama, for instance, was practical minded, looking to guarantee the immediate future with simplicity and clarity. Alabama's constitution required the state to establish "one or more schools" in each township and school district.[38] Florida went in the opposite direction, adding emphasis on the state's education duty. Florida, like most other states, required "a uniform system of Common Schools," but made it "the paramount duty of the State to make ample provision" for those schools.[39]

The other unmistakable thread running through these education clauses was their emulation of Charles Sumner's proposed condition for readmission—that states create a system of "public schools open to all, without distinction of race or color." States used some derivation of his language. South Carolina, of course, adopted Sumner's proposal wholesale, using both of its key concepts: "all" and "without distinction of race." Louisiana went a step further, extending integration beyond just the common schools. It provided that "all children of this State between the ages of six and twenty-one shall be admitted to the public schools or other institutions of learning sustained or established by the State in common without distinction of race, color or previous condition. There shall be no separate schools or institutions of learning established exclusively for any race by the State of Louisiana."[40] Pretty heady stuff for 1868.

The more common approach, however, was to just state that schools must be "open to all." "All" lacks the definiteness of Sumner's approach and, without it, later generations might argue that an education clause did not include an anti-discrimination principle at all. But the idea of schools open to all has a universal and potentially broader uncompromising meaning as well. States did not have to specify that schools be open to all. They could have left it at requiring a system of education. That would have implicitly countenanced the possibility of segregation and exclusion. The fact that they didn't indicate that they were aiming for the broader universal principle that encompassed anti-discrimination. States later reinforced this interpretation when they thought it necessary to alter their education clauses to provide for segregation during Jim Crow.

THIS RADICAL EDUCATION REVOLUTION, WHILE CONCENTRATED in the South, was not limited to the region. Sparks of that revolution could be seen in other states before the Civil War ended. Those prewar states, however, remained outliers and the nation's education future uncertain until the South acted. Once the South acted—as a whole by 1868—the education revolution had the clarity and strength to solidify expectations for the rest of the nation moving forward. The history of the right to education, quite simply, divides into the world before and after 1868. Uncertainty pervaded the preceding years and nothing would ever be the same again in the subsequent years.

The first hint of the coming change was with the four new states that joined the Union in the 1860s: Kansas, West Virginia, Nevada, and Nebraska.[41] All four entered with education clauses in their constitutions.[42] Kansas initially sought to enter the Union as a slave state, but Congress rejected Kansas's first three pro-slavery constitutions. On its fourth attempt, Kansas passed an anti-slavery constitution and Congress admitted it to the Union in 1861. The 1861 constitution also included an education clause modeled after Northern systems. West Virginia, of course, was born out of the Civil War itself, separating from Confederate Virginia and joining the Union. Its constitution also included an education clause. Nevada and Nebraska were less dramatic. They entered the Union with education clauses in 1864 and 1867—with Nevada removed further in distance and Nebraska further in time from the war.

The real drama occurred, however, in an existing state, not a new one: Missouri. Missouri originally petitioned to enter the Union as a slave state in 1819. Had Congress granted the petition, Missouri would have broken the national balance between slave and free states, tipping it toward slavery. The South would not stand for keeping Missouri out, and the North would not stand for becoming a minority. To keep the national peace, Congress devised the Missouri Compromise, admitting Missouri as a slave state and Maine as a free state. It also drew an imaginary line westward, separating free and slave territories. Slavery could exist below the line, but not above it. The peace, however, was short-lived. The Supreme Court declared the compromise unconstitutional in *Dred Scott v. Sanford* in 1857, triggering fears and tension that all but assured the Civil War.

As the Civil War neared its end, Missouri—the state that had generated so much controversy—took a major step away from its slave roots, foreshadowing what was hopefully to come in other states. Missouri's Constitutional Convention began on January 6, 1865, and wrapped up on April 10—the day after Robert E. Lee surrendered to Ulysses Grant at Appomattox and ended the war. At that momentous occasion, Missouri explicitly mandated that the state provide education for "all" children.[43] Missouri's rationale did not mince words. As one delegate explained, the state was "throw[ing] off the shackles of a system of domestic slavery" to ensure that all citizens could participate in a republican form of government.[44] It hoped to set an important example—one that could not have

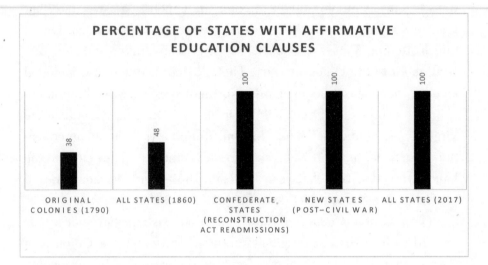

Percentage of states with affirmative education clauses.
Courtesy of the author.

been imagined just a few short years earlier. Once a slave state, Missouri would now be constitutionally free and educated, "a worthy pattern for all States."[45]

Missouri was prescient. Only one in five state constitutions affirmatively guaranteed education at the turn of the nineteenth century. At midcentury, that number was still only one in three. With four existing states and one new state adding an education clause in the 1850s, the number edged close to 50 percent.[46] In the three years immediately following the Civil War, that percentage jumped to over 80. And after 1868—the year the Fourteenth Amendment was ratified and the nation's constitutional reunification was no longer in doubt—no state would ever again enter into the Union of the United States of America without an education clause in its constitution. This was no accident.

Congress was no longer willing to leave public education to chance. Education's role in democracy was too central and the possibility that states might later backtrack on education too dangerous. Guarding against regression, Congress, as noted above, conditioned the final three Confederate states' readmission on them never taking away the education rights that they had just vested in their constitutions. While the importance of this fact has been almost entirely lost on historians, Congress did not forget it. Half a century later when New Mexico petitioned for statehood and failed to include an education clause in its constitution after the war, Congress rejected the petition.[47] New Mexico had somehow overlooked the education revolution that so rapidly spread in the aftermath of the war.

What New Mexico had missed, even Northern states—safe and secure in their standing—did not. Several Northern states revised their constitutions following the war. Congress had no leverage over them, but the recommitment to a republican form of government swept over them, too. As they revised their constitutions, they included education clauses, and, by 1875, every state except one had an education clause. Equally remarkable is the progressive conversation that pervaded those changes in the North.

Pennsylvania's 1874 constitution, in particular, offers a microcosm of the nation's education journey, marking just how far it had come and was still willing to go. At the dawn of the nation, Pennsylvania's 1776 constitution reflected the sentiment of the Northwest Ordinance. It called for one school per county for the "convenient instruction of the youth" and "encourage[d]" universities. In 1790, constitutional revisions forwarded the notion that the state's education responsibilities were discretionary and the schools that it might create were just for poor kids. Other families, the legislature must have assumed, could fend for themselves or seek education through religious organizations. Those assumptions were gross miscalculations. Education stalled in Pennsylvania. There was far from enough of it in the cities and none at all in many rural areas.

Against that backdrop, delegates to Pennsylvania's 1872–1873 convention proclaimed that "the section on education [was] second in importance to no other section to be submitted to this Convention."[48] Some believed that the very passage of the constitution rested on what they did with education. A lot of people would vote for or against the entire constitution based on whether it promised to meet their education needs. The vital importance of education inspired the convention to take exceptional steps—financially, structurally, and politically.

Pennsylvania's convention predictably reiterated the time-honored notion that public education is a necessity of a republican form of government, but it also emphasized the state's experience that grounded that mantra in reality. Delegates indicated that scores of uneducated voters went to the polls each election with no understanding of who or what they were voting for, leaving them vulnerable to fraud and bribes. To solve this and other problems, Pennsylvania went to a level of prescription not seen in other constitutions.

It was not enough to mandate public education; the convention sought to ensconce education as the state's primary function. Everything else paled in comparison. Even on the question of when and how often the legislature would meet, education took front stage. Legislatures have countless issues to manage, but the one thing the Pennsylvania legislature must do, one delegate emphasized, is convene regularly for the purpose of maintaining the education system: unlike other issues, "our system of common schools . . . require an annual appropriation and annual supervision."[49]

The convention also sought to build a special constitutional structure around education to separate it from the normal politics of lawmaking. Delegate Buckalew explained that "our common schools constitute a sort of neutral territory . . . where all our people stand on common ground," and they must stay that way.[50] The delegates' fear of political influence was palpable and distinct. In the South, the fear was that states would lack the resources to immediately fund a system of public education. In Pennsylvania, the fear was that the state would simply choose not to. For that reason, the convention moved its new education clause as far away from its old one as possible, eliminating legislative discretion and mandating specific actions.

One of the first steps was to make the state superintendent of education an independent constitutional officer. They did not want the superintendent to be an extension of the governor or the legislature. The superintendent should carry out the most important and basic function of government without fear of friend or foe.[51] Delegate Lear explained that the superintendent should be "characterized by official purity" and free "from all the contaminating influences of political manipulation and management."[52] So, unlike other state officers, the superintendent would not serve at the pleasure of the governor but would have a full four-year term.[53] The delegates were so adamant about the superintendent's independence that they resisted even having the description of the superintendent included in the part of the constitution pertaining to the executive.[54]

Ensuring independence also required a different approach to education funding. Rather than a funding bill that might vary in terms of when and how it was taken up each year, the constitution made public school appropriations part of the general appropriations bill for state government offices, placing school funding on the same plane as the courts and legislature.[55] Everything else that the state might spend money on would be in separate bills.[56] Even more poignantly, the convention mandated that the legislature appropriate no less than $1 million for education each year, a roughly 30 percent increase over the prior year. The important point, however, was not the dollar amount but that the convention was dictating education at such a detailed level.

Ironically, by dictating a specific dollar amount, the convention was also doing something that would necessarily be outdated in the near future. Some delegates claimed that such a measure was unbefitting of a constitution—and they were probably right. Others argued that the legislature could be trusted to carry out its most important function. But these objections were drowned out by those who emphasized that the importance of education required an exception to general rules. Sufficient funding for public schools could not be left to risk or political whim. A non-discretionary funding floor was necessary to solidify the superintendent's independence and alleviate the need to "beg and implore" the legislature for money each year.[57]

Yet for all their firmness, the delegates showed another side—the fear of getting education wrong. Their goal of devising a perfect education system led them down any number of rabbit holes. They intensely debated things big and small—things as big as the implications of using the word "uniform" to describe the education system to things as mundane as textbook selection and the frequency with which they would be purchased. The debate on textbooks alone spanned over thirty pages.[58] The outcome of these debates is beside the point. The debates themselves reveal an effort and seriousness far removed from the wishful thinking of the founders. The time had finally come when a state sought to devise an actual education system that might match the perfection of the republican form of government of which their forefathers had long ago dreamt.

When the people of Pennsylvania ratified that constitution in 1874, they effectively completed the revolution to secure education as a constitutional right (even if it would be toyed with later). At that point, every state but one had an education clause. And the single state without one, Connecticut,[59] was not in dire need. Its public education system predated the US Constitution and was in many respects a century or more ahead of most others. It established its first high school in 1638 (making it the second oldest in the nation), its first school law in 1650, its school tax in 1794, and its upgraded perpetual school fund in 1795.

IF ONE HAD STOPPED AT THAT MOMENT IN HISTORY—OR REALLY any moment in the few years before—and asked those in Congress or those who drafted and ratified the state constitutions and the Fourteenth Amendment to the US Constitution what the two most important rights of citizenship were, it is hard to imagine they would have left education out of their answer. If you had asked them what distinguished America from the rest of the world, they would have said a republican form of government in which everyone from the richest to the poorest can participate, and in which government provides public education so that all might participate intelligently. While that sentiment might have overstated reality, the facts were consistent with that general impression. Save Prussia, no other country in the world equaled the United States in terms of education access. Alexis de Tocqueville and James Bryce—both from Europe and two of the most noted commentators on our nineteenth-century democracy—separately observed that the common man's political engagement in the United States was a re-markable manifestation of the particular form of government the nation had fomented.

But if you asked modern legal scholars whether education is a fundamental right protected by the federal Constitution, they would tell you no, and they would be correct in one sense. The United States Supreme Court (in a 5–4 decision) refused to recognize education as a fundamental right in 1972, reasoning that the Constitution neither explicitly nor implicitly protects education. The Court feared that nothing distinguished education from the various other things that are important in life, like food and shelter. The foregoing history, however, reveals that education is far different than anything else government might offer its citizens (other than the right to vote). The nation's very concept of government is premised on an educated citizenry. From its infancy, the United States has sought to distinguish itself with education. More particularly, education has been the tool through which the nation has sought to perfect its democratic ideas. That, not our failures, is the real lesson to take from our history.

Yet, as the next chapter shows, restricting education can also subvert democracy. Democracy, citizenship, and education ultimately move hand in hand, whether the goals are good or bad. So education policy is never really just about education. The stakes are always much higher.

CHAPTER 6

THE FALL

RECONSTRUCTION AND THE CONSTITUTIONAL RECOMMITMENTS to democracy achieved a lot in the decade immediately following the war. Democracy, however, remained a work in progress in the collision between the ways of old and new, between white aristocracy and inclusive democracy. Inclusive democracy was an idea too bold for many to accept. The collision was so intense that the new democracy rested as much, if not more, on the presence of military force as it did on the power of the idea. In that context, democracy could just as easily retreat as expand.

The possibility of retreat became all the more likely with the contested presidential election of 1876 between Republican Rutherford B. Hayes and Democrat Samuel Tilden. Less than a decade after democracy had blossomed, it wilted from the compromise this election produced. In an election in which eight million votes were cast, Tilden reportedly won the popular vote by a margin of around 250,000, although the level of fraud and voter intimidation on election day made it hard to trust any number.

The problem was most poignant in Louisiana, Florida, and South Carolina. The vote margins in those states were razor-thin and results would be decisive in the electoral college. The presidency literally hinged on the disputed vote counts in those states. Sadly, the chicanery in those states was so pervasive that it was probably impossible to settle on a fair and accurate vote count. So the Republican Party brokered a truce that proved to be no less consequential than the Civil War itself. If the Democrats conceded the election to Rutherford Hayes, he would withdraw Union troops from the South and end Reconstruction.

That deal sealed democracy's and education's fate for much of the next century, particularly for African Americans. So much of what had been accomplished during Reconstruction began to vanish. African Americans were not reduced to slavery. To be clear, they continued making important economic and educational advances, primarily through self-help and Northern philanthropy. But their seat at the public decision-making table and the possibility of full citizenship were gone. With Northern political and military forces receding, Southern whites waged a full assault on the governmental structures that had elevated blacks into the body politic: voting and schooling.

That much cannot be denied or sugarcoated, but so much of the meaning that the historical details represent is in the eyes of the beholder. Appropriately eager to condemn the racist agenda to undermine black citizenship, the modern eye misses other deeper truths of the time. One is that while whites were completely unwilling to share political power with African Americans and squashed black voting at every turn, their attack on public education was nuanced in important respects.

A region where systematic public education, much less education for blacks, had been a foreign idea prior to the war was ironically conflicted in how to execute its attack on education. Yes, whites wanted to ensure blacks would not rise above an oppressed station in life, but most whites had come to see public education as a good thing. Many whites were not, so to speak, willing to throw the baby out with the bathwater when it came to education.

Public education in the South—which was really a black idea—had become too powerful to quash. Whites might not condone equal or integrated education, but they would not easily condone deep incursions into the idea of public education, either. Public schooling had taken hold in enough places and minds, even white minds, that the South could not go back. This allowed public education to move forward even after the 1876 election and the fall of Reconstruction. Public education moved forward as a conflicted institution beset by unreconcilable tensions—an idea too strong to abandon but too dangerous to faithfully implement. When whites regained political power, they retained public education while also going to extreme lengths to block the full citizenship that public education is otherwise intended to produce. This meant reifying public education on the one hand and insisting that it reinforce inequality on the other.

Because whites were disenfranchising blacks at the same time, blacks could do very little to resist. Blacks, however, retained their faith in the promise of education. Even as they saw legal impediments to voting and citizenship rising before their eyes, many did not fully accept or acknowledge that the doors of democracy would soon be entirely closed to them. They continued to believe they could overcome racist ideology and political exclusion so long as the public school doors remained open to them.

This faith was, in important respects, no different than the faith they and their forefathers had held during slavery. Just as literacy had offered the hope and possibility of freedom during slavery, public education could still offer the pathway to meaningful citizenship. Comparing the two periods, the odds would have surely seemed much better, if not reasonable, even after the North abandoned them in 1876. After all, the South could not eviscerate the Fourteenth Amendment's guarantee of equal protection, due process, and the privileges and immunities of citizenship. Nor could it change the Fifteenth Amendment's guarantee of racial equality at the ballot box. But what blacks surely could not have imagined was that judges would turn against them. The single institution designed to rise above politics and stay true to the Constitution's ideas faltered miserably in the face of a white assault on black citizenship. If anything, judges encouraged the assaults. Judicial failures reached all the way to the United States Supreme Court. When African Americans and democracy were in their time of need, the Court acceded to and blessed Reconstruction's reversal and African Americans' oppression.

But if one looks close enough, this dark period once again reveals the power of the idea of a right to public education—how it persevered against racist impulses. Because it persevered, public education has a longer, enduring story that survived for another generation to later call on its power once again.

IN THE 1870S AND 1880S, MANY SOUTHERN WHITES—PARTICULARLY elites—claimed that they were living under an illegitimate system of government. From their perspective, the state constitutions that they operated under had been improperly forced upon them. They would have never willingly adopted such a system themselves. Their constitutions were "alien document[s] unsuitable to local conditions."[1] Never mind the notion of democracy or the fact that those constitutions were a condition of reentering the Union. Powerful Southern elites held on to the idea of a political order rigidly stratified around the plantation system. The new constitutions were a threat to that system. With the Union soldiers finally gone, the time was long overdue to dismantle the constitutional system thrust onto the South through Reconstruction.[2]

Their specific gripes, however, boiled down to race. Those constitutions symbolized black power and a world in which blacks could aspire to opportunities on par with whites. It was this, more than anything, that they sought to undo. When reduced to specifics, they objected to the black vote, black education, and spending money on blacks.

In their minds, blacks had done nothing over the course of Reconstruction to prove themselves worthy of the right to vote or social advancement beyond that of field laborers. Universal public education was but a foolish attempt to reinforce both the vote and social advancement. Planters saw the value of competent workers but no value in "inflat[ing] the economic and political expectations of workers."[3] The only thing education would accomplish would be to "spoil good field hands."[4] Even worse, education would lead blacks to push for even more social and political equality. Moving any further down this road, they argued, was futile. Georgia's governor argued that "God made them negroes and we cannot make them white. We are on the wrong track. We must turn back."[5] South Carolina's governor similarly proclaimed that "the greatest mistake the white race has ever made was to educate the free Negro."[6] Whites also objected to the cost of black education. Paying taxes to educate people they had once held as slaves made no sense to plantation owners. It also made no sense to those who sought to disenfranchise them. Why pay taxes to educate citizens whom you planned to disenfranchise?[7] In that respect, money spent on black education, Mississippi's governor said, was "money thrown away."[8]

The tax issue, in particular, was complex—part racial, part financial. Whites blamed black lawmakers for taxes that they perceived as way too high. Taxes had, in fact, shot up following the ratification of new Southern constitutions. They were necessary to build a real system of public schools, as well as other smaller social service projects. But taxes also went up because the economy had tanked. Newspapers sympathetic to white tax frustrations, however, were not interested in nuance or democratic values. They helped direct those frustrations at education, running stories about education spending and arguing that it was excessive.[9] Whatever the truth or justifications, African Americans suffered the blame. Prior to the war, the planter class had kept government and taxes limited by completely ignoring the public commons. After the war, African Americans helped build the public commons. So those who wanted to reduce state expenditures as opposed to raising taxes found an easy target in education and African Americans.[10] Not only that, the solutions to black voting, black education, and high taxes were, in effect, all one and the same: defund public education.[11]

These white grievances morphed into a constitutional agenda that eventually spread across the entire South, just as surely as the pro-democracy agenda had spread at the close of the war. The new constitutional agenda was two-pronged: disenfranchise black voters and segregate and underfund public schools, at least for blacks. Those leading the agenda were unabashed in their motives. The president of Mississippi's 1890 Constitutional Convention, Solomon S. Calhoon, opened the convention in the bluntest terms: "We came here to exclude the negro. Nothing short of this will answer."[12] Reflecting back on the convention's work afterward, he similarly remarked that "while there are other important questions to settle, the question of paramount importance was that of suffrage, and it should be dealt with in a manner to leave no doubt of the effect."[13] South Carolina's 1895 Constitutional Convention carried the baton next, expressing the same goals. Soon enough, no Southern state was immune from the sickness. In 1901, in Virginia, for instance, constitutional delegates met "to eliminate the negro from political life."[14]

The world was, in effect, being intentionally turned upside down. Two decades earlier, Southern conventions produced constitutions that were markedly democratic in their aspirations. At South Carolina's 1868 Constitutional Convention, the proceedings opened with remarks from delegates who said they had come "to frame a new constitution, or to make such changes in the old one as were necessary to secure a Republican form of Government."[15] And when that convention ended, the delegates beamed with pride over the rebirth of republicanism: the education system they had created to prepare everyone for the responsibilities of citizenship would, if "carr[ied] out in good faith," obliterate "the stain of ignorance which now pollutes our history" and "in no distant time . . . elevat[e] of all our people to a social, political and religious eminence."[16] In contrast, South Carolina's 1891 convention began with the chair of the convention claiming that the prior constitution "was framed by a body that did not represent the people of South Carolina." It was instead a work of "despotism." We are here now, he said, to "blot out a Constitution made to perpetuate the reign of ignorance and vice over wisdom and virtue."[17]

Wiping out the progress of the prior era was not, however, without its barriers, most notably the Fourteenth and Fifteenth Amendments to the United States Constitution. These new conventions might undo part of the Reconstruction deal by rewriting their state constitutions, but they lacked the power to undo the Fourteenth and Fifteenth Amendments. By its explicit terms, the Fifteenth Amendment prohibited states from denying "citizens of the United States [the right] to vote . . . on account of race, color, or previous condition of servitude." Though less explicit in what "equal protection" meant, the Fourteenth Amendment was understood to prohibit at least some of the more extreme and explicit acts of discrimination, such as running two separate tax systems that spent white taxes on white citizens and black taxes on black citizens.

The Mississippi Convention debated its options for getting around these roadblocks at length. Some delegates were so bold as to argue that they could do whatever they wanted because those Amendments were illegitimate. But more calculating minds prevailed, cautioning that it was better to use indirect measures to exclude blacks from voting. Mississippi inserted two new voting provisions into its constitution to achieve that indirection. First, it adopted an "understanding" clause. Rather than a rigid literacy requirement—which would have also disenfranchised a substantial number of white voters—the constitution provided that "every elector shall . . . be able to read any section of the Constitution of this State; or he shall be able to understand the same when read to him, or give a reasonable interpretation thereof." This meant that illiterate citizens would still be allowed to vote if they could convince local election officials that they still "understood" the constitution. The real purpose, however, was not to excuse illiteracy but to establish a constitutional provision to racially discriminate against black voters. Local officials would quickly bless illiterate whites with the right to vote while scrutinizing blacks until they spotted an actual—and just as often invented—gap in understanding. As the *Raymond Gazette* almost laughingly assured voters, "there might be honest differences of opinion between a corn-field nigger and inspectors of the election."[18]

The second piece of the disenfranchisement puzzle was poll taxes. Notably, some Southern states had first introduced poll taxes in their 1867 and 1868 constitutions, not to disenfranchise anyone, but to fund education. Those citizens who couldn't pay the tax were still allowed to vote. Mississippi's new iteration of the poll tax was intended to remove this optional aspect, require back payment of past poll taxes, and double the current tax. For African Americans "who were increasingly being trapped in perpetual debt by the illegal misuse of sharecropping by

White planters," poll tax increases and back payment would make voting cost-prohibitive.

After Mississippi led the way on how to best disenfranchise blacks, the rest of the South followed. Prior to 1890, no Southern state required any proof of literacy or constitutional understanding to vote, but these devices quickly cropped up in one way or another throughout the South. South Carolina, North Carolina, Alabama, Virginia, and Louisiana joined Mississippi in adopting reading and/or writing requirements. The new idea even stretched beyond the South to Oklahoma. Mississippi, South Carolina, Virginia, Louisiana, and Georgia adopted understanding clauses or requirements. Alabama, Georgia, and Louisiana came up with a more blatantly subjective tool for discrimination: a legal requirement that voters be of good moral character.[19]

The practical results of these constitutional changes were stark. Mississippi used the poll tax and understanding clauses to disenfranchise well over 100,000 blacks.[20] By comparison, only 11,000 whites were excluded. Two years before the 1890 revisions to the Mississippi Constitution, voter turnout in the presidential election among the "eligible electorate" was 43 percent.[21] By 1902, electoral turnout was cut in half, slumping to 18.8 percent.[22] The decline fell almost exclusively on blacks, whose turnout fell from 29 percent in 1888 to 2 percent in 1892 to 0 percent in 1895.[23] There simply weren't that many remaining registered black voters anymore. In Louisiana, black voter registration fell from 95.6 percent before the constitutional changes to 9.5 percent after.[24] A few more years out, it fell to 1.1 percent.[25]

Shutting blacks out of the voting booth, however, was not enough. Whites wanted to block them from ever getting back in again. African American educational achievement had steadily risen following the war. Many African Americans continued to believe their education efforts would allow them to overcome the new literacy and understanding requirements. White delegates recognized that possibility, too. Dorothy Pratt explained in her comprehensive analysis of the Mississippi Convention, "No one missed the point that the future of disenfranchisement depended on an illiterate African American population."[26]

The new voting restrictions might work for a while, but long-term trends in African American education represented a larger "problem."[27] Newspapers made sure the average white citizen understood: "As soon as all the negroes in the state shall be able to read and write they will become qualified to vote," and then "they will demand their rights."[28] So just as education and voting had always gone hand in hand with the American theory of democratic expansion, delegates at Southern constitutional conventions believed that changing the educational status quo and trajectory was the means of shrinking democracy.

The constitutional changes to education ran the gamut—from crystal clear to obscure manipulations. The clearest change in the agenda was to segregate schools. While the constitutions in Mississippi and elsewhere would retain provisions about "uniform" or "common" systems of schools open to all, white delegates inserted a key caveat that left no mistake that those general principles only went so far. A new section of the Mississippi Constitution simply stated: "Separate schools shall be maintained for children of the white and colored races."[29] South Carolina's 1895 constitution was more emphatic: "Separate schools shall be provided for children of the white and colored races, and no child of either race shall ever be permitted to attend a school provided for children of the other race."[30] Other states adopted similar provisions, explicitly mandating segregated schools.[31]

The only way to be more oppressive would have been to eliminate African American education or public education in general altogether. Mississippi had the highest percentage of blacks in the South and contemplated something along those lines. Convention delegates "began to question the appropriate nature of [education's] inclusion" in the state constitution.[32] Again, from their perspective, education was only in the constitution at the behest of blacks and members of Congress, neither of whom had any legitimate claim on Mississippi's constitution.

Such a drastic change did not occur, but the convention was dead set on suppressing African American education as much as possible. The first sign of their anti-democratic agenda was subtle but unmistakable. Reconstruction-era education clauses, including Mississippi's, had recognized public education's role in democracy. The education clause in Mississippi's 1868 constitution had begun with an explicit reference: "As the stability of a republican form of government depends mainly on the intelligence and virtue of its people, it shall be the duty of the legislature" to establish a system of public schools. The 1890 constitution, however, excised that language, thumbing its nose at the democratic forces that had first placed public education in the constitution. But that alone wouldn't change anything in reality. The convention's task was to constrain black education as a practical matter. That required tinkering with the financial system itself.

The "best" solution was not immediately obvious. In the years leading up to Mississippi's convention, North Carolina and Kentucky had conducted their own experiments in undermining African American education. They did it by segregating tax dollars. Taxes paid by whites were spent only on white schools and taxes by blacks only on black schools. State and federal courts, however, declared the practice unconstitutional. The North Carolina Supreme Court, for instance, reasoned that segregating school dollars is "subversive of the equality and uniformity recognized in the system of public school." Segregation in the collection of taxes is, likewise, inconsistent with the constitutional mandate for a common and uniform system of public schools and taxes.[33]

A Kentucky federal district court was even more pointed in striking down the segregated tax and school expenditure law there. The state's position taken to its logical conclusion, the court reasoned, was nonsensical. It would mean the state could also segregate taxes based on "the nativity of the citizen" and essentially run separate systems for all government programs, even the criminal justice system. "Such distribution of taxes would entirely ignore the spirit of our republican institutions, and would not be the equal protection of the laws as understood by the people of any of the states of this Union at the time of the adoption of this amendment."[34] Equal protection meant something much different, explained the court: "The laws of the states must be equal in their benefit as well as equal in their burdens, and that less would not be 'the equal protection of the laws.'"[35]

A number of delegates to Mississippi's 1890 Constitutional Convention urged it to enact a tax segregation scheme anyway, but more astute delegates knew that putting such a scheme in the state constitution would just create federal constitutional problems.[36] They saw a more devious solution to the problem: get the state out of, or largely out of, the school funding business. Make school funding dependent primarily on local tax revenues and give local officials more discretion in operating their schools. This would do two important things.

First, it would make vast inequality possible. Wealthy areas could spend as much on education as they wanted, and poor areas—areas heavily populated by blacks—would remain, well, poor. Second, wealthy white communities would effectively be relieved of the duty of supporting black education. Again, they would keep their money local. And in heterogeneous areas, local officials would have the discretion to divide up funds between white and black schools any way they wanted. If local officials did it as a matter of practice rather than state law, the state could not be accused of segregating taxes or mandating differential treatment. These strategies could allow Mississippi to accomplish a result pretty close to the same as tax segregation. It might even accomplish something more unequal.

This work-around took hold in other states as well. Other states, however, devised additional creative strategies to further absolve the state of education responsibility and increase the capacity for local discrimination. These strategies involved changes to state superintendents' powers and state boards of education. Shrinking their powers would mean that local officers would have more discretion to act.[37] From a distance, the changes look like issues of mind-numbing education bureaucracy, but the conventions implemented them with the intent of further chipping away at the statewide education systems that Reconstruction constitutions created—and the opportunities they had promised blacks. Similarly, if the state reduced the mandated school-year length, local authorities could provide a shortened year for blacks while maintaining a longer one for whites.[38]

As with voting, the changes produced disastrous results. State funding for public education was roughly equal across schools until around 1880.[39] In fact, African American schools were funded at a slightly higher level than white schools in North Carolina and Alabama. But under the new constitutional system, inequality reached wild proportions. In Adams County, Mississippi, for instance, the district spent eleven times more on white students than blacks.[40] And at a statewide level, by 1915, South Carolina spent twelve times more on white students than black students.[41] Florida operated one of the "milder" inequality regimes, but still spent more than twice as much on white students' education as blacks'.[42]

Local counties and districts had to go out of their way to produce disparities this large. One strategy was to not even spend the funds allocated by the state. For instance, by 1937, three out of four Mississippi counties were spending less than what the state gave them for their black schools.[43] Nearly half of the counties were spending less than 75 percent of the state's appropriated education funds.[44] These counties, of course, did almost nothing to support black schools beyond what the state provided. The impacts on the classroom were huge. Black teachers were forced to teach much larger classes in dilapidated buildings with tattered textbooks. On top of being asked to do more work, districts paid black teachers much lower salaries than whites—sometimes only one dollar for every three that they paid to a white teacher.[45] Districts also structured black learning completely differently. While the one-room schoolhouse was vanishing for white students, black students of all ages were often taught by the same teacher in the same room. In the early 1900s, Mississippi, South Carolina, and Louisiana did not even operate high schools for African Americans.[46] Other Southern states only provided a few African American high schools.

In 1899, Mississippi's state superintendent, beaming with pride, summed up the new constitutional status quo: "It will be readily admitted by every white man in Mississippi that our public school system is designed primarily for the welfare of the white children of the state, and incidentally, for the negro children."[47] Whereas schools had once represented at least the symbolic possibility of pulling oneself up by the bootstraps, segregation and inequality in schools aimed to squeeze out that idea and any sense that African Americans were real citizens. Richard Kluger, who famously chronicled the NAACP's fight against school segregation, captured the psychological warfare: "How do you instill pride in segregated schoolchildren—indeed how do you imbue them with even rudimentary values of good citizenship—when the very fact of their separation overwhelms nearly every other aspect of their education and belies any claim of pride?"[48] But the practical impact was equally damaging. Charles Hamilton Houston, the architect of the NAACP's attack on segregation, explained: "Since voteless blacks had no voice in the administration of their schools, . . . discrimination had become far worse."[49]

Maybe the most unfathomable part of it all was that the US Supreme Court helped whites accomplish their scheme, abandoning black citizenship and education rights, even when the US Constitution plainly demanded otherwise. For instance, the Reconstruction-era Congress passed the Civil Rights Act of 1870 to enforce the Fifteenth Amendment's prohibition on racial discrimination in voting. The first two parts of the law specifically referenced "voter registration" discrimination based on "race, color, or previous condition of servitude." The last two parts of the legislation required that all votes be counted and barred voter intimidation.

William Garner, an African American voter, attempted to pay his poll tax, but the tax collector refused to accept it. Later, when he tried to vote, he was denied the opportunity due to the unpaid poll tax. The official blocking him from voting was indicted under the Civil Rights Act of 1870. But in 1876, in *United States v. Reese*, the Supreme Court reversed the indictment in a remarkable feat of logic.[50] The Court declared the Civil Rights Act itself unconstitutional, reasoning that Congress only had the power to prohibit racial discrimination in voting. Requiring that all votes be counted and prohibiting voter intimidation in general, the

Court said, went beyond racial discrimination because those later protections could theoretically benefit whites, too. Never mind that black voters were the ones being intimidated and their ballots the ones rejected. The Court clearly had no interest in judging the case based on reality. What the Court really did was waive a judicial flag of sympathy, if not encouragement, for those whites resisting African American voting—and maybe even more.

In 1883 in the *Civil Rights Cases*, the Court issued another similarly troubling decision. This time the Court invalidated an antidiscrimination law that protected African Americans in everyday life, the Civil Rights Act of 1875. The Act prohibited racial discrimination in "public accommodations," which basically means businesses that invite the general public inside to buy goods or services. This includes hotels, theaters, restaurants, stores, and railroads. The Court held that the law was beyond Congress's power. Congress had gone after private discrimination, but the Fourteenth Amendment only grants Congress the power to go after discrimination by states, reasoned the Court. Again, never mind that these businesses operated under state licenses and laws.

Had the Court stopped there, African Americans might have salvaged their legal rights and citizenship. After all, in striking down the Civil Rights Act of 1875, the Court had recognized that state discrimination was different from private discrimination. The Court never hinted that federal power was limited in its ability to block state-based racial discrimination. But the Court soon shackled the federal Constitution as a tool of combatting state-based discrimination, too. The case was *Plessy v. Ferguson*. Decided in 1896, it involved a Louisiana state law that required segregation on train cars. Homer Plessy argued the law violated the Fourteenth Amendment's guarantee of "equal protection of the law," but the Court reasoned the law treated everyone equally: both races were segregated and neither whites nor blacks could ride in each other's cars.

The entire point of Louisiana's law, of course, was to exclude blacks, not whites, because whites believed blacks were inferior. The Court swept this ideological motive away as little more than a figment of blacks' imagination:

The underlying fallacy of the plaintiff's argument consists in the assumption that the enforced separation of the two races stamps the colored race with a badge of inferiority. If this be so, it is not by reason of anything found in the act, but solely because the colored race chooses to put that construction upon it. The argument necessarily assumes that if . . . the colored race should become the dominant power in the state legislature, and should enact a law in precisely similar terms, it would thereby relegate the white race to an inferior position. We imagine that the white race, at least, would not acquiesce in this assumption.[51]

Then the Court threw salt on the wound, reasoning that it would be a waste of time for the law to try to promote equality in everyday walks of life. The Court wrote:

If the two races are to meet upon terms of social equality, it must be the result of natural affinities, a mutual appreciation of each other's merits, and a voluntary consent of individuals. . . . This end can neither be accomplished nor promoted by laws which conflict with the general sentiment of the community upon whom they are designed to operate. . . . Legislation is powerless to eradicate racial instincts, or to abolish distinctions based upon physical differences, and the attempt to do so can only result in accentuating the difficulties of the present situation. If the civil and political rights of both races be equal, one cannot be inferior to the other civilly or politically. If one race be inferior to the other socially, the constitution of the United States cannot put them upon the same plane.[52]

Having blessed state laws that require segregation in everyday aspects of life, the core function of government—public education—would be next. The Court in *Plessy* alluded to as much, justifying segregation on train cars based on pre–Civil War school segregation practices in the North. But in 1899, in *Cumming v. Richmond County Board of Education*,[53] the Court did more than just bless school segregation; it blessed the denial of educational opportunity to African Americans altogether. *Cumming* involved a school district that closed its high school for African Americans to save money during an economic downturn. It kept the high school for whites open. The district said that eliminating high school education for African Americans would conserve much-needed resources for other schools, including African American elementary schools.

The specific legal challenge in *Cumming* was not to school segregation itself or the closing of the African American school, but to the fact that the county collected taxes from African Americans to support a white high school that they could not attend. This framing of the problem highlighted the absurdity of what whites were doing here and elsewhere. Whites had previously attempted to segregate taxes and expenditures so that their tax dollars would not support African American education. If whites did not want to support African American education, surely African Americans could not be expected to support white education, particularly when African Americans were being denied their own school. Yet even this simple courtesy was too much to ask of the Court.

The Court papered over the case as an inconvenient economic decision that the board of education had to make. Economic decisions, the Court explained, are matters best reserved to the discretion of local officials, not federal courts. What the Court could not have missed, but refused to acknowledge, was that Mississippi and other states originally expanded local discretion with the precise goal of depriving blacks of education. The Court jumped over that history and focused on current circumstances, concluding there was not any evidence that the board's decision to close the school was "made with any desire or purpose . . . to discriminate against any of the colored school children."[54]

Yet for all the terrible moments and trends, one very important silver lining runs through this dark period that almost no one has ever stopped to consider: whereas attacks on public education were a centerpiece of the assault on black citizenship, the right to education (first vested in the immediate aftermath of the Civil War) nonetheless lived on. The fact that it did is a testament to how much the South changed in the decades immediately following the Civil War. The idea of public education had taken hold in a region where it was previously foreign. Once it took hold, it fundamentally changed the South—so much so that even staunch segregationists were unwilling to live with the consequences of taking it away. Public education's legacy was already too strong to break. This left the opponents of democracy to settle for separate and unequal education rather than the elimination of education. And if they settled for that, it could continue as an idea and institution with room for possible growth. It was an idea and institution that could remain in place and maybe even spark a second Reconstruction at some later date. As the next chapter reveals, it did exactly that in the 1970s, calling the nation once again back to its foundational ideas. But for now, the immediate silver lining.

Those seeking to oppress blacks in the late 1800s had to make a compromise of sorts. The thing they objected to most was black citizenship. They primarily objected to public education because it reinforced full black citizenship. Too many white constituents wanted education for themselves for white politicians to totally decimate the idea and institution of public education. The public education system that blacks demanded and helped build during Reconstruction had also been extended to poor and middle-class whites who never before had it. These everyday folks may have been completely on board with black disenfranchisement, but they wanted to keep public education.

The compromise, then, was segregated and unequal education. The compromise, however, created an unreconcilable tension between black oppression and the continuation of public education: If public education is a right of citizenship and the tool through which society prepares young people for citizenship, how can the state provide public education and not expect it to aim toward citizenship? The odd answer, I suppose, would be simply to reinforce white superiority at every turn and insist on second-class citizenship for blacks.

North Carolina and Mississippi provide two of the clearest examples of the deep and unretractable roots education took and which forced the contradiction. Charles Dabney, a scholar of the period, was highly critical of North Carolina's Reconstruction government. He would have been one of the first to argue that the South needed to be "redeemed" from the Northern influences and the state constitutions they had imposed on the South. Yet Dabney still reflected the evolved thinking on education among the "redeemers." After outlining a litany of critiques of North Carolina's Reconstruction-era government, Dabney allowed that North Carolina's Reconstruction government had made at least

> one important contribution to the school laws of North Carolina, which became an example for the South. The southern states had usually depended for school support on the income from the Literary Funds or other permanent endowments. Their laws were fatally defective in that they did not require taxation for the schools. Confused as it was, the legislation of the Reconstruction Government tended to correct this. These changes in the methods of school support were the most lasting and helpful of all the legislation of this period in these states.[55]

This sentiment also showed up in the laws that whites passed after retaking control of North Carolina's state government. The post-Reconstruction government recognized that the state could not fully finance the public education system that had been constitutionalized a few years earlier due to oddities in the balance of power between local and state government. Those oddities stymied education growth.[56] When the redeemers reclaimed power, they could have easily allowed education to wither. They could have even killed education if they wanted.

They did the exact opposite. "There was a revival of interest in the schools and new leaders appeared to support them"[57]—even Confederates. Zebulon Vance, who had served two terms as the Confederate governor of North Carolina and as a colonel in the Confederate army, was elected to a third term as governor in 1876. He was the furthest thing from a black, republican, or Reconstruction sympathizer. Yet Vance and the new state government that took office with him made it a point to press forward with the state's public education project, including addressing the tax problems that limited education growth. They passed new state laws directing localities to pass property taxes and additional poll taxes (beyond the existing state poll tax) to support public schools. They also established a training school for teachers to make sure that new schools could be properly staffed.

Thomas Jarvis, who followed Vance as governor, did even more for education. Dabney called him the "really first 'Educational Governor' in the South."[58] In his 1881 inaugural address, Jarvis called on everyone in the state, regardless of faith or political affiliation, to commit to the development of its education system. "No scheme for the advancement of North Carolina and the development of her resources can be successful or permanent that does not encompass the education of her children. This I regard as of the very first importance, for without it all our efforts will be in vain."[59]

Mississippi did not press forward with North Carolina's education fervor, but context matters. Mississippi's 1890 Convention walked right up to the edge of eliminating public education and pulled back, which raises the question: Why did a group so hostile toward blacks and black education stop short? At its 1890 Convention to disenfranchise blacks, Mississippi delegates complained about the cost of public education in general and the cost of educating blacks in particular. The answer to why they stopped short lies in the fact that they knew public education was an appropriate and key function that belonged in the state constitution.[60]

Delegates conceded that there was simply no way to escape the public education demands of the times. Some reasoned that if Mississippi did not educate its citizens, the federal government likely would, and that was a fate far worse. But it was not just practical political calculation. Former Governor Alcorn, for instance, appealed to the state delegates' better instincts. He called "for sanity and conscience" on the question of education. Another delegate, H. J. McLaurin from Sharkey County, seconded Alcorn's point and spoke even more directly, saying that "the convention had gone far enough against [blacks] and should call a halt."[61] Notwithstanding the overwhelming stench of racism in the air, these voices found an audience, and a full-scale attack on public education fell flat. It was enough to segregate education and change the financing method—at least for the politicians.

The other irony was that the constitutional changes that affected education funding later proved pretty unpopular among regular folk. For the most part, the convention's fervor to reduce blacks to second-class citizenship and limit expenditures on them drowned out any sensible assessment of what the state was really doing to its overall education system. But when everyday whites came to appreciate how little money was available for their schools under the new system, they were upset. The new constitutional system drew "pervasive" and "unexpected attacks" because of the changes to education funding.[62]

In fact, one of Mississippi's most prominent white Democrats, Wiley Nash, tried to undo an aspect of the constitutional system he had just helped erect. Nash was a native Mississippian of humble beginnings who went on to serve in the Confederate army and later as a state legislator and the state attorney general. According to his obituary, he "did as much as any one man to assist in gaining control of the state government and accomplishing the overflow [sic] of carpet bag and Negro rule."[63] Again, this man was no black or Reconstruction sympathizer. Yet it was this very man who was so dismayed with how the new constitutional system depleted the state of school resources that he devised a legal strategy to change how the poll tax (which supported schools) worked. And he did it in his official capacity as state attorney general, acting on behalf of the people of the state.

Most read the 1890 constitution as making the poll tax a voluntary measure that a local community could adopt or reject because it indicated that "no criminal proceedings shall be allowed to enforce the collection of the poll tax."[64] Nash wanted to make the collection of the poll tax mandatory to ensure more funds for public education. His plan was to find a poor person who was delinquent in paying the poll tax. The local sheriff would then confiscate the person's property to be sold to cover the back taxes. When the person resisted, the legal issue of mandatory poll taxes would be before the courts, along with Nash's creative legal theory. The constitution, Nash reasoned, may have prohibited criminal proceedings to collect back poll taxes, but he emphasized that the constitution also specifically provided that the tax was "to be used in aid of the common schools, and for no other purpose" and that liens could be imposed to collect the tax.[65] This meant the tax had to be collected.[66] By his logic, all the constitution did was rule out criminal prosecution. In the end, the Mississippi Supreme Court disagreed, leaving the tax optional and the schools underfunded—probably as the convention had intended.[67] The larger significance of the case, however, is the revelation of how much white support remained for public education—a support that was, at times, at odds with what the 1890 constitution had done.

The general sentiment supporting education did not die in Mississippi or much of anywhere else. Southern power brokers disenfranchised blacks during the late 1800s, but they did not disenfranchise poor and middle-class whites. Those regular white folk would soon carry the banner for public education themselves. Blacks had provoked an interest in public education that could not be undone. In the late 1800s and early 1900s, middle-class whites, in particular, campaigned for public education, building on African Americans' prior foundational work.[68] In other words, what had begun as a black education movement in the South morphed into an education movement led by whites.

Even if that movement was primarily in the service of white education, it maintained and drew on the themes of universal access to public education that preceded it. Support for those themes was sufficiently widespread that the South's planter class—those who held so much power and otherwise had little interest in supporting public education for all—eventually came around, too.[69] In the end, even though the whites who regained control of state government were determined to reverse almost everything that Reconstruction achieved, "they kept the central features of educational governance and finance created by the ex-slave-republican coalition."[70]

That silver lining, as the next two chapters detail, became the foundation for a second reconstruction—the civil rights movement in the mid-twentieth century—and the rebirth of the constitutional right to education in the 1970s and 1980s, which is continuing to this day. The

simple notion that education should be a vested right in state constitutions—a notion that secured uniform acceptance across all states, North
and South, following the war—resulted in the Reconstruction generation removing certain aspects of public education from public debate.
Constitutions settle certain matters. It matters not what the racist legislator or the changing compositions of a legislature want across time.
Constitutional principles call them back to central truths and principles.
This is why constitutions are so crucially important. And this is what
allowed the right to education to live to fight another day. Even if racism
disregarded and trampled on the right to education for decades, so long
as it remained on the books, a latent power would lurk.

CHAPTER 7

THE SECOND RECONSTRUCTION

I F SEGREGATED EDUCATION WAS THE LYNCHPIN OF DISCRIMINA-
tion and second-class citizenship, dismantling school segregation was
the key to forcing America's recommitment to the democratic path first
envisioned following the Civil War. The civil rights movement of the
mid-twentieth century has so many parallels to Reconstruction that
scholars often called the movement the "Second Reconstruction." Just
like the freedmen following the Civil War, the NAACP and its allies
later thought that if they could secure equal education for African Americans, equal citizenship would follow.

In 1922, the NAACP got a huge boost when a group of wealthy
white liberals pulled together $100,000 to donate to the cause. The
donors wanted to support "a large-scale, widespread, dramatic campaign to give the Southern Negro his constitutional rights, his political
and civil equality, and therewith a self-consciousness and self-respect
which would inevitably tend to effect a revolution in the economic life
of the country."[1] The very first step, the group believed, was making segregated public schools too expensive to operate. Courtroom victories,
in particular, would "give courage" to African Americans and focus the
nation's attention "like nothing else . . . upon vicious discrimination."[2]

The NAACP, however, not white liberals, was the appropriate group to execute the campaign.

With money in hand, the NAACP began detailing strategy and soliciting counsel from some of the nation's best legal minds. The NAACP's legal committee asked Felix Frankfurter, who later became a Supreme Court justice, what he thought of a litigation strategy. Frankfurter told them to ask Charles Hamilton Houston, the dean of Howard Law School, first.[3]

Houston's family was steeped in history, practical experience, and legal expertise. Born in 1895, the year before the Court decided *Plessy v. Ferguson*, he saw firsthand the devastation that segregation worked on African Americans and American democracy. But he was also born into a remarkable family. Houston's father, William LePré Houston, grew up during Reconstruction, graduated from Howard Law School in 1892, and founded Washington DC's first black law firm.[4] Charles Hamilton Houston's grandfather, Thomas Houston, was born into slavery in Kentucky and an amazing man in his own right, teaching himself to read and write and escaping to freedom in Illinois. He later worked as a conductor in the Underground Railroad and then as an assistant to Ulysses Grant. He even served as "an honorary pallbearer" when President Lincoln's body was brought home to rest in Springfield.

His family surely had even higher hopes for Charles, and he did not disappoint. He achieved things early in life that most African Americans would never dare dream of. He went to Amherst College and graduated as one of six valedictorians in 1915. A few years later, he went to Harvard Law School, becoming the first black editor of the *Harvard Law Review* (the better part of a century before Obama became the president [i.e., editor in chief] of *Harvard Law Review*). Just six years after graduation, Houston became the dean of Howard University School of Law. The school was a part-time evening program graduating a dozen or so students each year when he started as dean. In less than a decade, he took it to a fully accredited and nationally recognized institution for the training of the nation's finest black lawyers. Charles Hamilton Houston was the perfect first ear to bend before activists ran off to the courts on a crusade. Houston told the NAACP to study the legal issues further and devise a long-term strategy. Don't just jump in headfirst. The NAACP took Houston's advice and hired Nathan Margold in 1930 to write a report that laid out the differing potential strategies in detail. Margold projected that taxpayer lawsuits—the approach suggested by the white financiers—would be a never-ending and largely pointless endeavor. Taxpayer lawsuits would require the NAACP to go after unequal school funding one district at a time on factual grounds. Margold tweaked the strategy, proposing instead to challenge "the constitutional validity of segregation if and when accompanied irremediably by discrimination."[5] The best target for that strategy was state statutes that allowed districts to divide school funds unequally. A win in that type of case would assure statewide results. In states where no such statute existed, Margold suggested that the NAACP target state and district practices and policies that systematically provided fewer resources to African American schools than white schools.

While logical on paper, the strategy would have looked like a pipe dream to most. *Plessy* remained in full force and its promise of separate but equal had never been enforced in any meaningful way. To the contrary, the Court had regularly found excuses for schools that failed to provide equal education. A failing economy in the 1930s only dimmed the NAACP's prospects further. State governments were already struggling to fund separate and unequal education, much less equal education. The stock market crash also depleted resources that the NAACP was counting on to fund their litigation effort. As a result, Margold's report largely remained on the proverbial shelf for a couple of years. Without the resources for a full-time legal staff, the NAACP was limited to small and more random cases.

It wasn't until Walter White took over as the head of the NAACP in 1933 that things changed. He believed that nothing would improve for blacks without a legal attack on segregation, and he knew the exact man to execute it—the man whom Frankfurter had first told the NAACP to consult: Charles Hamilton Houston. Houston initially served as a part-time counselor to the NAACP, remaining dean at Howard. But when Houston left Howard in 1935 to become the NAACP's full-time special counsel, the school fight was finally on. The NAACP's formal announcement said Houston was coming "to handle a legal campaign against unequal educational facilities."[6] Houston would also have a crucially important person at his side: Thurgood Marshall. Marshall later became one of the brightest legal stars in the nation's history and the US Supreme Court's first African American justice.

Houston knew Marshall well. Marshall was one of Houston's students at Howard Law School. Marshall attended Howard in large part because the all-white Maryland School of Law refused to admit blacks. As a student, Marshall immediately caught the attention of Howard's faculty and dean. A professor in one of Marshall's first-year classes recognized his writing as already better than a lot of practicing attorneys'. Marshall soon came under Houston's tutelage and began helping Houston with NAACP legal work while he was still in law school. Taking on this important extra work, Marshall still graduated first in his class in 1933. He was not the type of student the movement could afford to lose. In 1934, the NAACP cobbled together the money to bring Marshall on staff.

Houston and Marshall were cautious in the cases they filed in those early days. The segregation edifice erected during Jim Crow and blessed by the Supreme Court in cases like *Plessy* was too entrenched to attack immediately with a wide-ranging legal claim. The Court had never offered so much as a hint that it saw anything wrong with segregation. The best Houston and Marshall could initially hope for was to force states to make good on *Plessy*'s standard of "separate but equal." Rather than challenge segregation, the NAACP demanded that black schools have the same resources as white schools. And rather than attack unequal education at the K–12 level, the NAACP attacked it in higher education.

Inequality in K–12 involved so many schools that attacking it would pose enormous costs and raise serious normative questions about African Americans' place in society—dangerous issues given that white power brokers still could not envision a world in which African Americans might aspire to full citizenship. Higher education offered a venue to ask

Houston at oral argument.
Courtesy of Charles Hamilton Houston Jr.

for relatively cheap changes that involved a small number of students and were less likely to trigger widespread controversy. Yet the beauty of a higher education strategy, from the NAACP's perspective, was that good higher education cases could establish general principles on which to launch and win much larger K–12 victories. Those larger victories could change government and society.

The NAACP filed its first higher education case against the Maryland School of Law—the one that Marshall would have gone to had it been open to him. Houston chose to file the case in state rather than federal court. The plaintiff in the case was Donald Gaines Murray. Murray had applied to Maryland's law school in 1935. His rejection letter offered a blunt explanation: "The University of Maryland does not admit Negro students and your application is accordingly rejected."[7] Maryland did not offer Murray a shot at a legal education anywhere else, either. This fatal flaw went to the beauty of the NAACP's higher education strategy, which had narrowed even further to attacks on professional schools in higher education. In this type of case, a plaintiff would not need to show that funding and opportunities in a black school were unequal. With no black law school, for instance, education was not even segregated and unequal. Legal education for blacks was simply nonexistent. Any reasonable court ought to recognize it as a violation of *Plessy*. The Maryland Court of Appeals did just that. No grand new theory was necessary.

The Maryland Court of Appeals began its January 15, 1936, opinion with the most basic principle: the Fourteenth Amendment requires a state to "extend to its citizens of the two races substantially equal treatment in the facilities it provides from the public funds. . . . 'To single out a certain portion of the people by the arbitrary standard of color, and say that these shall not have rights which are possessed by others, denies them the equal protection of the laws.'"[8] The only real mental hurdle for the Maryland Court of Appeals was the notion that blacks and whites were destined for different types of careers and lives. If so, the lack of a black law school might be no big deal. A state might, for instance, claim that educational opportunities in the state were equal because the state spent $100 a student on an agricultural school for blacks and $100 a student on a law school for whites.

The Maryland Court Appeals did not go for this type of mental gymnastics. It kept its eyes on white and black students pursuing the same education degrees. So-called fiscal equality between a black farmer education and a white lawyer education, reasoned the court, did "not justify the exclusion of colored citizens alone from enjoyment of any one facility furnished by the state." The court, however, offered a clear caveat. Equal opportunity in legal education, or any other type of degree for that matter, does not require the state to provide that education to "members of the two races in the same place. The state may choose the method by which equality is maintained."

The NAACP was not reaching for that principle anyway. The court was just reassuring society. The NAACP got exactly what it wanted out of the case—maybe even a little more. First, the court issued an order and a basic legal precedent requiring that blacks receive equal education opportunities. Under that precedent, the court reasoned that, because "no separate law school is provided by this state for colored students,"

Maryland failed in its constitutional duty. But the court went one step further. It could have just ordered Maryland to build a separate law school for blacks. Instead, the court ordered the state to admit African Americans to the Maryland School of Law. "If [black] students are to be offered equal treatment in the performance of the function, they must, at present, be admitted to the one school provided."[9] When Maryland waived its right to appeal to the US Supreme Court, the NAACP's victory was sealed, though an important limitation remained. The decision was binding precedent only in Maryland. A national change would have to wait for a trip to the Supreme Court.

Another case that could do that was already in the works in Missouri. Lloyd Lionel Gaines applied to Missouri's law school and, like Murray, was rejected based on his race. Missouri, however, was ahead of Maryland, at least in terms of a legal defense. Missouri indicated that it would establish a black law school when blacks started applying in sizable numbers. The problem, according to the state, was timing. It could not open a black law school overnight or before it had students to fill it. So, in the meantime, Missouri said African Americans could attend law school outside the state and it would pay the extra costs associated with their out-of-state tuition. That interim promise was enough to satisfy the Missouri Supreme Court. It rejected Gaines's challenge in 1937. That loss gave the NAACP its shot at the Supreme Court, and it took it.

Charles Hamilton Houston argued Gaines's case before the Supreme Court on November 9, 1938, and got an exceptionally quick response—just four weeks after the argument. Houston's careful strategy of asking the Court to do nothing more than enforce *Plessy v. Ferguson* was paying off. The Court wrote a short decision and, by a vote of 6–2, agreed that Missouri was violating *Plessy*. The Court commended Missouri for promising to build a law school for blacks, but that "unfulfilled" promise, the Court said, was not enough. What mattered, the Court said, was "that instruction in law for negroes is not now afforded by the State, either at Lincoln University [the college for blacks] or elsewhere within the State, and that the State excludes negroes from the advantages of the law school it has established at the University of Missouri."[10]

The failure to provide blacks legal education within the state, while providing it to whites, "is a denial of the equality of legal right to the enjoyment of the privilege which the State has set up, and the provision for the payment of tuition fees in another State does not remove the discrimination."[11] The fact that only a few blacks might pursue legal education does not change the state's duty. Gaines had "an individual [right] to the equal protection of the laws, and the State was bound to furnish him" with legal education regardless of what education other blacks in the state might seek.[12] The only remedy on these facts, the Court reasoned, was for Missouri to admit Gaines to its law school.

As important as the legal victory in *Gaines* was in terms of precedent, very little changed elsewhere in the real world. Not in higher education and definitely not in elementary and secondary schools. Richard Kluger wrote of the decade following *Gaines*, "There was still no institution in the South where a Negro could pursue a doctorate."[13] There was only one accredited medical school for blacks (compared with twenty-nine for whites), only one provisionally accredited law school (compared with forty for whites), and not a single engineering school.[14] So in 1946, the NAACP legal team (which Thurgood Marshall was then leading) decided to press for more robust doctrine, to go beyond the most minimal enforcement of separate but equal.

Rather than attacking the fact that a state didn't operate a law school for blacks, it began attacking the very concept of segregation. It chose Oklahoma as its battleground. Oklahoma said it was in the process of building a law school for blacks. While the NAACP clearly cited its victory in *Gaines* as controlling precedent that demanded equal educational facilities, the NAACP's briefs in Oklahoma emphasized a new idea that "segregation in public education helps preserve a caste system . . . designed and intended to perpetuate the slave tradition."[15] Formed and operated with this purpose, the NAACP made, for the first time, the audacious claim that separate schools could not be equal.

The Supreme Court did not bite. Technically, the Court ruled in the NAACP's favor in *Sipuel v. Board of Regents of the University of Oklahoma*,[16] but the only thing the Court ordered Oklahoma to do was to comply with *Gaines*. Oklahoma's obligation was simply to provide a legal education for Ada Lois Sipuel (not to integrate its schools). Oklahoma did what the Court asked and rushed to open a law school for blacks, though to call it an actual law school is a gross overstatement. What Oklahoma really did was rope off a section in the state capitol building and assign three faculty members to teach evening classes there.

This sham of an attempt to provide African Americans equality gave the NAACP the facts it needed to potentially push a little further than *Gaines*, even without directly striking down segregation. Since Oklahoma had established a law school for blacks, the NAACP could petition the Court to hear the case again and ask it to weigh in on what equality in segregated law schools might or might not look like. But the Court passed on the opportunity, reasoning that the only proper issue before it was the prompt provision of legal education for blacks, not whether that education, once provided, was qualitatively equal. At best, the outcome was a disappointing draw for the NAACP. It forced Oklahoma to do something and got the Court to reaffirm *Gaines*, but it did not get the new precedent and remedy it wanted. That type of victory would have to wait. But the NAACP planned for that contingency and had two other cases in the pipeline that would force the Court's hand.

The first case was in Texas. Texas, relatively speaking, was a leader in complying with the Court's *Gaines* decision. Texas appropriated money to create a real university for blacks: Texas State University. The University even built a law school. When the law school opened, it set up the issue in a way the Court could no longer skirt. The issue was not just access to black schools, but how "the educational facilities at the newly established school . . . compared with the University of Texas Law School."[17]

The other case was back in Oklahoma but did not involve a challenge to segregation in professional schools. Instead, the NAACP chose a case with facts that could move the law one slight step closer toward their overall goal of desegregating public elementary and secondary education. The case involved a student, G. W. McLaurin, seeking a doctorate degree in education. In that context, the NAACP could try out its theories about the role of education in broader society without squarely asking the Court to decide on those grounds. Rather than setting up some sham of an education school, Oklahoma agreed (after a trial court loss) to admit McLaurin to its all-white school of education. More than that, Oklahoma changed its laws "to permit the admission of Negroes to institutions of higher learning attended by white students, in cases where such institutions offered courses not available in the Negro schools."[18] But this concession came with an enormous caveat.

Black students attending the formerly all-white schools would still receive instruction on a "segregated basis," whatever that meant. The president of the University of Oklahoma said it meant that McLaurin would "sit apart at a designated desk in an anteroom adjoining the classroom; . . . sit at a designated desk on the mezzanine floor of the library, but not . . . use the desks in the regular reading room; and . . . sit at a designated table and . . . eat at a different time from the other students in the school cafeteria."[19] The school actually put a railing around McLaurin's chair and hung a sign proclaiming that it was "Reserved for Colored."[20]

Together, the Texas and Oklahoma cases forced the Court to answer two crucial questions: What does it take to make separate institutions of higher education equal? And if a state chooses to run a technically integrated institution, what does equality within those walls require? The NAACP made its strongest stand against segregation to date in the Texas law school case, *Sweatt v. Painter*, arguing that a separate law school for blacks, even if well-funded, could not be equal. It wrapped its arguments in democratic theory: "Enforced racial segregation aborts and frustrates the basic purposes and objectives of public education in a democratic society."[21] For that reason, segregated education served no legitimate government purpose (a key question in equal protection challenges).

The NAACP's full rationale could have just as easily been pulled out of John Adams's and Thomas Jefferson's notes on education, Congress's readmission debates, or the states' constitutional conventions. Drawing on the traditions found in those discussions, the NAACP simplified the myriad problems of segregation into the democratic challenge that public education is intended to solve. In its brief before the Supreme Court, the NAACP wrote:

> We have come to realize that democratic processes can only operate effectively where there is an alert and enlightened citizenry. In order to make certain that our citizens are equipped to make rational decisions and thus maintain and preserve our democratic institutions, it is vital that their individual skills and values, as well as a pragmatic belief in the basic tenets of democracy, be developed through the medium of education. This function of education has become so important that it is no longer left solely in the hands of the parents or philanthropists. It is one of the highest functions of state government. In order that Americans may develop their intellectual capacities and ethical principles to the fullest, and thus participate most effectively in the responsibility and duties of citizenship, all the forty-eight states have uniformly undertaken to provide educational benefits at a minimum cost to the individual citizen.[22]

In making this broad claim, the NAACP was still careful to offer the Court a narrower way out of the case that did not involve striking down school segregation altogether. The NAACP argued that segregation's threat to democracy was possibly most acute in the context of legal education. Law schools train the lion's share of individuals who render many of the highest acts of public service: to form and execute the policies of democracy. Law schools train "policy makers for the even more complete achievement of the democratic values that constitute the professed ends of American policy."[23]

The NAACP then went to lengths to explain how democracy, education, and the law are part of an interconnected whole—a whole in which segregation cannot play a role. If "the role of education in our society today is one of equipping our citizens with information and specific skills in order that they may productively enjoy the benefits of democracy," segregated education will corrupt our democracy and undermine the "very ideals which education is supposed to instill."[24] A "segregated citizen cannot give full allegiance to a system of law and justice based on the proposition that 'all men are created equal' when the community denies that equality by compelling his children to attend separate schools. Nor can a member of the dominant group fail to see that the community at large is daily violating the very principles in which he is being taught to believe."[25] Legal education and the issues it raises, argued the NAACP, made this case "fundamentally different" from *Plessy v. Ferguson*; *Plessy* "cannot help this Court in making a proper determination of petitioner's complaint."

The Court bit this time. It didn't overrule *Plessy* or adopt a wide-ranging view of desegregated education in democracy, but the Court moved one major step closer to where the NAACP wanted it to go. The Court began its opinion with the basics. In terms of faculty, curriculum, and resources, the University of Texas was superior to the new law school at Texas State. That inequality alone was theoretically enough to order the admission of black students to the University of Texas. Yet the Court, for the first time, reasoned that education was about more than access to quantifiable resources. Resources are not the full measure of educational opportunity. More important, the Court explained, are "those qualities which are incapable of objective measurement but which make for greatness in a law school," things like "reputation of the faculty, experience of the administration, position and influence of the alumni, standing in the community, traditions and prestige."[26] As to these things, the comparisons were not worth rehearsing: "It is difficult to believe that one who had a free choice between these law schools would consider the question close."[27] But lest Texas think it might try to solve that riddle, the Court's final point about segregation signaled the possibility that the Court might just strike down segregation entirely in the coming years.

Hewing dangerously close to the NAACP's argument about the intersection of democracy, law, and education, while leaving the NAACP's conclusion about the incompatibility of segregated education with democracy unstated, the Court wrote that legal education is "an intensely practical one" and "cannot be effective in isolation from the individuals and institutions with which the law interacts. Few students and no one who has practiced law would choose to study in an academic vacuum, removed from the interplay of ideas and the exchange of views with which the law is concerned."[28]

These vacuums were exactly what Texas had created. At Texas State, Herman Sweatt would be denied interaction with whites, who constitute "85 percent of the population of the State and include most of the lawyers, witnesses, jurors, judges and other officials with whom he will inevitably be dealing when he becomes a member of the Texas Bar."[29] The same was true for white students, though the Court didn't explicitly proclaim it. But the Court was steadfast for black students: the denial of interaction with one's peers is itself a denial of equal opportunity. The Court added a dig at *Plessy* to boot. The notion that excluding blacks from the University of Texas "is no different from excluding white students from the new law school . . . overlooks realities."[30] Whites were not beating on the doors of black law schools any more than they tried to ride the black train car with Homer Plessy. They and everyone else knew that the opportunities for blacks were subpar and, more important, intended to symbolize the second-class citizenship of blacks.

With that, the Court made the NAACP's point about legal education as a microcosm of democracy itself. If our constitution, laws, and democracy claim to be inclusive, they cannot operate an education system that does the opposite, that splinters citizens into in-groups and out-groups. Those types of practices are simply incompatible with the ideas on which our laws stand—at least in the context of legal education. Legal education demands one singular opportunity and one single proving ground where democracy's future leaders and technicians rise or fall on their own merit, rather than on the color of their skin.

The Court's rationale in *McLaurin* was more cursory but rested on the same premises. Admitting McLaurin to a white school but segregating him within those walls was not enough to achieve equality. Such practices would still harm him because, as the Court explained, segregated restrictions "impair and inhibit his ability to study, to engage in discussions and exchange views with other students, and, in general, to learn his profession." The Court also pointed out that far more than just McLaurin's education was at stake. Those pursuing degrees in education want "to become, by definition, a leader and trainer of others" and those students whom McLaurin would someday teach will "necessarily suffer to the extent that his training is unequal to that of his classmates."[31]

With those decisions—issued on the same day in 1950—the NAACP had gone about as far as it could without directly asking the Court to overrule *Plessy* and the doctrine of separate but equal. The NAACP had spent two decades pointing out how separate was not equal, but it had not fundamentally challenged the doctrine that separate *could* be equal. Either the NAACP would use *Gaines*, *McLaurin*, and *Sweatt* to demand, one case at a time, that separate be equal or the NAACP would go for broke.

Leading figures in the NAACP legal orbit advised against a direct attack on segregation. As impressive as the NAACP's victories had been so far, they thought it was just too early to expect more from the Court. If the NAACP forced the Supreme Court's hand, the Court might very well reaffirm *Plessy*, which might cause separate but equal to hang around even longer, worsen the political environment, and zap the civil rights movement's growing momentum. But when called to a vote, the NAACP board of directors threw caution to the wind. This meant abandoning the narrow higher education context and going after segregation at the foundation of democracy—elementary and secondary education. So, in late 1950, the fight that would ultimately culminate in the *Brown v. Board of Education* decision began.

It started in an auspicious corner of the South. The Court's decision in *Brown v. Board of Education* was actually a consolidation of four different cases—one from Kansas, one from Virginia, one from Delaware, and another from South Carolina. Each one proceeded through the lower courts separately before the Court consolidated them. The NAACP filed the first of those cases in South Carolina, the site of the nation's last major education experiment. It was in South Carolina's Sea Islands that the Union had given African Americans autonomy, autonomy that they had immediately used to establish schools. It was in South Carolina that African Americans had dominated the state constitutional convention and envisioned an incredibly progressive system of public

Segregated Clarendon County South Carolina School, 1938.
Courtesy of South Caroliniana Library.

education modeled in important respects after Massachusetts. And it was also in South Carolina that the NAACP found a uniquely receptive federal district judge in 1950: Julius Waties Waring. Waring was born in 1880. He once remarked that he spent his life growing up around ex-slaves who "you loved and were good to."[32] Talk of that sort, of course, can be cheap, but his sympathetic sentiment had shown up in the way he handled the NAACP's earlier attempts to enforce separate but equal.

Still, South Carolina was also where the opening shots of the Civil War were fired, where the Confederacy drew much of its strength, and where one of the two most influential segregationist constitutions of the late 1800s sought to redeem the South and constitutionalize Jim Crow. Richard Kluger wrote: "It would have been hard to find a more perilous test case. How much wiser it would have been to launch the attack on segregation in a border state."[33]

At trial, the NAACP made an interesting change in strategy. The soaring ideology of education, democracy, and the law are not necessarily the thing of fact-intensive trials. Sure, ideology brings a case together, forms a narrative, and animates closing arguments and appeals, but winning a trial requires cold, hard facts. If the NAACP was no longer fighting for resource equality, what type of facts could reveal the intangible harms of segregation? For that, the NAACP turned to evidence that might establish, as a matter of fact, that segregation imposed a psychological badge of inferiority on blacks. The NAACP commissioned experts and a famous doll study to show that segregation not only symbolized black inferiority but also had tangible effects on blacks. The doll study, although later the subject of serious methodological critiques, tugged at the heartstrings. Young black children said they preferred white dolls over black dolls—that white dolls were pretty and black dolls ugly.

The NAACP hammered this evidence all the way to the Supreme Court. In its first briefs before the Court, the argument was simple: segregated schools necessarily harm black students. More specifically, the NAACP's uncontradicted evidence "conclusively demonstrate[d] that racial segregation injures infant appellants in denying them the opportunity available to all other racial groups to learn to live, work and cooperate with children representative of approximately 90 percent of the population of the society in which they live . . . and to adjust themselves personally and socially in a setting comprising a cross-section of the dominant population."[34] It "interferes with his motivation for learning; and instills in him a feeling of inferiority resulting in a personal insecurity, confusion and frustration."[35]

The brief's only allusion to democracy involved two references, submerged within larger arguments, that segregated education also affects students' ability "to develop citizenship skills."[36] And when the Court ordered a second round of briefs and reargument in the case, the Court posed a specific issue to the litigants: whether the Fourteenth Amendment was originally intended to prohibit school segregation. So the NAACP's second brief naturally focused on demonstrating that the Fourteenth Amendment was intended to eliminate all forms of racial caste, distinction, and discrimination. On that point, education played even less of a role in the NAACP's brief because it argued the framers' intent regarding equality was all-encompassing. The NAACP's two-hundred-page brief devoted no more than a couple of paragraphs to democratic education theory.

Those few paragraphs, however, were powerfully placed at the beginning of the brief, framing everything else. The NAACP wrote that "the substantive question [in the case] is whether a state can, consistently with the Constitution, exclude children, solely on the ground that they are Negroes, from public schools which otherwise they would be qualified to attend. . . . The importance to our American democracy of [this] question can hardly be overstated."[37] Even the states fighting to keep segregation "recognize the accepted broad purposes of general public education in a democratic society." They accept the "burden of educating [their] children" because "in a democracy, citizens from every group, no matter what their social or economic status or their religious or ethnic origins, are expected to participate widely in the making of important public decisions. The public school, even more than the family, the church, business institutions, political and social groups and other institutions, has become an effective agency for giving to all people that broad background of attitudes and skills required to enable them to function effectively as participants in a democracy."[38] The remainder of the brief laboriously detailed the framers' general thoughts on discrimination and segregation and the extent to which states understood that the Fourteenth Amendment prohibited them from segregating schools.

In the end, the Supreme Court's decision in *Brown* returned to role of education in democracy as a central thesis. As to original intent regarding school segregation, the Court declared it a wash: "What others in Congress and the state legislatures had in mind cannot be determined with any degree of certainty."[39] As to its own precedent in *Gaines*, *Sipuel*, *Sweatt*, and *McLaurin*, the Court said they were of little help; the issue was no longer one of comparing the "tangible factors in the Negro and white schools." The only way the Court could decide *Brown*, it wrote, was to "consider public education in the light of its full development and its present place in American life throughout the Nation." The Court answered that inquiry with its most often quoted passage:

Today, education is perhaps the most important function of state
and local governments. Compulsory school attendance laws and the
great expenditures for education both demonstrate our recognition
of the importance of education to our democratic society. It is required in the performance of our most basic public responsibilities,
even service in the armed forces. It is the very foundation of good
citizenship. Today it is a principal instrument in awakening the child
to cultural values, in preparing him for later professional training,
and in helping him to adjust normally to his environment. In these
days, it is doubtful that any child may reasonably be expected to succeed in life if he is denied the opportunity of an education. Such an
opportunity, where the state has undertaken to provide it, is a right
which must be made available to all on equal terms.[40]

That understanding of public education combined with the evidence of segregated schooling's detrimental effects on black children
convinced the Court that separate but equal in education "has no place.
Separate educational facilities are inherently unequal."[41]

In the decades since, *Brown* has been subject to any number of
valid critiques. Even if black students suffered from a sense of inferiority, for instance, it was a huge leap in logic to lump the entire blame
on schools. The Court also ignored the harm of segregation to whites
and shirked the opportunity to challenge the ideology of white superiority. One might even say the Court focused too much on the facts and
ignored the law. The Court could, and maybe should, have declared
that explicit racial distinctions (or distinctions designed to disadvantage
a racial group) are unconstitutional regardless of their effect. If equal
protection of the law means anything, it ought to mean that legislators
cannot write laws to treat people differently based on race.

Yet those critiques, though valid on some level, ignore social reality.
No matter the grounds on which the Court decided the case, enormous
political and social backlash would surely follow. The Court thought the
best chance of acceptance, partial acceptance, or just weathering the
storm was a narrowly written decision that appealed to whites' better

George Hayes, Thurgood Marshall, and James Nabrit Jr. (Howard law professor and attorney) after winning *Brown v. Board of Education*. *Courtesy of Getty Images.*

angels and did not declare segregation in every facet of life unconstitutional. History proved the Court was overly confident in its powers of persuasion or naive in its sense of possibility, but one can appreciate the instinct.

If one were going to fairly criticize the Court in *Brown*, it would not be on those grounds but in its omission of a single phrase from its May 17, 1954, opinion: "fundamental right." *Brown*'s famous democracy paragraph did everything but explicitly declare education a fundamental right, drawing within a heartbeat of the right but no further. That paragraph offered the rationale as to why education should be a fundamental right, and then stopped, leaving education as an "opportunity" that, if afforded to citizens, must be equal. The fine line was no accident.

The full depth of the Court's decision to avoid recognizing a fundamental right to education is even clearer in the backstory behind *Bolling v. Sharpe*—a companion case to *Brown* that involved segregation in Washington, DC's schools. *Bolling* required its own separate opinion because Washington, DC's schools are creatures of the federal government rather than a state, and the Fourteenth Amendment's prohibition on state discrimination cannot technically constrain discrimination, or anything else, in DC's schools. If the Constitution was to restrict federal segregation, it would be under the Fifth Amendment's guarantee of individual liberty (against federal interference), not the Fourteenth Amendment's guarantee of equal protection.

Records show that Chief Justice Warren's initial draft of the *Bolling* opinion did, in fact, declare education to be a "fundamental liberty" and struck down school segregation as "an arbitrary deprivation of [that] liberty."[42] But when he circulated the draft, two other justices were reluctant to use that language—primarily because the Court's prior invocation of fundamental rights in the early 1900s had proved to be a grossly misguided attempt to second-guess legislative prerogatives. The Court later overturned those mistakes, but it had left a bad taste in the mouths of some justices for any talk of fundamental rights. They did not want to make the same mistake twice. Warren was more concerned with unanimity than anything and simply deleted the word "fundamental."[43] A sentence that had once declared education a "fundamental liberty" now called it a "liberty" without assigning any special protection to it.

In the context of the immediate case, these omissions, deletions, and distinctions did not matter much. The battlefield was segregation. No matter how connected the right to education, democracy, and segregation were to one another, the right to education was not in serious jeopardy in *Bolling* or *Brown*. Pitchforks had never been drawn against education itself and there was no reason to expect it now, either. The pitchforks would be drawn over segregation, whether in schools or at Woolworth's lunch counters. And in the current context, the concept of integrated education was the springboard to achieving everything that the right to education was meant to achieve for the freedmen eighty years earlier. In fact, the Court's opinion in *Brown v. Board* became the ideological foundation for a new democratic revival. But first, the Court wanted to decide the case as narrowly and decisively as possible. The day for pressing further would come later. So after deciding *Brown*, the Court paused in developing new doctrine and waited for the rest of society and government to catch up, hoping that the symbolism of *Brown* would serve as a beacon.

Whites and government officials were slow to draw near, but civil rights activists were invigorated. The decision in *Brown* helped fuel the civil rights protest movement in the 1950s and 1960s. Protestors knew, or hoped, that a Supreme Court recommitted to the Constitution and its democratic equality roots would not turn its back on them as they boycotted, marched, and protested for their rights. And the combined social pressure of those protests and the Court's decision in *Brown* demanded a legislative response. When the responses finally came, they came in rapid succession.

In 1964, Congress passed the Civil Rights Act, barring discrimination in public accommodations, employment, and federally funded programs (particularly public schools). Equally important, the Act authorized the Department of Justice to litigate school desegregation cases. The burden of making reality and constitutional reason rhyme would no longer fall solely on the NAACP's shoulders. In 1965, Congress passed the Voting Rights Act, creating robust protections against voting discrimination and requiring states with a history of disenfranchising blacks to preclear any changes in their voting laws through the Department of Justice. This process ended several decades of continually evolving discriminatory voting practices that always left Congress and the courts playing catch-up. The Voting Rights Act also undid the nefarious link between education and voting that Southern states used to exclude blacks from the ballot box: literacy tests. Just weeks short of the 100th anniversary of the Fourteenth Amendment, Congress passed the Fair Housing Act of 1968, prohibiting discrimination in the sale, rental, advertising, and financing of housing. It even required local authorities to affirmatively further housing integration.

Once the stars of democracy aligned between the executive, legislative, and judicial branches in the late 1960s, the Court set even more ambitious goals in its school desegregation decisions, attempting nothing short of a complete reconstruction of public education. Such a rebuild, the Court hoped, might wipe out inequality. In 1968, in *Green v. New Kent County*, for instance, the Court held that schools had to do more than just stop discriminating. They had an "affirmative duty to take whatever steps might be necessary to convert to a unitary system in which racial discrimination would be eliminated root and branch."[44] Having waited on schools to act for more than a decade following *Brown*, the Court finally lost its patience, announcing that "the time for mere 'deliberate speed' has run out. . . . The burden on a school board today is to come forward with a plan that promises realistically to work, and promises realistically to work now."[45] Then, in 1971, in *Swann v. Mecklenburg*, the Court gave district courts enormous power when schools failed in their affirmative duty. District courts could, in effect, take over school districts, order attendance zones redrawn, reassign students, require the busing of students, and mandate finely racially balanced schools. Most important, courts could do this on a metropolitan and countywide basis without getting into the nuances of what had caused segregation in individual schools.

In 1973, the Court pushed desegregation into the North. In the North, segregation had occurred as a matter of local practice. It was not etched in state or local law. But in *Keyes v. School District No. 1*, the Court held that if plaintiffs could show acts of intentional discrimination, they could demand the same remedies as in the South. To make matters easier, the Court held that if plaintiffs could show intentional segregation in a "substantial portion" of a district, courts should presume that all segregation in the district stemmed from discrimination. This presumption went on to have wide-ranging effects in the North and the South as courts applied this presumption to all aspects of schools' education programs: student assignments, teacher assignments, transportation, facilities, discipline, ability grouping, and more. This meant courts demanded not only that schools be racially balanced at the building level but that they ensure equality in most everything they did. Until they achieved that equality, courts would continue to presume the problem was discrimination.

But like the demands of the nation's first Reconstruction, this recommitment to democracy provoked a troubling response.

CHAPTER 8

THE CIVIL RIGHTS BACKLASH

*B*ROWN AND ITS PROGENY SET DEMOCRACY ON A SECOND collision course with entrenched racism. The question was whether democracy might prevail this time around—or at least persist better than it did after Reconstruction. Less than two years after the decision in *Brown*, the forces against it aligned at the highest levels. The most obvious example was the so-called Southern Manifesto, a document signed by nineteen US senators and eighty-two US representatives. Formally known as the Declaration of Constitutional Principles, the Southern Manifesto charged that the Court in *Brown* had abused its power. Its first premise was that states are free to enact any system of education they want, including having none at all. In other words, the Constitution and the nation's democratic norms did not apply to education.

"The original Constitution," the Southern Manifesto emphasized, "does not mention education. Neither does the 14th Amendment nor any other amendment. The debates preceding the submission of the 14th Amendment clearly show that there was no intent that it should affect the system of education maintained by the States." The Southern Manifesto also boldly claimed that the Supreme Court had created the race problem, not Southern states. *Brown v. Board* was "destroying the amicable relations between the white and Negro races that have been created through 90 years of patient effort by the good people of both races. It has planted hatred and suspicion where there has been heretofore friendship and understanding." So it was the intent of those who signed the Southern Manifesto to use "all lawful means to bring about a reversal of this decision which is contrary to the Constitution and to prevent the use of force in its implementation."[1]

State leaders took this final charge to heart in the late 1950s in what was called "massive resistance." State leaders passed legal work-arounds where they could and encouraged resistance where they couldn't. In Little Rock, Arkansas, the governor and legislature took the position that the state was not bound by an illegitimate Supreme Court ruling and refused to do anything to desegregate their schools. They went so far as to amend their constitution, "flatly commanding the Arkansas General Assembly to oppose 'in every Constitutional manner the Unconstitutional desegregation decisions of May 17, 1954 and May 31, 1955 of the United States Supreme Court.'" Acting on that command, the legislature "reliev[ed] school children from compulsory attendance at racially mixed schools" and "establish[ed] a State Sovereignty Commission."[2]

The Little Rock School District was caught in a bind. The state was telling it to keep schools segregated and the local federal district court was demanding action. The school district decided to move forward with a plan to admit nine African American students at the previously all-white Central High School in September 1957. But the governor headed the district and the students off, ordering the Arkansas National Guard to stand outside the school and block African American students from entering for three weeks. The governor's action also emboldened local citizens who opposed desegregation. They began actively interfering with the desegregation plan.[3] It took President Eisenhower ordering federal troops to Central High School for its doors to open to the African American students.[4]

Presidential action also emboldened the courts. When the case got to the Supreme Court, the Court made it clear that this type of behavior would not be tolerated. The underlying merits of the desegregation plan did not even warrant discussion. For the Court, the case had become a matter of respect for the rule of law. Channeling its own anger, the Court wrote:

> The Constitution is the "supreme Law of the Land. . . . It is emphatically the province and duty of the judicial department to say what the law is.". . . That principle has [for more than a century and a half] been respected by this Court and the Country as a permanent and indispensable feature of our constitutional system. It follows that the interpretation of the Fourteenth Amendment enunciated by this Court in the *Brown* case is the supreme law of the land, and Art. VI of the Constitution makes it of binding effect on the States "any Thing in the Constitution or Laws of any State to the Contrary notwithstanding.". . .
>
> No state legislator or executive or judicial officer can war against the Constitution without violating his undertaking to support it. Chief Justice Marshall spoke for a unanimous Court in saying that: "If the legislatures of the several states may, at will, annul the judgments of the courts of the United States, and destroy the rights acquired under those judgments, the constitution itself becomes a solemn mockery."[5]

The other threat, however, did not involve violence at all. The other threat was that states would just do away with public education altogether—that they would finally unwind that great American constitutional commitment to public education, the commitment that the freedmen and the Union had fought so hard for during Reconstruction. Ironically, it was Virginia—one of the three states that had its readmission to the Union explicitly conditioned on the provision of education and the state that was the most reluctant to adopt an education clause—that tested those waters.

Virginia concocted a two-part strategy to prevent school desegregation from happening as a practical matter, but did so without directly contesting any court order to desegregate. The first step was to fund private school vouchers, including religious schools. This alone was no

small task and required Virginia to amend its constitution in 1956. With
that change, white families who wanted segregated schools did not need
to protest around the public school doors and risk arrest. They could just
exit the public school system altogether for a segregated private one.

The problem, though, was that those whites who were not so staunch
in their views might just willingly attend integrated public schools with
no fanfare. What would the state then do with them? Fixing this problem required a second step. Virginia called a special session to pass a law
"to close any public schools where white and colored children [were]
enrolled together [and] cut off state funds to such schools."[6] The state
would then reroute that money to private vouchers and even "extend
state retirement benefits to teachers in newly created private schools."[7]
Another work-around came later. The state repealed its compulsory
attendance laws, meaning local officials could decide for themselves
whether kids had to attend any school at all.

Prince Edward County School District, one of the four districts in
the consolidated case that made up *Brown v. Board*, was to be Virginia's
resistance test case. After the Court's decision in *Brown v. Board II*, each
school district went back to its respective local federal court. The federal district courts were to work through the details of desegregating the
schools. The Virginia District Court ordered Prince Edward County to
admit African American students to its white high school in September
1959. The school district refused, saying it "would not operate public
schools 'wherein white and colored children are taught together.'"[8] To
ensure that schools remained segregated, the county followed the state's
legislative strategy. The county stopped levying school taxes and closed
its public schools. In conjunction with those actions, a "private group,
the Prince Edward School Foundation, . . . formed to operate private
schools for white children in Prince Edward County and, having built its
own school plant, [was] in operation ever since the closing of the public
schools." A year later, state and local tax dollars began rolling into the
private school. The local district even gave property tax breaks to individuals who donated to the private school. Someone offered to open a
private school for black students, but black families declined, believing

they had to fight for their right to public schooling. Sadly, this meant they went without any formal education from 1959 to 1963. Finally, in 1963, federal, state, and county officials worked out a compromise. Classes for white and black students would be offered in a building that the county owned, but it was not officially a public school.[9]

The issue of whether the state and district had to provide public education was foremost a state constitutional issue and was litigated in state court first. The Virginia Supreme Court blessed everything the state and local school district did. According to Virginia's Supreme Court, "the closing of the Prince Edward County public schools, the state and county tuition grants for children who attend private schools, and the county's tax concessions for those who make contributions to private schools"[10] were all completely fine. The court reasoned that the state constitutional mandate to provide "an efficient system of public free schools throughout the state" only applied to the state; local counties had "an option to operate or not to operate public schools."[11]

Virginia's strategy, and the state supreme court's validation of it, left the US Supreme Court in a pickle. While Virginia's motivation was awful, it had not actually denied African Americans admission to any public school that whites attended. Whether Virginia funded private education was generally its own business. Nothing in the federal Constitution explicitly mandated public schools, and state courts are the definitive final word on their state constitutions. If the Virginia Supreme Court said its constitution does not require counties to operate public schools, the US Supreme Court can't second-guess that conclusion. Of course, the nation's history offers many reasons why the Court should recognize an implied federal right to education, as does the explicit condition on Virginia's readmission to the Union, but those issues had not been briefed and were not before the Court. Going out of the way to reach those issues would have been a highly unusual and controversial move.

This quandary revealed the Court's folly in failing to deal with the issue of a fundamental right to education in *Brown*, but in the context of the Virginia case, it was not the time to correct the error. The Court had dug its own hole in *Brown* and had to find a different way out in

Virginia. If the Court did nothing, showed the least bit of weakness, or even hinted that complex issues were at play, states and districts would exploit the opening and the promise of *Brown* might be lost. With the future of desegregation still in doubt, the Court could not run that risk. So the Court focused on the narrative surrounding what Virginia was doing and put legal niceties largely to the side. That was its way out. It detailed Virginia's shenanigans and then just repeated what two lower courts had previously said about the illegality of closing public schools and funding private schools to evade desegregation. The Court's only contribution was to say that it agreed with their conclusion that those actions are unconstitutional. After that, Virginia and local districts continued to plot out integration-evasion strategies, but the Court had shown it would not break. There was just no way the Court would tolerate anything but fidelity to *Brown*.

With that show of resolve, white moderates soon enough conceded that the Court had won and so moved closer to the Court than its resisters. Legal scholar James Ryan explained that white moderates themselves helped "defeat[] massive resistance by pushing for schools to remain open" in major metropolitan areas, even as Prince George was doing the opposite.[12] "These parents did not subscribe to a particular ideology, nor did they endorse extremists at either end of the spectrum. They rejected the cause of massive resistance as well as that of massive integration. They acted instead to protect their own interests. Desegregation was less threatening to their interests than shuttering the schools, so they chose the former over the latter."[13] Once again, the state constitutional right to and provision of education lived on despite major headwinds.

At that point, the fight against desegregation shifted away from massive resistance, violence in the streets, or blatant obfuscation. The new fight was to be on the facts, on practical reality, and the idea that desegregation had to have its limits. The task of resisters was to find pressure points in the facts and convince the Supreme Court that they were constitutionally significant. Don't fight the Court. Don't fight education. The rule of law and democracy had proved too strong. Better to get the Court on their side.

Given the Court's numerous unanimous decisions siding with the NAACP over the past two decades, this was a tall order, but one that became possible sooner than anyone could have imagined. It all turned on the election of Richard Nixon and the four new justices he appointed to the Supreme Court between 1969 and 1974. In the lead-up to his election, Richard Nixon campaigned aggressively against the Supreme Court, including on hot-button desegregation issues. While some debate lingers about Nixon's true feelings about desegregation, those feelings don't matter much. Through his words and actions, Nixon made every attempt to woo and pacify the South. He told "southern delegates to the Republican National Convention that when children were bused 'into a strange community . . . I think you destroy that child.'"[14] He added: "It is the job of the courts to interpret the law, and not make the law."[15] Judges are not "qualified to be a local school district and make the decision as your local school board."[16]

As president, he was more nuanced. He claimed to be a rule-of-law man, so he could not just openly thwart the Court. But right out of the gate, he made excuses for districts that were slow to desegregate. Most notably, in 1968, the Nixon administration intervened in the NAACP's desegregation suit against thirty-three Mississippi school districts. But rather than siding with the NAACP and the Supreme Court's demand for immediate plans to desegregate schools, the Nixon administration requested a one-year delay under the premise that immediate desegregation was a bad idea. The symbolism was enormous. It was the first time the Department of Justice had opposed the NAACP in a school desegregation case. Observers said Nixon was nodding to the South, if not paying it back, for its support in the presidential election. From then on, "Nixon had to be hauled kicking and screaming into desegregation on a meaningful scale, and he did what he did not because it was right but because he had no choice."[17] The most generous reading of Nixon's approach was that he just wanted the school desegregation issue to go away. He did not want to have to choose between Southern pacification and judicial compliance.

The best way to navigate that problem was by appointing a new breed of judges. Between 1969 and 1974, Nixon handpicked four Supreme Court justices whom he thought would move the Court in a very different direction from Warren, if not overturn the prior era's precedent. His picks proved to be monumental. He appointed Warren Burger as chief justice and William Rehnquist as an associate justice (who would later also become chief justice). Burger replaced Chief Justice Warren, the architect of *Brown*'s unanimous decision and the one who carefully stayed the course when the Court's authority was challenged. Burger had been on the DC Circuit since 1956 and was a known Warren critic. Rehnquist was more than just a critic. Rehnquist was a Supreme Court clerk when *Brown v. Board of Education* first arrived on the docket. He wrote a memorandum titled "A Random Thought on the Segregation Cases," imploring Justice Jackson to rule against the NAACP. Rehnquist wrote, "I realize that this is an unpopular and unhumanitarian position for which I have been excoriated by 'liberal' colleagues, but I think *Plessy v. Ferguson* was right and should be re-affirmed."[18]

Once on the Court, Burger and Rehnquist quickly began outlining the limits of school desegregation, limits that capitulated to and threw fuel on the fire of the civil rights backlash. Just as the moral and federal force of Reconstruction overrode countervailing forces during the 1860s and 1870s, the moral and federal force of *Brown* and its progeny overwhelmed segregationists in the 1960s and early 1970s. And just as the underlying resistance persisted, shifted tactics and arguments, and found ways to civilly undo much of what had been won during Reconstruction's recommitment to democracy, so, too, did the Burger Court help undo much of what had been won in *Brown* and its progeny.

The first chip into *Brown*'s legacy came in *Keyes v. School District No. 1*. The opinion in *Keyes* was a mixed bag. As noted above, *Keyes* ordered a desegregation remedy and adopted a presumption that eased plaintiffs' litigation burdens in some cases. But the Court splintered over what plaintiffs had to show to trigger that presumption. A minority on the

Court believed that basic proof of racially imbalanced schools should be enough to require desegregation, but the majority demanded that plaintiffs show the state's intentionally discriminatory acts caused the segregation. Since evidence of intentional discrimination was present in *Keyes* (and all Southern districts as a matter of law), the distinction had no immediate effect there. But with the requirement of intentional discrimination, the Court drew a line that would define the rest of school segregation's history.

School segregation caused by private housing choices, demographic shifts, socioeconomic inequalities, or anything else not explicitly connected to state action was beyond the reach of the Constitution. Lower courts could no longer assume the state had played a role in segregation. Plaintiffs would have to establish the link, and that link would necessarily fade or evade proof as time passed. The Court, in other cases, also required the intent standard outside the school segregation context, using it as a limit on remedies for all of society's racial inequalities—employment, zoning, environmental dangers, and healthcare.

Advocates could not fully see that future in 1973, but a few suspected that school desegregation doctrine alone would not ensure equal opportunity. They thought the realization of full educational equality rested on the issue that *Brown* skirted: the fundamental right to education. Advocates finally and squarely raised that issue in a school funding case, *San Antonio v. Rodriguez*, rather than desegregation. They had more than a few reasons to believe they would win on the issue this time. Other courts, including the lower court in *Rodriguez* and state courts in separate cases, were already holding that education was a fundamental right. *Brown* itself had declared education the "most important function of state and local governments" and an "opportunity" that "must be made available to all on equal terms." And while *Keyes* had adopted an intent standard, plaintiffs still won that case. In fact, the Court had not rejected an education equality case since the NAACP started bringing them in the 1930s. Yet the Court in *Rodriguez* made it clear that the good old days of expanding education rights were behind it.

Responsibility for writing the opinion in *Rodriguez* fell to another of Richard Nixon's Supreme Court appointees, Lewis Powell. Justice Powell was an enigma of sorts. From one perspective, Powell was a moderate or reasonable pragmatist. Yes, he served on the Richmond School Board in Virginia during a time when it did nothing meaningful to desegregate its schools, and his firm represented Prince Edward County, one of the defendant districts in *Brown v. Board*. But Powell's defenders emphasized that he never did anything to interfere with desegregation. He simply oversaw gradual, peaceful desegregation in accordance with the demands of the time. In his Supreme Court confirmation proceedings, the Congressional Black Caucus told a much different story of Powell. They charged that Powell's role as chairman of the Richmond School Board was disgraceful:

> What the very words of the United States Court of Appeals, Fourth Circuit, indicate beyond a shadow of a doubt is that Lewis Powell's eight-year reign as Chairman of the Richmond School Board created and maintained a patently segregated school system, characterized by grossly overcrowded Black public schools, white schools not filled to normal capacity, and the school board's effective perpetuation of a discriminatory feeder or assignment system whereby Black children were hopelessly trapped in inadequate, segregated schools. . . . Under his guidance, the Richmond School Board maintained a "discriminatory 'feeder' system, whereby pupils assigned initially to Negro schools were routinely promoted to Negro schools." To transfer to white schools, they had to "meet criteria to which white students of (the) same scholastic aptitude (were) not subjected."[19]

Powell left the Richmond Board of Education to serve on the Virginia State Board of Education. There, the plot only thickened. Powell was present during meetings in which the board unanimously voted to give money to white families attending private schools to avoid desegregation. This included financial grants in Prince Edward County when the district entirely shut down its public schools in defiance of court-ordered desegregation. Powell even voted for retroactive reimburse-ments for white families in Prince Edward.[20]

Maybe Powell had mixed motives. Maybe he was playing a longer game in the service of a moderate, peaceful transition. Maybe he was "just following the law" that Virginia had passed. Virginia statutes blocked integrative reassignment when he was on Richmond's board and state law authorized private tuition grants when he was on the state board. Harder to explain was his own writing in *Swann*. Powell submitted an anti-busing brief in *Swann* on behalf of Virginia.[21] The brief argued that busing was "disruptive" and that the lower courts placed too much weight on "racial balance" among the schools. Bordering on inflamma-tory, if not crossing the line, Powell called the lower court's desegrega-tion order "simplistic racial mixing pursuant to formula" and argued that school districts had to instead be allowed "reasonable discretion . . . in the assignment of pupils and the administration of a school system."[22] If one credits these details as representing the real Lewis Powell, Powell looked like another perfectly cast character in Nixon's script to pacify the South and redirect the Court.

Whatever Powell's racial politics may have been, he was always stead-fast on one thing: his fidelity to state and local education policymaking discretion over educational equality through the federal Constitution. He put that bias on full display in *Rodriguez* when it mattered most. Powell was the fifth and decisive vote to deny students the fundamental right to education. While *Rodriguez* never attained the symbolic cultural status of *Brown*, it was just as consequential in terms of the education resources and protections that students had then and now. It did not just seal the constitutional fate of minority children across the nation; it sealed the fate of poor kids.

The facts in *Rodriguez* were abysmal. Texas's school funding system left predominantly minority and poor school districts with literally half as much money as other districts. How could Powell turn his head from such an egregious, undeniable fact? His rationale rested on two ideas: the sanctity of state discretion in running schools and the notion that a right cannot be fundamental if it isn't explicitly spelled out in the Constitution.

The trouble with treating state discretion with sanctity is that not all state prerogatives are the same. Sure, if a state prefers big school districts over small ones or prefers that students take four math courses rather than three in high school, those issues are up to the state (or local district). But if a state wants to run a finance system that year in and year out gives students in one district fifty cents for every dollar that students in a neighboring district get, surely equal protection would raise its eyebrows.

Powell swept the distinction away and took on the role of state government apologist and factual skeptic. Powell said Texas's intentions were good. It was, according to him, trying to make progress toward a fairer system. Even if Powell's characterization of Texas's motivations was correct, it begs the question: Why don't students deserve a fair system right now? Powell swatted that concern away, too, saying he wasn't sure money affected educational quality anyway. He stopped short of the audacious claim that money never mattered, conceding that at some point funding might be so low that students would not receive the most basic aspects of education—safe buildings, core curriculum, literacy, and teachers, for instance. But Powell emphasized that plaintiffs had not made the claim that Texas's funding system was so grossly inadequate as to deprive students of those things.

After downplaying the facts on funding inequality, Powell revealed his general bias against recognizing a fundamental right in education. Powell, again, had to disregard a lot of counterpoints and evidence, but this time he had to sweep aside the Court's own history. The Court had long recognized education's importance to citizenship, democracy, and personal autonomy. Cases in the early 1900s, for instance, recognized that "the American people have always regarded education and acquisition of knowledge as matters of supreme importance which should be diligently promoted."[23] *Brown* and other cases later pronounced that "education is perhaps the most important function of state and local governments."[24]

Powell said these cases didn't matter. While they express "an abiding respect for the vital role of education in a free society," he thought they

were little more than puffery and did not support a constitutional rationale for recognizing education as a fundamental right. "The importance
of a service performed by the State," he reasoned, "does not determine
whether it must be regarded as fundamental."[25] The only thing that mattered to Powell was "whether there is a right to education explicitly or
implicitly guaranteed by the Constitution." And since "education" does
not appear in the text of the Constitution, the remaining question was
whether the Constitution implicitly protects education. Powell said no.
His logic on that question is hard to swallow, too, but went like this:
education isn't comparable to other rights the Court has recognized as
fundamental; and if we recognize education as fundamental, what other
rights come next?

Powell's argument falls apart pretty easily if you scratch at it. If
"importance" doesn't matter, what does? Powell did not answer that
question. He just said it couldn't count. If importance mattered, he
claimed the Constitution would have to protect food, water, and housing, too, and the Constitution clearly does not protect that. But that
just isn't so. The importance of those things is distinct from education.
Yes, those things are vitally important to basic survival, and formal education is not. Yet, at the same time, education is crucially important
to literacy, political understanding, self-government, and the like; food,
water, and housing are not (though they certainly keep people alive so
they can learn and exercise political rights). In fact, government has
long made the provision of public education its central mission because
of education's direct reinforcing effects on citizens' ability to carry out
their duties, whereas government has never done that in regard to those
other "important" things for individuals' lives and survival.

Powell's other point—that implicit constitutional rights are very
closely connected to rights explicitly protected by the Constitution—
makes some sense. The problem for him, though, is that the general rule
sounds like a winner for education. Plaintiffs already argued that public education is closely connected to the exercise of explicit constitutional rights like freedom of speech and voting. That argument, moreover,
sounds like the thinking of the founding fathers, Congress and the states

during the Reconstruction era. On this score, education is undoubtedly distinct from food, water, and housing. Powell's response was not that plaintiffs were wrong, but that they were asking for too much:

> We have never presumed to possess either the ability or the authority to guarantee to the citizenry the most effective speech or the most informed electoral choice. That these may be desirable goals of a system of freedom of expression and of a representative form of government is not to be doubted. These are indeed goals to be pursued by a people whose thoughts and beliefs are freed from governmental interference. But they are not values to be implemented by judicial instruction into otherwise legitimate state activities.[26]

In other words, with Powell at the helm of the opinion, the Court was not going to recognize education as a fundamental right—no how, no way. Compelling arguments and evidence be damned.

As a testament to how much the world had changed only to move backward, Thurgood Marshall was a member of the Supreme Court when it decided *Rodriguez*. But unlike all the cases Marshall brought to the Court as a litigant, his voice was relegated to a minority position as an actual member of the Court. From there, he was forced to dissent and took the opportunity to call the Court out for the mockery it was making of everything the Court had stood for (and he had worked for) over the prior decades. The opening lines of his *Rodriguez* opinion made no bones about what the Court was doing: "The Court today decides, in effect, that a State may constitutionally vary the quality of education which it offers its children in accordance with the amount of taxable wealth located in the school districts within which they reside." That, Marshall said, was "an abrupt departure from the mainstream of recent state and federal court decisions" and "a retreat from our historic commitment to equality of educational opportunity." The net result would be to "depriv[e] children in their earliest years of the chance to reach their full potential as citizens."[27]

Marshall then chided the majority for moving the goalposts. Had it applied the same approach of other recent Supreme Court cases, it would protect education. By the same token, had those prior cases applied the *Rodriguez* majority's standard, they would have rejected any number of fundamental rights that the Court now holds dearly. Throwing the Court's recent decisions in the majority's face, Marshall said, "I would like to know where the Constitution guarantees the right to procreate, or the right to vote in state elections, or the right to an appeal from a criminal conviction." Nowhere explicitly is the answer. Yet "the Court has displayed a strong concern with the existence of discriminatory state treatment" in regard to all of these rights. To have done otherwise would shock the conscience now.

Sure, Marshall wrote, "some interests which the Court has deemed to be fundamental . . . are themselves constitutionally protected rights," but some are not.[28] That means the test for recognizing fundamental rights cannot be whether a right is explicitly in the Constitution. Likewise, the fact that some interest is not mentioned in the Constitution does not answer whether it is firmly rooted in the Constitution. The task, Marshall reasoned, is "to determine the extent to which constitutionally guaranteed rights are dependent on interests not mentioned in the Constitution. As the nexus between the specific constitutional guarantee and the nonconstitutional interest draws closer, the nonconstitutional interest becomes more fundamental and the degree of judicial scrutiny applied when the interest is infringed on a discriminatory basis must be adjusted accordingly."[29]

Under that approach, education is undeniably fundamental. "The fundamental importance of education is amply indicated by the prior decisions of this Court, by the unique status accorded public education by our society, and by the close relationship between education and some of our most basic constitutional values."[30] As to citizenship, which the Constitution explicitly guarantees, *Brown v. Board* made education's connection clear. Just a year before *Rodriguez*, the Court in *Wisconsin v. Yoder* reiterated the point, writing that "providing public schools ranks at the very apex of the function of a State" and that "some degree of education is necessary to prepare citizens to participate effectively and intelligently in our open political system." That opinion drew only a single dissent, and it was on other grounds. As to free speech, which the Constitution also explicitly protects, Marshall emphasized the Court's opinions recognizing education's connection to the right "to inquire, to study and to evaluate, to gain new maturity and understanding." As to the democratic processes our Constitution explicitly enshrines, Marshall quoted one of Justice Brennan's prior opinions: "Americans regard the public schools as a most vital civic institution for the preservation of a democratic system of government."[31] And as to voting, which the Constitution explicitly protects in more than one place and the Court treats as fundamental, evidence in recent presidential elections and other data "clearly demonstrate a direct relationship between participation in the electoral process and level of educational attainment."[32]

Marshall then went to the facts in *Rodriguez*. Though Powell tried to muddy the waters with uncertainty as to whether money matters in schools, Marshall cut to the "inescapable fact that if one district has more funds available per pupil than another district, the former will have greater choice in educational planning than will the latter." Nuanced social science debates over school funding practices were beside the point. The issue for the Court was "an objective one that looks to what the State provides its children, not to what the children are able to do with what they receive. That a child forced to attend an underfunded school with poorer physical facilities, less experienced teachers, larger classes, and a narrower range of courses than a school with substantially more funds—and thus with greater choice in educational planning—may nevertheless excel is to the credit of the child, not the State."[33]

The raw power of Nixon's new votes on the Supreme Court nonetheless overtook reason and reality in *Rodriguez*. The next Supreme Court term only got worse for education. If the intentional discrimination standard seemed inconsequential in *Keyes*, its decisiveness was painfully obvious in *Milliken v. Bradley* in 1974. *Milliken* involved school desegregation in Detroit. The trial court had established two undeniable facts: Detroit's core city school district segregated its schools by race years ago and now the overall metropolitan area was so segregated that Detroit's city schools could not be integrated without including suburban districts in the desegregation plan.

On one level, desegregating Detroit's schools should have been no different than desegregating Charlotte, North Carolina, in *Swann*. Both metropolitan areas included a core city where primarily African Americans lived and primarily white neighborhoods that surrounded the city. The Supreme Court in *Swann* did not distinguish between the various parts of the city. It just ordered school attendance boundaries redrawn and, if necessary, busing to facilitate metropolitan-wide desegregation. It never asked whether segregation in any particular Charlotte neighborhood was the result of intentional state action. Nor did it overly concern itself with neighborhood or school district autonomy. It did not matter, for instance, that the city of Charlotte and the county of Mecklenburg had run separate school districts until 1959, only merging five years after *Brown*.

But in *Milliken*, school district independence and boundaries mattered more than anything to the court. The Court emphasized that the suburban school districts ringing Detroit's central city district were independent school districts. According to the Court, merging or coordinating these small districts was too complicated and would upset too many expectations in local communities. Never mind that these districts were still agents of the state or that their size, shape, and autonomy were more an accident of history than an inherent aspect of education. By a vote of 5–4, the Court insisted that plaintiffs needed to show intentional school segregation, not just in Detroit's city schools, but in its suburban districts, too. Absent that, lower courts could not order metropolitan-wide school desegregation.

That simple idea—that school desegregation remedies could not cross school district boundaries—sealed desegregation's future before it ever began in earnest in much of the country. The Court was, in effect, telling families who did not want to be part of desegregation that they could just move to a new neighborhood, maybe just a mile away in the same county. The school district line would protect them. All too soon this possibility became reality and earned the name "white flight." The

Court's opinion stopped desegregation dead in its tracks in many areas, and white flight later reversed integration's gains elsewhere. The combined effect of the funding inequality that the Court had already blessed in *Rodriguez* made the picture even bleaker: schools could once again be racially separate (so long as there was no proof of intentional action) and financially unequal (even if it was intentional). In other words, the Court, as a practical matter, had moved the bar below *Plessy*. *Plessy*, at least, said that separate should be equal.

Those sad truths were too much for Thurgood Marshall to abide. His historical recitation bluntly highlighted the detour the Court was taking:

> This Court recognized [in *Brown*] that remedying decades of segregation in public education would not be an easy task. Subsequent events, unfortunately, have seen that prediction bear bitter fruit. But however imbedded old ways, however ingrained old prejudices, this Court has not been diverted from its appointed task of making "a living truth" of our constitutional ideal of equal justice under law.[34]
>
> After 20 years of small, often difficult steps toward that great end, the Court today takes a giant step backwards. . . . The Court's answer is to provide no remedy at all for the violation proved in this case, thereby guaranteeing that Negro children in Detroit will receive the same separate and inherently unequal education in the future as they have been unconstitutionally afforded in the past.

This detour and failure to uphold the Constitution, Marshall worried, was not one the nation's future could bear. He called on the democratic theory that had propelled education from the nation's founding through *Brown*—the same theory he invoked a year earlier in *Rodriguez*—to make his point.

> The rights at issue in this case are too fundamental to be abridged on grounds as superficial as those relied on by the majority today. We deal here with the right of all of our children, whatever their race, to an equal start in life and to an equal opportunity to reach

their full potential as citizens. Those children who have been denied that right in the past deserve better than to see fences thrown
up to deny them that right in the future. Our Nation, I fear, will
be ill served by the Court's refusal to remedy separate and unequal
education, for unless our children begin to learn together, there is
little hope that our people will ever learn to live together.[35]

Subsequent history has depressingly affirmed the wisdom of Marshall's warning. The work of *Brown*, both practically and in hearts and
minds, ended too soon. There is no other way of saying it: we left the job
undone. Left undone, *Brown*'s short-term gains could only hold for so
long. The instincts that had first called for segregation persisted in some
places and morphed into subtler forms elsewhere, eventually overtaking
Brown's promise and the gains that lower courts and communities tried
to secure. In fact, by the late 1990s, school districts were as segregated
as they had been in the late 1960s and early 1970s, when serious desegregation efforts first began.

Though *Milliken* was the mightiest blow against integration and
equality, it was not the last. Over the next twenty years, the Burger
Court and then the Rehnquist Court further chipped away at desegregation, regularly issuing decisions that curtailed lower courts' desegregation orders and powers, even if it did not entirely foreclose them. The
final nail in the coffin came in 1992. In *Freeman v. Pitts*, the Court held
that demographic shifts, which inevitably happen over time, absolve districts of continuing desegregation efforts. Private housing choices rather
than state action, the Court reasoned, were the real cause of school segregation. The time had come for courts to release school districts from
desegregation.

The full blame, however, doesn't rest solely with the Court. The
Court was as much a sign as a cause of the times. The Court in *Brown*
was a catalyst in ushering in a new era of fidelity to constitutional rights,
minority rights, and democratic equality through education. But the
Burger Court was a product of the political forces that put President
Nixon in office. In 1960, John F. Kennedy defeated Nixon in his first

bid for the presidency. Kennedy, ironically, dominated the Deep South, winning six Southern states and splitting the electoral votes in a seventh. Lyndon Johnson was even more dominant in the next election, taking 486 of 638 electoral votes. But just as the civil rights movement took hold in Congress, the White House, and the courts, a growing segment of the public worried things were going too far. That segment, along with staunch segregationists, formed a large anti–civil rights bloc.

Richard Nixon seized on the shift in his second presidential campaign in 1968. It carried him to his own landslide victory. The only place he didn't dominate was in the Southern Black Belt. But he didn't lose to someone to his political left. He lost to someone further right. The segregationist George Wallace took the South. But in his 1972 reelection campaign, Nixon "corrected" that, too, tacking even further to the political right and taking the South handily. In fact, Nixon only lost a single state in the country: Massachusetts. The American political landscape effectively flipped in less than a decade. "At the highest levels of government, emotionally laden terms like 'law-and-order' were backlash code words for a cynical strategy that appealed to white fear and distrust—splitting communities and further polarizing the nation."[36] Nixon took full advantage.

The shifting political winds were also reflected in legislation. For instance, less than a year after the Court's decision in *Swann* authorized student reassignment and busing, Nixon sent proposals to Congress to "place firm and effective curbs on busing."[37] The first proposal, the Equal Educational Opportunities Act, included positive measures unrelated to desegregation, but prohibited federal agencies and courts from ordering desegregation plans that increased school bus travel times or distance. In some places, a court could theoretically carry out the Supreme Court's proscribed ruling without running afoul of Nixon's proposal, but in other places the constitution was unreconcilable with the proposal.[38] Nixon's second proposal made no pretense of moderation or constitutional compliance, boldly claiming the authority to stay "all federal court orders that require new busing of any student, or that require any student to be bused to a school other than the one he is currently attending, until July 1, 1973."[39]

Congress passed Nixon's first proposal, the Equal Educational Opportunities Act, by a wide margin: 323–83 in the House and 81–15 in the Senate. While the final bill took a slightly narrower stance in restricting busing, it was no less symbolic. It was a backlash against desegregation. Under no circumstances could the Act's funding be used "for the transportation of students or teachers (or the purchase of equipment for such transportation) in order to overcome racial imbalance in any school or school system . . . to carry out a plan of racial desegregation."[40]

Congress's stated rationale was flimsy at best. It said it wanted to curb school segregation, but forbade the best methods for doing so. Congress claimed that "desegregation plans that require extensive student transportation has, in many cases, . . . deplet[ed schools'] financial resources available for the maintenance or improvement of the quality of educational facilities and instruction."[41] It also claimed that desegregative busing "creates serious risks to [students'] health and safety, disrupts the educational process . . . , and impinges significantly on [students'] educational opportunity."[42]

In short, desegregation and the commitment to the American idea of equal educational opportunity started dying in the 1970s—in the White House, in Congress, and in the courts. The deepest wounds were inflicted in *Keyes*'s intent standard, *Milliken*'s prohibition on metropolitan desegregation, and *Rodriguez*'s rejection of a right to education. Constitutional standards entail a power and definiteness that is hard to match and tend to live long after those who issue them are gone. But those blows were a result of what had already occurred in the White House and Congress. The result was school resegregation, political party realignment, and stalled progress in terms of educational and democratic equality.

Yet as troubling as those reversals were, something strange happened. This backlash to America's second Reconstruction had an important underbelly you would have never seen coming.

CHAPTER 9

REDISCOVERING THE
CONSTITUTIONAL RIGHT TO EDUCATION

WHILE THE SUPREME COURT'S EFFORTS TO DESEGREGATE schools and other facets of life sparked a backlash that eventually unraveled hard-won gains, *Brown v. Board* also reawakened a consciousness toward public education that did not go away. That education consciousness, however, was not as closely tied to race or political parties as it had been during the first Reconstruction of the 1860s and 1870s. This broader consciousness allowed a general education movement to spread at the same time that cultural tensions and political fights around race were retracting civil rights and school desegregation.

Not even the Supreme Court's decision in *Rodriguez*, refusing federal constitutional protection for education, could squash the idea that education was a fundamental right. The idea of a right to education was too strong, the history too long, and the roots in state constitutions too deep. If the Supreme Court would not validate the idea, advocates would just seek out another venue. They sought it in the most unlikely of places: state courts. Equally surprising, geography and political leanings did not define or limit the places where they won.

A movement to secure a constitutional right to education swept across the nation following *Rodriguez*. Plaintiffs fought and won from California and Washington to New Hampshire and Connecticut. They fought and won from Wyoming, Minnesota, and Ohio to Alabama and, of all places, Texas—the very place where the Court had stopped the federal constitutional movement dead in its tracks. The legacy and legal precedent that advocates established in these states continues in full force today, a legacy that has outlived *Brown* in many important practical respects, even if not nearly as well known by the average person.

The state movement for a constitutional right to education began almost by happenstance. When plaintiffs were filing suit in federal court in *Rodriguez*, two other groups were also filing in state courts in California and New Jersey. The state court claims were not all that different from *Rodriguez*. They made the same claim that education was a fundamental right under the federal Constitution and, almost as an afterthought, added that education was a fundamental right under their respective state constitutions as well.

To even be in a state court raising state constitutional claims flew in the face of conventional wisdom. Federal law has long been seen as the only source of meaningful individual constitutional rights and the federal government as the only one willing to uphold those rights. It was, after all, state government that passed laws and constitutional amendments to institute Jim Crow. It was state courts that validated those laws and the violation of individual rights since the late 1800s. It took nothing short of overwhelming federal force and constitutional doctrine to end that era. Yet in the early 1970s, plaintiffs took another shot at state courts and constitutions anyway.

The California Supreme Court was the first to take on the question of whether education is a fundamental right. In a case called *Serrano v. Priest*, it delivered an opinion on the subject before the US Supreme Court decided *Rodriguez*. The California Supreme Court, however, did not offer any serious thought about an independent state constitutional right to education. Its analysis centered on the idea of a federal right. The only hint of a relevant state constitutional right was buried in a

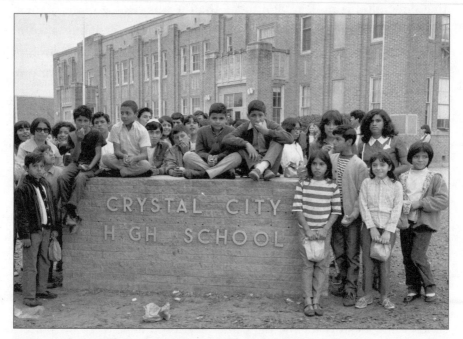

Latino students walk out to protest unequal resources in San Antonio schools in December 1969, hekping spark federal and state litigation.
San Antonio Light/ZUMA Press.

footnote. The footnote simply stated: "Our analysis of plaintiffs' federal equal protection contention is also applicable to their claim under these state constitutional provisions."[1] Regardless, the court's rationale recognizing a right to education was spot on.

The court evoked the same democratic maxims that have always sustained public education. "Education," it wrote, "supports each and every other value of a democratic society—participation, communication, and social mobility, to name but a few."[2] Like voting, education "is 'preservative of other basic civil and political rights.'"[3] And the court had really hard ground to stand on. Unlike a federal court, it had a state constitution that specifically referenced education and incorporated a democratic imperative. The text of the California Constitution justifies the state's duty to provide public education on the notion that "a general diffusion of knowledge and intelligence [is] essential to the preservation of the rights and liberties of the people."[4] The court made it clear that education is no less vital today than it was two centuries earlier: "The need for an educated populace assumes greater importance as the problems of our diverse society become increasingly complex. . . . The public school has been termed 'the most powerful agency for promoting cohesion among a heterogeneous democratic people at once the symbol of our democracy and the most pervasive means for promoting our common destiny.'"[5] For these and other reasons, the Court said it was "convinced that the distinctive and priceless function of education in our society warrants, indeed compels, our treating it as a 'fundamental interest.'"[6]

A year and a half later, when the US Supreme Court rejected the federal right to education in *Rodriguez* and thereby overturned the federal aspects of California's decision in *Serrano*, the entire fate of the right to education rested on that previously insignificant footnote mentioned above. Plaintiffs returned to the California Supreme Court, asking that it set a new destiny for the right to education independent of the federal Constitution, a destiny the court had not fully considered last time. The California Supreme Court stood by its earlier footnote, writing that "the fact that a majority of the United States Supreme Court have now chosen to contract" the right to education "can have no effect upon the existing construction and application afforded our own constitutional provisions." And all the reasons—or excuses—the US Supreme Court gave for not getting involved in education simply did not matter. As the California Supreme Court wrote:

> The constraints of federalism, so necessary to the proper functioning of our unique system of national government, are not applicable to this court in its determination of whether our own state's public school financing system runs afoul of state constitutional provisions. Moreover, while we cannot claim that we have achieved the perspective of "expertise" on the subjects of school financing and educational policy, our deliberations in this matter have had the benefit of a thoughtfully developed trial record . . . comprehensive if not exhaustive findings on the part of an able trial judge, and

voluminous briefing by the parties and no less than nine amici curiae, among which are included the state Superintendent of Public Instruction. We believe that this background amply equips us to undertake the searching judicial scrutiny of our state's public school financing system which is required of us under our state constitutional provisions guaranteeing equal protection of the laws.[7]

The California Supreme Court further noted that it had a duty to scrutinize the state's school funding because of its "impact on those individual rights and liberties which lie at the core of our free and representative form of government, are properly considered 'fundamental.'"[8]

The New Jersey Supreme Court was a bit luckier than California. New Jersey's court was just slow enough—by just a few days—in issuing its education decision that it did not have to backtrack or clarify itself. By its own admission, the New Jersey Supreme Court, in *Robinson v. Cahill*,[9] had already prepared but not released its decision upholding a federal right to education when the US Supreme Court issued its opinion in *San Antonio v. Rodriguez*. That minor delay allowed the New Jersey Supreme Court to add a couple of paragraphs to its decision, largely offering the same rationale as the California Supreme Court in its second education rights case.

The New Jersey Supreme Court reasoned that state constitutions can be "more demanding" than the federal Constitution because federalism concerns don't exist in state court.[10] But the New Jersey Supreme Court also took the opportunity to lodge a dig at the US Supreme Court's rigid, if not disingenuous, approach to individual rights. New Jersey cast its lot with Justice Marshall's way of thinking in his *Rodriguez* dissent. New Jersey's court explained that it flies in the face of logic and reality to say, as the *Rodriguez* majority did, that the level of protection the Constitution affords a right rests solely on whether the right is explicitly or implicitly guaranteed in the Constitution. For instance, "the right to acquire and hold property is guaranteed in the Federal and State Constitutions,"[11] but the US Supreme Court doesn't treat it as fundamental—and for good reason. Even once the Court declares a right fundamental, it makes judgment calls as to what state interests are "compelling" enough to justify infringing on a fundamental right. So the outcomes in these cases are in no respect cut and dry. The problem with *Rodriguez's* "mechanical approach," the New Jersey Supreme Court said, is that it "divert[s] a court from the meritorious issue. . . . Ultimately, a court must weigh the nature of the restraint or the denial against the apparent public justification, and decide whether the State action is arbitrary."[12] But rather than go down the rabbit hole of how best to determine what rights are fundamental (or not) and what state interests might override the rights, the New Jersey Supreme Court simplified the issue. In its constitution, the education clause requires a "thorough and efficient" system of schools.[13] That made the question it would answer much easier: Is the state's funding scheme sufficient to deliver such a system? The Court found that it was not.

With those cases in California and New Jersey, cases that were originally more a part of *Rodriguez* than something distinct, an entirely new set of possibilities opened for the right to education. Rather than securing the right to education with one fell swoop in the federal courts, advocates now would go one state at a time, developing arguments based on each state's own unique history, not the larger American story. Yet the national revolution that *Brown* started and the idea of education that it had articulated still loomed large. It inspired them to be as bold, or nearly so, as *Brown* had once been. State courts answered the call.

While deciding cases entirely on state grounds, state court after state court invoked *Brown's* famous lines about the importance of education to justify their own actions. State courts routinely quoted *Brown's* citizenship passage at the beginning of their opinions, before they wrote anything themselves, so as to say that *Brown's* basic idea framed everything that would follow in support of the constitutional right to education. By my count, at least fifteen courts in more than twelve different states directly quoted *Brown's* passage that way. Opinions in another ten or so cases called on that same *Brown* passage to chide some result in a case that judges thought fell short of vindicating students' right to education.

Still, many of the earliest state-level cases outside of California and New Jersey struggled to find footing for a fundamental right to education. During the 1970s and 1980s, plaintiffs won a handful of cases beyond those two states, but nothing approaching a clear overall positive trend emerged. Some courts copied California and New Jersey's reasoning while several others said *Rodriguez* was correct—that the problem of and solution to school funding inequality were too uncertain for judges to get involved. "What did equality of educational opportunity mean in terms of funding anyway?" they would ask. Spending the same amount on all students. Spending the amount necessary for each student to achieve equal results with his peers. Was such an outcome even possible? Does a court make policy if it declares education a fundamental right and then affixes some particular equity requirement to the right?

The solution to these problems came when courts began to search for and rediscover the reasons why states first enacted their education clauses. Courts did not need to pull answers out of thin air or theory. They needed to go back to their constitutional roots. Those roots could answer the question of what a constitutional system of schools should look like, what an adequate education should consist of, what effort the state owes its children. West Virginia—a state that had literally been born out of the conflicts that led to the Civil War—provided an early glimpse of this possibility.

In 1979, the West Virginia Supreme Court was tasked with deciding the constitutionality of its school financing system. The court turned to the constitutional convention debates of 1861 and 1872 "to find whether the words [requiring a 'thorough and efficient' education] were hyperbole or were meant to have legal significance."[14] The debates pointed to the latter. The Court pointed out that the West Virginia education clause had been modeled after Ohio's. And the constitutional delegates to Ohio's convention had explained that the purpose of a "thorough and efficient" mandate was

to see common schools advance, not only to meet such demands as are now made upon them, but to meet higher and greater requisitions.

Then the common of the future will need to be far above the common of the present. He wanted to see a system of schools as perfect
as could be devised, and to see it improve so as to keep pace with
the most rapid progress of the most rapid element of our social or
political constitution.[15]

These ideas of immediacy, perfection, and modernization were further reflected in specific decisions that the West Virginia convention
made: the decision to expand the school year, to ensure state funding
for the system, and to require the state to establish a system of schools
immediately. On that basis, West Virginia's Supreme Court revalidated
the state's constitutional duty to its kids in 1979.

West Virginia, however, remained an outlier until 1989, when the
Kentucky Supreme Court dug even further into its history for a deeper
meaning of the constitutional right to education in *Rose v. Council for
Better Education*. The evidence being amassed regarding inequality in
places like Kentucky and elsewhere was just too massive to sweep aside
with the flimsy or fearful logic found in other state court opinions. In
Kentucky, the facts were clear: "The quality of education in the poorer
local school districts is substantially less" in terms of "classroom teachers' pay; provision of basic educational materials; student-teacher ratio;
curriculum; quality of basic management; size, adequacy and condition
of school physical plants; and per year expenditure per student."[16] And
the problem went beyond inequality. Evidence "indicated that not only
do the so-called poorer districts provide inadequate education to fulfill
the needs of the students but the more affluent districts' efforts are inadequate as well, as judged by accepted national standards."[17] Money was
the cause. Witnesses and data "showed a definite correlation between
the money spent per child on education and the quality of the education
received" and that the state was underfunding its schools—often to the
tune of thousands of dollars per student per year.[18]

The Court said the issue was whether the state constitution's explicit mandate for the state to "provide an efficient system of common
schools throughout the state" demanded something better from the

state.[19] Long-forgotten history said yes. Kentucky's current education clause dated back to 1890. The framers of that education clause were "cognizan[t] of the importance of education and, emphasized that the educational system in Kentucky must be improved. Referring to the education of our children, [a leading voice in the constitutional convention] admonished the delegates, 'do not let us make a mistake in dealing with the most vital question that can come before us.'"[20]

The Court relied heavily on Delegate Beckner's fuller explanation of the clause's purpose and the education committee report on the clause. Beckner said that "if . . . we forget the children, and, in the slightest degree, fail to appreciate the obligations of the State to provide sufficient facilities for training them to be good citizens, we will deserve and receive in the great hereafter anathema, and not ascription of praise."[21] Beckner pointed out that Kentucky's "common schools" dated back nearly seventy years to 1822. Those common schools were originally created to support a "'system of practical equality in which the children of the rich and poor meet upon a perfect level and the only superiority is that of the mind.'"[22]

The real guidepost in Beckner's remarks, however, was in those that looked to the future:

> If public schools have come to stay, if they are a part and parcel of our free institutions, woven into the very web and woof of popular government; and if they are in the future to be the dependence of the people of Kentucky for the instruction of their youth, what is the logic of the situation? Manifestly to encourage and improve them, to seize every opportunity to make them more efficient, to treat them with no niggard or stinted hand, but just in so far as we love our children, to try to make their training-places fit nurseries of immortal spirits that have divine purposes to fulfill on earth, and cannot hope to succeed, unless their intellectual powers be properly developed.[23]

Based on Beckner's and other delegates' commentary, the Court concluded the education clause ensconced education as one of the state's "most 'vital'" functions.[24] The constitution made education the duty of the state, required state supervision to ensure that the schools were continually becoming more efficient, required learning opportunities that leveled the lifelong playing field for students, and required the state to provide the financial support necessary to achieve those ends.[25] The Court then reduced these duties and principles to a simple overarching constitutional demand "that each and every child in this state should receive a proper and an adequate education, *to be provided for by the General Assembly*."[26]

The Kentucky Supreme Court delivered its decision just a few years after another important marker in education history: the publication of *A Nation at Risk*—a report by the National Commission on Excellence in Education. The report, along with a host of studies, warned of a "rising tide of mediocrity" in American education and stoked the idea that the country was suffering a national "crisis in education."[27] The concern was so widespread that President Bush called a National Education Summit in 1989, bringing together state governors to address America's school problem.[28] The "standards-based reform" movement, which demanded that states set high academic standards in core subject areas, grew out of this summit and era.

Seizing on this new receptivity to education standards, the Kentucky Supreme Court did something no other had. Rather than rest on broad education principles and language, it looked to experts for help in defining an "adequate" education in the modern context. While the education standards this interaction produced are mundane to the modern eye, the fact that they were mandated by a constitutional clause was revolutionary. The Court wrote that

an efficient system of education must have as its goal to provide each and every child with at least the seven following capacities: (i) sufficient oral and written communication skills to enable students to function in a complex and rapidly changing civilization; (ii) sufficient knowledge of economic, social, and political systems to enable the student to make informed choices; (iii) sufficient understanding of governmental processes to enable the student to understand the issues that affect his or her community, state, and nation; (iv) sufficient self-knowledge and knowledge of his or her mental and physical wellness; (v) sufficient grounding in the arts to enable each student to appreciate his or her cultural and historical heritage; (vi) sufficient training or preparation for advanced training in either academic or vocational fields so as to enable each child to choose and pursue life work intelligently; and (vii) sufficient levels of academic or vocational skills to enable public school students to compete favorably with their counterparts in surrounding states, in academics or in the job market.[29]

With that, the constitutional education adequacy movement was born, drawing on specific constitutional language and the historical roots that had demanded it. Following Kentucky's lead, high courts in at least eight other states issued similar decisions over the next decade, changing the trajectory of the constitutional right to education.[30] The movement grew even more from there. Whereas plaintiffs only won about a third of the time in the years between *Rodriguez* and *Rose*, in the two decades following *Rose*, plaintiffs "prevailed in twenty of twenty-seven final decisions of the highest state courts or unappealed trial court decisions (74 percent)."[31] Not until the Great Recession did any signs suggest the movement might slow.[32] Those signs, however, seemed more like temporary pauses once the recession was clearly over. State supreme courts once again were intervening to enforce the constitutional right to education, including in states like Pennsylvania, where the courts never before had. And as the movement matured, other important things became all the more clear, like the right to education is about far more than money. Money is certainly relevant, but the real issues in these cases had always been students' access to quality teachers, safe school facilities, small class sizes, modern curricula, and support services. But the right to education also supports less obvious, but equally crucial, interests—things like freedom from segregation, access to preschool, and fair school discipline.[33]

To be clear, however, a number of state supreme courts still refuse to validate their education clauses or find flimsy excuses for legislatures that fail their students. The constitutions in these states are no less compelling, nor the facts on inequality any less troubling. Florida and Illinois, for instance, have very specific and powerful education clauses. Their constitutions don't stop with concepts like an "efficient" education. Instead, they have updated their constitutions and mandate "high quality" education. Yet the courts in both states refuse to enforce the mandates. It's not that the courts lack tools to measure the quality of education. They just reason—under the concept of separation of powers—that those questions are left completely to legislatures; courts should not intrude on legislative discretion. As a result, those states in particular have maintained some of the most distressing educational inequalities in the nation. The funding gap between school districts in Illinois has long been among the largest in the nation.[34] Florida's effort to fund its schools has been among the most minimal in the nation. Even worse, Florida chopped almost $3,000 per pupil out of the education budget during the recession—one of the largest cuts in the nation. Yet, Florida and Illinois courts have refused to do anything, making a cruel reality obvious: in the absence of a federally recognized right to education, students' access to equal and adequate education depends on the state in which they happen to live.

The larger global story of the right to education, however, remains one in which courts aim to recognize and enforce the right to education. The particulars of state education clause text and history, judicial interpretations, and effective enforcement necessarily vary. But courts' understanding and explanation of those education clauses revolve around a common set of principles. The first one is that students have a constitutional right to an adequate or equal education—or both. An adequate education can just as easily be described as a quality education, and some states call it just that. Others call it a thorough education. The particular phrase a state uses is not all that important. The important point is what the phrase is attached to. It could be called an education adequate to prepare students for high school graduation, for college, for jury duty, for citizenship, or for the workplace. Even if termed a "minimally adequate" or "basic education," the key is not those minimalist-sounding phrases but the long-term goal or purpose to which education is tied. A basic education sufficient to prepare students to succeed in college and later pursue graduate school would, after all, be a really great "basic" education, whereas a "high quality" education that prepares students for manual labor might not be.

Courts, to their credit, have consistently tied students' right to education to more ambitious goals. When the state of New York, for instance, argued that a sound basic education meant an eighth-grade education, the state's highest court was beside itself. It said students' right to education entailed far more than just an eighth-grade education. In fact, it rejected the idea that the right could "be pegged to the eighth or ninth grade, or indeed to any particular grade level."[35] The court said that if it was going to peg education quality to anything, it would be "voting and jury service because they are the civic responsibilities *par excellence*."[36] Students are entitled to an education that "prepares them to function productively as civic participants," and that preparation can be quite rigorous.[37] Whether in terms of voting, jury service, self-government, or all of the above, at least thirty state courts have found that "preparation for capable citizenship is a primary purpose or the primary purpose of the education clause."[38]

State courts recognizing a right to an equal education are distinct from these adequacy courts but invoke similar concepts. An equal education could mean that all students have exactly the same resources. Some early cases moved in that direction, but the threat that a state might give everyone an equally underfunded education soon prompted a more sophisticated understanding of equality. Equality could, for instance, mean that all students have the resources they need to achieve the same outcomes as their peers. This would mean that students with disabilities are constitutionally entitled to more funding per pupil than their peers because extra funding is necessary for those students to graduate from high school. From this perspective, the key question is again the particular outcome that all students need to achieve for a court to conclude that the state has delivered equal opportunity. Courts tend to set the baseline for that outcome on some level similar to adequacy. In other words, it might be an equal opportunity to become proficient in the state's high school curriculum or participate as an effective citizen. That baseline does not require that all students achieve the same outcome, but it does require that they have the same shot at achieving that baseline outcome.

The second common principle in these cases is that the duty to ensure quality or equal educational opportunities rests with the state, not local communities or districts. So much education history and development has occurred at the local level. Many local communities have, no doubt, achieved incredible things. But that local story is also the source of vast inequality because some communities can't raise the funds, attract the teachers, and provide the services students need. While the Supreme Court in *Rodriguez* was willing to treat local control as an end unto itself, state supreme courts have reasoned that there is nothing special about local control as a state constitutional matter. State constitutions are crystal clear. They make it the explicit "duty of the state" to provide education.[39] Recognizing this distinction, state courts have effectively inverted the standard way of doing business and thinking about education in many states. As the Kentucky Supreme Court wrote, maintaining constitutionally appropriate educational opportunities throughout the state "is the sole responsibility of the General Assembly."[40]

A related theme in this education movement is that states' education duty is an absolute one.[41] It is one thing to say a state has a duty in education. It is something else to say the duty is absolute. Calling education a state duty could be dismissed as nothing more than rhetorical flourish. Or state legislators might be allowed to decide how deep the state's commitment to education runs and whether it is substantive. If so, the strength of lawmakers' duties, like the vows of a husband or wife, rely on the good faith of the individuals making them more than judicial enforcement. In recognizing education as an absolute duty, however, courts reject that way of thinking. States and their lawmakers don't really have any choice in the matter. The constitution mandates fidelity to certain aspects of education.

This notion is crucial when states make excuses for their failures in education. "Failure is the local district's fault," the state might say. "Teacher pensions are out of control." "Money doesn't matter." "Financial exigencies or depressions have reduced tax receipts." "We are working on it." "Give us time." Some version of: "It's too hard." Or the best one: "Poor students face too many challenges to do any better in school, and those challenges aren't our responsibility." And to all these excuses, courts have said, it does not matter because the state's duty is absolute. "If local government fails, the state government must compel it to act, and if the local government cannot carry the burden, the state must itself meet its continuing obligation,"[42] wrote the Arkansas Supreme Court. The Kentucky Supreme Court similarly explained that local mismanagement reflects on the state as much as anyone. It is the General Assembly's duty to monitor local districts "to assure that they are operated with no waste, no duplication, no mismanagement," not pass the buck to them.[43] Another court was more blunt: "We reject the argument . . . that funding should not be supplied because it may be mismanaged and wasted."[44] Courts have similarly rejected financial exigencies and depressions as excuses: "Financial reasons alone [do not excuse] the constitutional command that the State must guarantee sufficient funding to ensure . . . a constitutionally adequate education."[45]

The practical importance of treating the state's duty as an absolute one was clearest in New Jersey. That absolute duty dictates just how far the state must go to serve its most vulnerable students. It is the state's duty, reasoned the New Jersey Supreme Court, to help students overcome academic challenges, no matter the cause. Poor students, the Court said, have a right to succeed or fail with all the help the state can muster because the ultimate duty of the state is to see that every student has the opportunity to receive an adequate education. Even when the path to improvement is uncertain, the constitution must side with forcing the state to act to provide students with the most plausible chance to succeed. Otherwise, we would "strip all notions of equal and adequate funding from the [state's] constitutional obligation."[46]

Other states convey the point through the principle that education is the state's foremost duty. This means the state must put education ahead of its other priorities. If it does this, the state won't breach its absolute duty in education. The idea of education as the state's foremost duty is embedded explicitly in the very text of some state constitutions. Florida's constitution declares that education is the state's "paramount duty."[47] Georgia's constitution says education is the state's "primary obligation."[48] Other state constitutions use analogous language, leading courts to conclude that "the constitution has created a 'duty' that is supreme, preeminent or dominant."[49] Some state constitutions even incorporate technical structures that ensure states don't put other things ahead of education. Nevada's constitution, for instance, requires the state to make the public education budget the very first appropriation of each session of the legislature.[50] To act on anything else other than education in the first appropriation, the Nevada Supreme Court held, is unconstitutional. Making education a state's first priority may only increase in relevance in the coming years as states increasingly expand alternatives to public education in the form of charters and vouchers. When those alternatives are funded before or at the expense of public schools, it raises the question of where a state's priorities in education lie. It is not enough to be committed to education in general because the state's duty is to *public* education.

The third major principle in these cases is that money matters. In nearly every school funding case litigated, the state claims at some point that money does not correlate with educational quality. And they have major political figures cheering them on from the sidelines. President George H. W. Bush famously proclaimed in 1991: "Dollar bills don't educate students."[51] Governor Andrew Cuomo used an annual state address to argue that New York was "spend[ing] too much" on education and "get[ting] too little in return."[52] Sure, politicians overstate their rhetoric, but even the US Secretary of Education has claimed money doesn't matter. In 2017, Secretary Betsy DeVos told Congress that "the notion that spending more money is going to bring about different results is ill-placed and ill-advised."[53] Two years later, justifying her proposal to cut federal education funding by 10 percent, she made a more audacious claim: "Students may be better served by being in larger classes, if by hiring fewer teachers, a district or state can better compensate those who have demonstrated high ability and outstanding results."[54] In other words, states don't need to spend money on schools to improve teaching and student services. They just need to get rid of some teachers, pay a few a little more, and pocket the rest of the money.

Courts have sided with data over the self-serving claims of politicians and government officials. A 2006 examination of the issue found that twenty-nine of the thirty courts to consider the evidence "determined that money does indeed matter."[55] One judge found the evidence so overwhelming that he remarked: "Only a fool would find that money does not matter in education."[56] Bruce Baker, a leading school finance scholar, recently reviewed all the relevant studies available. He said the collective research establishes three simple points. First, the amount a district spends per student is "positively associated with improved and/ or higher student outcomes."[57] The extent of the improvement varies, but "direct tests of the relationship between financial resources and student outcomes [show] money matters."[58] Second, the major things that schools spend money on—reducing class sizes and increasing teacher pay—are "positively associated with student outcomes."[59] Third, the "adequate and equitable distribution" of financial resources is "a necessary underlying condition for improving [student] outcomes. That is, if the money isn't there, schools and districts simply [cannot] support strategies that might improve student outcomes."[60]

The sophistication of the studies also continues to increase. One of the best to date, relying on more than three decades of school funding data and student outcomes, makes a very specific finding: a 20 percent increase in per-pupil funding, if maintained over the course of students' education careers, results in low-income students completing almost a full additional year's worth of learning.[61] That additional learning "is large enough to eliminate the education attainment gap between children from low-income and non-poor families."[62]

With this type of evidence, courts have routinely ordered states to reform the way they fund schools. Their duty, their absolute duty, their paramount duty, is to "provide funding which is sufficient to provide each child . . . an adequate [and equal] education."[63] This, as suggested above, means going the extra financial mile for needy students. New Jersey's Supreme Court captured the intersection of money and the state's constitutional duty beautifully: "Money can make a difference if effectively used, it can provide the students with an equal educational opportunity, a chance to succeed. They are entitled to that chance, constitutionally entitled. They have the right to the same educational opportunity that money buys for others."[64] Ohio's Supreme Court echoed that same basic ethic: "Although a student's success depends upon numerous factors besides money, we must ensure that there is enough money that students have the chance to succeed because of the educational opportunity provided, not in spite of it."[65]

Yet it is just as important to understand that these cases are about far more than just money, and sometimes not about money at all. They are first and foremost about equal and adequate educational opportunities. Money may help secure those opportunities—quality teachers, technology, facilities, and support services—but the opportunities themselves are what guide the constitutional inquiry. And any number of educational policies have the potential to deny students adequate and equal educational opportunities. If they do, students can use the right to education to challenge those policies just as surely as they can challenge the state's school funding practices.

In Connecticut, for instance, plaintiffs showed how racial segregation, even if unintentional, created unequal educational opportunities.[66] Although the case was the first of its kind, the Connecticut Supreme Court said the constitution was clear: "The state has an affirmative constitutional obligation to provide all public schoolchildren with a substantially equal educational opportunity. *Any* infringement of that right must be strictly scrutinized."[67] The court said the state's claim that it had "substantially equalized school funding and resources" was irrelevant because the constitution's education mandate was "broader" than that. When "extreme racial and ethnic isolation in the public school system deprives school children of a substantially equal educational opportunity," the constitution demands the "state to take further remedial measures."[68]

The West Virginia Supreme Court faced a similar crossroads in 1996. A quarter century earlier it had recognized education as a fundamental right in the context of a school funding claim, but the 1996 case involved school discipline: When can schools expel a student, and does the state have a responsibility to provide some form of education thereafter? The court said the fundamental right to education cannot be limited to any single context. Regardless of context, infringements on the right to education require the strictest of scrutiny. Exclusion from school is about the clearest infringement one can imagine. The court didn't question whether a school could legitimately exclude students who posed serious safety risks from regular public school, but the court said such students' right to education of some kind remained:

> Without alternative education, children similar to J.P.M. become orphans, abandoned by the educational system, without anyone to educate them and give them the opportunities inherent in being an educated person. . . . If the West Virginia Constitution makes education a fundamental right, then children similar to J.P.M. must be afforded an education and services. J.P.M., and other similar children, are not orphans of the educational system because the West Virginia Constitution bars their abandonment, unless the State can demonstrate a compelling State interest.[69]

The fourth major principle in these cases is that the delivery of educational opportunity must stand outside or above the political forces and debates that drive other issues. State constitutions are actually designed toward this end. Yes, states need enormous discretion in myriad different education policy issues because, after all, much of education involves judgment calls: Should schools focus more on science, math, and technology? Are higher salaries or job security the best bet for promoting teacher quality? Are Common Core standards better than traditional ones? On these and many other questions, courts must defer to legislatures. And politics will surely come into play to some extent when legislatures make these decisions. But as to a state's fundamental commitments and obligations in education, state constitutions have made their best attempt to separate the shifting whims of politics and public opinion from education.

Two of the most obvious examples of such constitutionally protected commitments are common school funds and state education officers. Our constitutional framers knew hard economic times would arise and, at other times, the public would divert its attention toward other pressing goals with the assumption that education was secure. They also simply knew that people are generally self-interested and won't always see the greater good. Even worse, some won't care about the greater good. As Senator Morton cautioned in the aftermath of the Civil War, "We cannot expect the men who own the property voluntarily to tax themselves to provide education for the others."[70] Guarding against these problems, states (and the federal government) acted to create constant sources of school funding that would persevere across time. States did this by constitutionalizing what they called a common school fund.[71] By 1870, 80 percent of all state constitutions created or protected a common school fund. State constitutions also often established nonnegotiable methods for distributing these and other school funds.[72] To be clear, these school funding plans were not foolproof. If they were, this book would read a lot differently. The resources that those common school funds generated proved insufficient to support a full system of education, but the intent behind the funds was unmistakable. And even in recent years, courts have relied on constitutional common fund rules to prevent some states from redirecting public school resources to some other end, such as vouchers or charter schools.[73]

States also guarded against the politicization of education by vesting constitutional authority in the hands of education professionals (or at least people solely focused on education). As a general principle, government agencies function under the direct and complete control of the legislature and governor. There are just two exceptions—criminal justice and education. Criminal justice is pretty obvious. Constitutional rights require state legislatures to do a number of things they may not like, and judges and juries decide who goes to jail and who does not, no matter what anyone else thinks. Just like the judicial system, schools are run by state officers who are not subject to the political process—at least not the same political process as other government agencies.

Following the Civil War, state constitutions increasingly established a state superintendent and/or state board of education. Doing so ensured that the individuals entrusted with administering education and setting various education policies would not be wedded to any geographic or political constituency. They were to act on behalf of all the state's children and exercise their best judgment, hopefully devoid of the normal politics of the state house. And unlike the heads of transportation, agriculture, commerce, and police, for instance, these education officials would not serve at the pleasure of the governor or legislature. Even today, the constitutional reservation of power in the hands of state officers limits the extent to which the political whims dictate education policy. In Indiana, for instance, then-Indiana Governor Mike Pence tried to force his education policies on the state department of education. The courts blocked him, holding that the state superintendent had independent constitutional authority over the issue. Similarly, the North Carolina legislature transferred certain powers from the state board of education to the state superintendent of education because it thought his politics better matched their own. But again, the courts said that the constitution, not the legislature, controlled the division of education power and reserved important ones for the state board of education that could not be changed.

Implicit in cases like these and others is that the right to education operates as a check on legislatures, governors, and state and local education officers. Of course, the most important check is on the legislature. Rather than "a grant of power" to wield as a legislature sees fit, one state supreme court explained that the education clause is "a mandate to the Legislature."[74] Courts have their own duty to enforce the mandate. This means that students can seek help from an independent judiciary when a state fails to do its job in respecting students' right to education. Without this check, nothing restrains states from allowing politics rather than student needs to dictate education policy.

There is, though, a powerful argument a state legislature can make during school litigation. Because only the legislature has the duty to provide education, states argue that it is entirely within the legislature's

discretion how best to provide it. In other words, courts lack the authority to override the legislatures' education policies and judgments.
This argument—not that the state is somehow doing its job well—has
allowed some legislatures to escape accountability for their failures.

Most courts, however, reject this assertion, relying on the US Supreme Court's famous rejoinder to President Thomas Jefferson more
than two centuries ago in *Marbury v. Madison*: "It is emphatically the
province and duty of the judicial department to say what the law is," not
those charged with executing it.[75] "Where there is a legal right, there is
also a legal remedy by suit or action at law, whenever that right is invad-
ed."[76] The same is true in education. When the constitution creates an
education right or duty, courts have no legitimate choice but to enforce
it. The Kentucky Supreme Court explained it best:

> We are asked—based solely on the evidence in the record be-
> fore us—if the present system of common schools in Kentucky
> is "efficient" in the constitutional sense. It is our sworn duty, to
> decide such questions when they are before us by applying the
> constitution. The duty of the judiciary in Kentucky was so deter-
> mined when the citizens of Kentucky enacted the social compact
> called the Constitution and in it provided for the existence of
> a third equal branch of government, the judiciary. . . . To avoid
> deciding the case because of "legislative discretion," "legislative
> function," etc., would be a denigration of our own constitutional
> duty. To allow the General Assembly (or, in point of fact, the Ex-
> ecutive) to decide whether its actions are constitutional is literally
> unthinkable.[77]

When courts get involved, they are not being political or asserting
the legislature's education authority as their own. Again, the Kentucky
Supreme Court emphasized in its seminal education decision:

> We do not question the wisdom of the General Assembly's deci-
> sion, only its failure to comply with its constitutional mandate. In

so doing, we give deference and weight to the General Assembly's enactments; however, we find them constitutionally deficient.

The judiciary has the ultimate power, and the duty, to apply, interpret, define, construe all words, phrases, sentences and sections of the Kentucky Constitution as necessitated by the controversies before it. It is *solely* the function of the judiciary to so do. This duty must be exercised even when such action serves as a check on the activities of another branch of government or when the court's view of the constitution is contrary to that of other branches, or even that of the public.[78]

It boils down to this: if we are a constitutional democracy and education is vested in those constitutions, courts serve as the "final" guard, enforcer, and protector of the right to education.[79] The failure of a court to fill that role is a "severe disservice to the people."[80] Judicial enforcement of the right to education is quite simply the only way to ensure "the Legislature . . . fulfill[s] [its] constitutional mandate."[81] The people who framed the constitutions were fully aware of the difficulty of making sure government carried out its education duties, so they assigned "different roles to different entities . . . to ensure that the education of school children in their state is not entirely dependent upon political influence or the voters' constant vigilance. . . . Matters intended for permanence are placed in constitutions for a reason—to protect them from the vagaries of politics or majority."[82]

THE FOREGOING PRINCIPLES—THE RIGHT TO AN ADEQUATE AND equal education, making education the state's absolute and foremost duty, requiring states to exert the necessary effort (financial or otherwise) to provide quality educational access, placing education above normal politics, and expecting courts to serve as a check—are all in the service of something larger: the original idea that education is the foundation of our constitutional democracy. Education is the means by which citizens preserve their other rights. Education gives citizens the tools they need to hold their political leaders accountable. Education allows children from all stations of life a fair shot at the American dream. Education, when provided for all, embodies the idea (even if it is no more than an idea) that America is the land of opportunity where individuals can become "self-made" men and women who set their own destiny. Democracy simply does not work well without educated citizens.

So if that is the education to which we aspire, constitutions must remove education from the normal rules of politics, legislation, social welfare, changing circumstances, and market economies. Constitutions must construct education systems that remain solid through good economic times and bad, through politically conservative, liberal, libertarian, and progressive times. Thank goodness our forefathers enacted constitutions premised on those principles. Thank goodness modern courts rediscovered those principles and were committed enough to the rule of law to stand up for them in the face of enormous political headwinds.

The question today is whether constitutions are enough, whether courts can, in effect, protect and save that right for the rest of us. Might it be, as it has always been, that constitutions are just ideas, the force of which ultimately depends on how deeply they penetrate our cultural psyches and how faithfully we pass those ideas along? How strong is the commitment to the right to education and a system of public schools for all in the public's mind today? There are now forces afoot, like there were during Reconstruction and the civil rights movement, aiming to overwhelm public education. If it comes down to it, can public education persevere once again, or is something different this time?

CHAPTER 10

THROUGH HISTORY'S EYES

THIS BOOK HAS TOLD THE STORY OF A NATION FOUNDED ON THE idea of a self-governing citizenry, bound together and prepared by public education. The idea is so central that public education became a right and delivering it the constitutional duty of states. The nation, of course, had major setbacks—economic and racial—but those setbacks, even when they aimed to, never overcame the fundamental commitment to public education. Education policies of the last decade, however, do not fit well within the nation's historical arc.

The setbacks of the last decade are, in many respects, attempts to go straight at public education itself as the problem. Jim Crow and the civil rights backlash saw attacks on public education, too. But those attacking public education did not claim public education was the problem. Rather, black people and the cost and inconvenience of extending equality to black people were the problem. Many of today's education policies and fads are premised on—and sometimes explicitly claim—that public education is fundamentally flawed and government ought to scrap it for something else. At the very least, government ought not be the primary provider of education.

This idea permeates states' decade-long disinvestment in public education and major new investment in private alternatives. Public education cuts initially looked like a response to the recession—overzealous and foolhardy, but understandable. In retrospect, the cuts look sinister. They came while states exponentially grew charters and vouchers—and remained in place well after the recession passed and state revenues were booming. To add insult to injury, various legislative mechanisms driving charter and voucher growth come at the direct expense of public schools. The contrasting reality of public schools and their private alternatives looks like a legislative preference for private school choice over public school guarantees.

Public school teachers have also been on the defensive for at least a decade. Once near and dear to the public's heart, teachers were cast as villains—paid too much and wedded to a set of self-serving rights and avoiding accountability. Unions made sure it stayed that way, so the new story went. The recession and changes in the courts created an opening to make this caricature of teachers stick this time. Those attacking teachers pushed further than they had ever before dared. Teacher salaries fell, classroom sizes swelled, and state and federal leaders redrew their relationships with teachers, altering tenure and imposing naively unrealistic evaluation systems. Those teachers who did not perform well could lose their jobs. The increasingly toxic environment prompted good teachers to flee the profession and college students to look for other careers. The pipeline of new teachers slowed to a trickle—not even enough to staff advantaged districts, much less all schools.

The federal government—once the strong voice to insist on more equality, more adequacy, and more commitment to public education—adopted a different role. Arne Duncan demanded more charters, more teacher accountability for test scores, and nodded with approval while others attacked tenure. Betsy DeVos shifted Duncan's charter school agenda into overdrive and pushed private school vouchers as an even better alternative. She made no bones about it: she wants to change education funding as we know it. Education should not operate around a system of public schools. Education should be about individual choice, and private schools are best suited to facilitate it. She would have state and federal dollars make it happen.

The last decade of education debate and change represents something very troubling within our larger historical context. At the very highest level, it involves states reneging on constitutional commitments, principles, and structures that have been with them for a century and half or more. Public schools never have and never will run without adequate financial resources. The recognition of that fundamental challenge explains why states put such precise language in their constitutions during Reconstruction. Of course, the exact amount of money a school needs and how it can best spend it involve deeper analysis of real facts, but wholesale efforts to defund or underfund public schools fly in the face of the principle that the state has a constitutional duty to provide adequate and equal public education—a duty that comes before all others.

Public schools never have and never will run without a positive relationship between schools, teachers, and students, either. Yes, we need to improve teacher quality and more fairly distribute the teachers we have. But neither can be accomplished if states run off the teachers they have, scare off new ones, and expect the ones who stick with it to do more. I hope it goes without saying that private schools, even when funded with public dollars, do not amount to public education. Similarly, common sense ought to tell us that charter schools, no matter how many we create, will not operate as the system of uniform schools for all students that state constitutions require.

The most troubling thing is that it doesn't take a constitutional scholar or education historian to recognize that something strange has happened. Politicians and advocates have taken on an unsettling aggressiveness toward public education. Political leaders talk about public education and teachers differently now. Governors spread the notion that teachers are "selfish," "lazy," and "ineffective." They say the people who represent teachers need a "punch in the face," are the "single most destructive force in public education," act like "terrorists," and operate with a "thug mentality."[1] The president of the United States characterizes public schools as "inferior" and uses pejorative phrases coined by the far-right privatization crowd, like "government schools," as part of his standard talking points about education. He even pits public schools against the American dream, saying that "failing government schools . . . deny [minorities] the opportunity to join the ladder of American success."[2]

People who should know better and are charged with being stewards of public education—secretaries of education—have even gotten in on the act. Betsy DeVos claims we cannot expect much improvement out of public schools; it is a waste of money to give them more resources. President Trump and Secretary DeVos say the "civil rights agenda of our time" is access to private "school choice," not adequate and equal public schools.[3] They claim private choice will "get America back on track . . . to improv[ing] education for the poorest among us." Maybe they have no idea that private school choice was conceived as a tool for resisting racial desegregation, but it is hard for those who do know to watch without feeling that they are part of a movie rather than witnessing reality. Arne Duncan, to his credit, was not explicitly hostile to the idea of public education, but he played into the hands of those who are. He made states' access to much needed federal money during the Recession depend on states' willingness to expand charters, not shore up their public school budgets.

The more civil approach involves dressing up public school critiques with economic jargon and logic. But too often it remains an attack nonetheless. It starts with the common refrain that schools are "failing," then moves to claim that they are failing because they are a "monopoly." The next logical step must then be obvious: break the public school monopoly. On the surface, it sounds accurate. A lot of schools are, in fact, "failing" on standardized tests. Those "failing" schools are also often the only option for the students who attend them.

But as astute observers pointed out decades ago, the point of standardized testing (for those who were not so naive as to think testing would improve schools by itself) was to develop an objective looking measure to show public schools were failing. This would build the narrative for their destruction. And "monopoly"? If trying to ensure every kid in the country gets a baseline shot in life is a monopoly, the label might make sense. But the dictionary definition of a monopoly entails concerted action by a business to control the supply of a commodity or service so that it can maximize profits to the disadvantage of consumers. Free public schools don't fit that narrative at all. Even if public schools have never completely fulfilled their legal obligations to students, they exist to discharge states' constitutional duty to reinforce democracy, not as some sinister governmental plot. What could such a sinister end be? To make America worse?

This new rhetoric feeds into equally coarse legislative behavior. In Kansas and Washington, for instance, the state legislatures flat out refused to comply with court orders to meet their constitutional obligations. Courts first found the states were providing inadequate and unequal education, which was bad enough. Then the states refused to do anything about it and things devolved into the constitutional equivalent of a gunfight at the O.K. Corral. In Kansas, the legislature eventually did something unheard of since *Brown v. Board*. It did not just resist reform. It took active steps to undermine the judiciary as an institution. It threatened the judiciary's budget and changed the process for appointing judges. The Kansas Supreme Court bravely held its ground and the legislature blinked at the last minute, but not without legislators filibustering the statewide education budget and insisting on a constitutional amendment to block court involvement in future school funding issues.

Other states have manipulated the political process, twisted arms, and threatened reprisals, all in the service of charters and vouchers. That level of effort (not that these specific tactics are appropriate for any purpose) is nowhere to be found in the service of public education. Kentucky and North Carolina offer perfect examples of manipulation. In Kentucky, teacher protests forced the legislature to put more money into the education budget. Governor Matt Bevin vetoed the bill—a bill his own party passed. His rationale? It did not include "comprehensive tax reform." He was also still peeved at teachers: "It's illegal for them to strike," and the Kentucky Education Association has been a "problem. . . . They've been very vocal, very loud, refusing to be a part of the solution even though in reality their members are going to be the beneficiaries of all of us getting this right."[4] Fortunately, the legislature marshalled the super-majority necessary to override his veto. But Bevin continued to press his positions anyway. Unable to do anything legislatively, he worked behind the scenes for changes at the state department of education. He wanted his own man to head the department. Even though the power to appoint and remove the superintendent rests with the state board of education, Bevin nonetheless pressured the board to do his bidding. It caved, removing the current superintendent without cause before his term expired. The board filled the position with someone from Bevin's office, someone Bevin knew would promote charter schools. In short, Bevin pulled all the political levers he could to subvert the normal education and legislative process.

Similarly, when Republicans lost the governor's mansion in North Carolina in 2016, the lame-duck legislature stripped the state board of education of power and transferred it to the newly elected Republican state superintendent. Just like Bevin, the legislature wanted to exercise education power no matter the state's constitutional structure. Fortunately, the courts later blocked the move as unconstitutional; but in 2018, the legislature was back at it again, searching for work-arounds. This time it was pandering to privileged communities that wanted to run their own schools separate and apart from their countywide school districts.

The legislature's first idea was legislation to break up school districts into smaller ones. The problem was that it did not serve any real educational purpose and looked like a legislative greenlight for good old-fashioned white "secession" from black districts, something already happening and drawing negative attention in places like Alabama. That reality led supporters to stand down on that bill and shift to another. Rather than secession districts, they proposed a bill to allow local communities to use their taxing power to directly fund charter schools. County school districts would continue collecting taxes for public schools, but individual communities within districts could impose a separate tax to operate their own charter school—a scheme yet unseen in school funding.

Governor Roy Cooper vetoed the bill. "Municipal charter schools set a dangerous precedent that could lead to taxpayer funded re-segregation," he said.[5] That's when things got really strange. The legislature found a loophole to exploit. North Carolina's constitution has an arcane provision to fast track certain narrow legislation. As long as the legislation does not apply statewide and is, in effect, special regional legislation, it does not require the governor's approval. So the legislature just changed its statewide charter bill to one aimed at Charlotte's suburbs, the communities it most wanted to help anyway. The change, however, made the resegregative effect and intent impossible to miss. The four communities receiving the chartering power were overwhelmingly white and submerged in a larger and far more diverse school district. As one commentator noted, the state went into "unchartered [legislative] territory" and "pioneer[ed]" a new way to resegregate schools.[6]

Tennessee offers the perfect example of arm-twisting and horse trading. In 2019, Betsy DeVos and President Trump were campaigning for a new voucher bill in Tennessee. Presidential and secretarial involvement in local legislation is highly unusual on its own. Presidents and secretaries press for federal legislation, but state legislation is a matter for state representatives and senators (unless it conflicts with federal law and policy). The relevant voices on vouchers for Tennessee are the people of Tennessee, not Washington. That anomaly, however, was just the beginning.

The legislature initially voted against the voucher bill. The Speaker of the House, however, would not accept defeat. He held the vote open for two more hours and went around pressuring representatives to change their votes. One representative claimed the Speaker offered him a promotion in the Tennessee National Guard (he rejected the offer). Another representative said the Speaker offered to exempt the representative's home district from vouchers if he would just vote yes. That's right. The Speaker was saying: *I know you don't believe in vouchers, but can you help me impose them on other parts of the state?* That representative, for whatever reason, changed his vote. The shenanigans were so bad that the FBI investigated the matter.

When the constitution got in the way too much, some political leaders have even tried to change the constitution. In Arizona, Governor Doug Ducey pressed for a voucher bill that could have eviscerated public education. Teachers beat that bill back, in part, by pointing out that a similar bill was declared unconstitutional in Nevada, which has a constitution similar to Arizona's. But just when education advocates thought the issue was behind them, Ducey and the privatization lobby worked as hard as ever on a referendum to put vouchers in the state's constitution. To top it off, the language they used was so confusing that voters who were staunchly against vouchers initially did not know whether they were supposed to vote yes or no on the ballot.[7] I guess if you can't beat 'em, trick 'em.

Florida's leaders also tried to change their constitution to remove its limits on vouchers and charters. They stacked the state commission on constitutional revisions, which automatically convenes once every twenty years, with members who would support putting measures on the statewide ballot to overturn a prior Florida Supreme Court decision striking down vouchers and to give the state independent authority to approve new charter schools (even when local communities voted against them). Some of the referendum language they proposed, like that in Arizona, was so confusing—presumably intentionally so—that the courts struck it from the ballot.

State constitutions long ago included any number of safeguards— from dedicated funding sources and uniform systems to statewide officials who aren't under the thumb of politicians—to isolate education from these political manipulations and ensure education decisions are made in service of the common good. The larger point was to ensure that democracy's foundation was not compromised. But the fact that politicians keep trying and sometimes succeed in their manipulations suggests these constitutional guardrails are not always enough to discourage or stop powerful leaders. This also reveals something deeper: modern-day incursions into public education are so unusual that our framers did not imagine them.

They anticipated that legislatures might favor schools in their home communities at the expense of a statewide system of public education. They anticipated that public education might suffer from benign neglect when legislatures, from time to time, became preoccupied with other issues. But they did not anticipate that legislatures would go after public education itself, treating it as a bad idea. That line of thinking died with the Civil War. Near unanimous support for the education clauses spoke of a new era from which the framers of those constitutions could reasonably assume we would never turn back.

But it is not just what today's leaders have said and done. Also telling is what they haven't said. Increasingly missing, if not entirely absent, is any discussion of education's purpose and values—reinforcing democracy and preparing citizens to participate in it. What they miss is that charters and vouchers, for instance, involve an entirely different set of premises about education—and for that matter an entirely different set of premises about government.

Charter and voucher advocates downplay this value divide and scoff at the idea that their policies threaten public education or democracy. We are all on the same side, they would say. They just want better educational opportunities, which is the pivot to their policy claim that charters and vouchers outperform traditional public schools. A full response to that claim here would just fall into the trap of distracting you yet once again. It is enough to say that those claims don't hold water. From the US Department of Education's first comprehensive study of charters through the Stanford University Center for Research on Education Outcomes' multiple studies, overwhelming evidence demonstrates that charter schools do not outperform public schools.[8] Roughly 80 percent perform the same as or worse than traditional public schools. In the average charter school in Ohio, for instance, students complete "14 fewer days of learning in reading and 36 fewer days in math."[9] Charter advocates that claim otherwise are juicing the data or comparing apples to oranges. The evidence on vouchers is no better. Students tend to fall behind and stay there when they transition from public school to private.[10]

Choice advocates fund their own studies to try to counter these empirical facts, but at its core, the choice movement is not really about improved educational opportunity. It is about ideology—an ideology that is not about democracy and public education values as we know them, which is why they don't lead with that discussion. Yes, those ideological positions hide under a thin veneer of faulty empirical claims about public education, charters, and vouchers.

So what is that ideology? First, they think of education as a commodity. That means education isn't special in all the ways that our traditions claim. It is like day care, housing, groceries, cars, and internet access. It is something of value, but consumers are best suited to determine the value of the product, what type of product they want, and the cost-benefit analysis of picking one product over another. Bad purchases, false advertising, and defective products are just part of the process of moving toward better results over time. The market, they say, will sort it all out in the end.

While that claim may sound like it is grounded in fact, it is really just a dressed-up version of another value belief: the market is always better at delivering services than government, and education is no different. Nancy MacLean's work, however, suggests the bias goes even deeper than just unflinching fidelity to the notion of market efficiency (which to be clear has its merit in the right context). MacLean details how a far-right movement of wealthy elites has been working for decades to fundamentally alter American democracy, including several of its constitutional principles. In many respects, they managed to transform conservative politics (i.e., the Republican Party) from within.[11]

They believe American democracy legitimizes highway robbery, giving a mere 50.1 percent of the public the power to pass laws that take money away from the minority and spend it on themselves. Such a system all but incentivizes insatiable base human instincts. Those most at risk of victimization are the wealthy minority. Over time, society will devour itself if allowed. The only check, they say, is rigid protection of property rights and rigid limits on government's ability to increase taxes.

What does this have to do with public education? Well, if one looks at state government, public education has always consumed the most resources—by a large margin—and redistributed them among the masses. And if education is a commodity rather than a pillar of democratic government, public education is just another way voters tax the wealthy to fund personal benefits for themselves. From this perspective, robust public education systems are a core problem of our majority-rule government system.

Yet arguing that public education, democracy, and our constitutional system are illegitimate is not the way to make friends, influence people, and change the system. These ideologues made the smart choice to find allies under other banners to push their agenda. They found their first major allies, ironically, in the ongoing segregationist movement in the 1960s and 1970s. As explored in chapter 2, segregationists at the highest levels of government saw vouchers as a way to avoid desegregation. They would just shut down public schools and subsidize families in their choice of segregated private schools.

The individual rights ideologues did not necessarily care so much about desegregation itself, but fully supported resisting desegregation if it could help shrink government. A voucher system prodded by segregation could go a long way toward getting government out of the education business. Even if the government helped fund private education, the government would not control and regulate private schools like they do public schools. Education decisions would largely be left to private actors. Equally important, a widespread voucher system would change government's financial responsibility in education. Voucher costs are easier to cap and shrink. Doing that eventually means shifting more fiscal responsibility for education to individuals and the market. Also, when a private voucher system interacts with the taxes an individual pays, the system begins to look more like individually financed education in which the government is just reimbursing costs rather than redistributing wealth through public education. This type of system operates as a hedge against slim majorities imposing their education costs on the wealthy minority.

The elite individualists' alliance with segregationists died, however, when middle-class Americans saw the voucher movement for what it was—a threat to public education itself, not just a segregation tool. Over the next few decades, one of the ideological leaders of the individualist movement, James McGill Buchanan, laid the foundation for vouchers' later rebirth. Buchanan was an award-winning economist who taught and ran policy centers at several prominent universities, including at the University of Virginia during massive resistance to desegregation and much later at George Mason, where conservative economic and public choice theory was taking hold. Through his policy centers, he was able to map out and play-test rhetorical and political positions to transform "the way people think about government" in America—away from the view that government served as a benevolent safety net and toward the notion that government coerced taxes from the wealthy and created dependency among the rest.

On his own, Buchanan's message just as easily would have been consigned to library stacks and lost to history. Academics were skeptical of the methods he used to validate his arguments and the conclusions he drew. Spreading his message beyond them was equally challenging. Once massive resistance to desegregate failed, his views did not have a natural audience of any size. His notion, for instance, that Social Security is a "Ponzi scheme" was not what most people wanted to hear. But what his audience lacked in size, it made up for with resources. A few notable and wealthy benefactors made sure that his position in the academy was secure and his message circulated, as wide as money could buy.

Buchanan's most recognizable benefactor was Charles Koch.[12] Koch had enormous resources and a keen interest in changing politics. Koch took over his father's business at a relatively young age and turned it into one of the most profitable in the world. His libertarian sensibilities and belief that government was extracting his hard-earned wealth drew him to Buchanan's ideas. In the late 1970s, they built a friendship, and Koch began writing checks. Over time, Koch did more than just write personal checks. He and his brother built a network of like-minded wealthy donors. Today, their political network donates hundreds of millions of dollars a year to remake American democracy one brick at a time—sometimes through huge federal lobbying efforts and other times through things as small as local school board races. Koch's network includes 700 donors. Their contributions start at $100,000.

In 2018, the Koch brother network's three-day annual summit identified education as their main priority and named Arizona as ground zero in the effort to privatize education. Speaking of the charter school and voucher changes detailed in chapter 2, Charles Koch told the audience that "we've made more progress in the last five years than I had in the last 50. . . . The capabilities we have now can take us to a whole new level. . . . We want to increase the effectiveness of the network . . . by an order of magnitude. If we do that, we can change the trajectory of the country."[13] One of the donors at the summit explained that education is "the lowest hanging fruit for policy change in the United States today. . . . I think this is the area that is most glaringly obvious."[14]

Let that sink in for a moment: change the trajectory of the country and do it through education. In other words, the agenda is not to improve education. The agenda is to change America. Education is, on one hand, the bystander. On the other, it is, as it has always been, the pathway to democratic change, for good or bad. The trouble is that when this new education agenda gets down to specific policy advocacy, those pushing it are not up front about their larger agenda. Rather than fess up to trying to fundamentally change our democracy, they try to borrow democratic language and bend it toward their own ends. For instance, they frame charters, vouchers, and school choice issues as educational civil rights. They tap into natural sympathies toward seemingly powerless parents and claim the goal is to allow disadvantaged families to exercise the same choices as wealthy families. They tap into our constitutional commitments to parental autonomy and religious freedom by framing charters and vouchers as issues of personal liberty and religion. They even evoke the nation's constitutional commitment to a right to education as they blur the lines between private and public education.

The radical individualist-libertarian movement has been so successful that it has our governors spouting their message. Governor Jeb Bush of Florida was an early, prominent cheerleader. In 2006, he appeared at a voucher rally and claimed: "This is a fundamental right, this is a civil right, this is as American as apple pie."[15] Someone had even made shirts for the rally emblazoned with SAVE OUR STUDENTS. More than a decade later, Florida Governor Ron DeSantis used similar but more modernized rhetoric. Vouchers would "empower" parents, not government, and create "equal opportunity" through the private sector.[16] When DeSantis signed a new voucher bill, you might have thought he was a public school advocate if you read his statement with no context: "At the end of the day, your success shouldn't be limited by family income, by what ZIP code you live in. It should be based on you working hard and getting the most out of your God-given talents. This [voucher program] gives you the opportunity to do that."[17] But as the *Orlando Sentinel* editorial board wrote, Florida's "new voucher program isn't about choice, it's about sabotaging public schools." Bush's earlier voucher program may have had some saving graces, but the new one crossed the education Rubicon. The state's first voucher program was "developed as a means of helping students from low-income families—often minority students—escape failing public schools. . . . The new program mainstreams vouchers by offering them to middle-class families [and taking the money straight out of the state treasury]."[18]

Yet what those who push back against vouchers and charters have not fully articulated is that these measures also cross the Rubicon for our democracy. As new voucher and charter bills lock in the privatization of education, they lock in the underfunding of public education. As they do this, they begin to roll back the democratic gains Congress sought during Reconstruction and then recommitted to during the civil rights movement. A few pictures on this score are worth a thousand words.

The first map below measures how much each state has privatized— or is open to privatizing—public education. Privatization, as measured on this map, means two things: (a) the existence of a voucher program (or some scholarship or tax credit variant) and the number of students the state authorizes them for; and (b) the existence of charter schools, the ease of creating new ones, and how many students attend them. The states in black are those that have above-average levels of privatization.

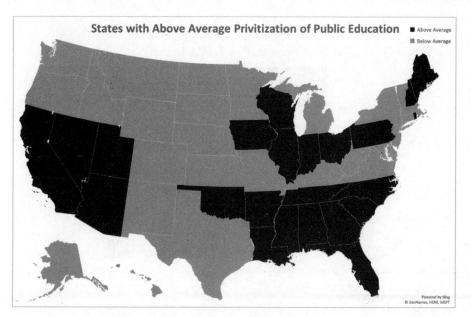

States with above-average privatization of public education.
Courtesy of the author.

Those states in grey are those with below-average levels of privatization. This grey group includes both states that have resisted privatization and those that have not resisted privatization but are no more open to it than the average state. North Dakota, South Dakota, and Kentucky, for instance, have resisted voucher and charter expansion, whereas Texas has allowed privatization, just not to an enormous degree. All four of those states, however, appear in grey.

The map tells a global story that sadly aligns with the nation's long-term racial and democratic stories. The Northeast, Upper Midwest, and Northwest—the parts of America with the fewest racial minorities—have only suffered modest privatization. Their public school systems, for the most part, do not face major privatization threats. The rural mountain states of Kentucky and West Virginia reflect a similar story—primarily white and uninterested in privatization. But the Southeast—the Confederacy's old stronghold—tells the exact opposite story: large percentages of African American students and, save one state, their public schools are facing deep privatization forces.[19]

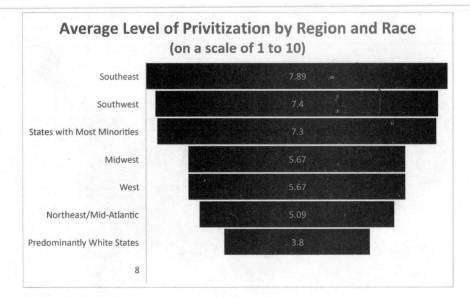

Average level of privatization of public education by region and race.
Courtesy of the author.

The map, however, does not capture the full depth of the distinction between these states, so the chart above goes one step further. It calculates each state's openness to privatization on a scale of 1 to 10, with 10 being the most open to privatization. It then combines the results from each state by geographic region, calculating each region's openness to privatization. It does the same with race, combining the results from the ten states with the highest percentage of racial minorities and comparing them with the ten states with the highest percentage of whites. The Southeast is more open to privatization than any other region in the nation. In fact, its rating is 55 percent higher than the Northeast's. Likewise, states with the highest percentages of minorities have twice the level of privatization as predominantly white states.

Public school funding, or the lack thereof, is the flipside of this privatization movement. One of the nation's foremost school funding scholars, Bruce Baker, led a national study of what it would cost for students to achieve "average" outcomes.[20] Average outcomes are not the same as adequate outcomes, proficiency, equality, or any other laudable goal we

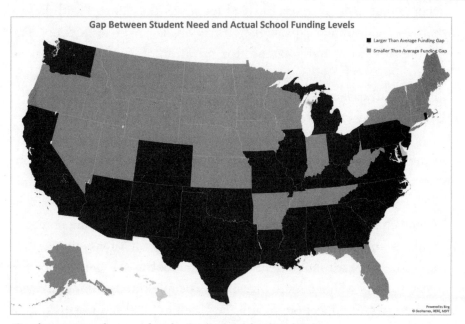

Gap between student need and actual school funding levels.
Courtesy of the author.

might pursue. Average means reaching the level that the average student is currently at—a level that many scholars and measures suggest is below adequate or proficient. The point of estimating the cost of average outcomes, though, is to remove subjectivity from the equation. Average does not require judgment calls or debates about what good education should look like. Relying on that notion, Baker and his colleagues identified the cost of achieving average outcomes and then measured that cost against the resources that are actually available to students across the country.

They found that when it comes to districts serving primarily middle-income students, most states provide those districts with the resources they need to achieve average outcomes. In fact, a lot of states spend several thousand dollars more per pupil in these districts than they actually need. But only a couple states provide districts serving predominantly poor students what they need. The average state provides districts serving predominantly poor students $6,239 less per pupil than they need. The map below does not even challenge the reality that the nation—and nearly every one of its states—is failing its students. The map above accepts that as a given and instead identifies those states with larger-than-average funding gaps in districts serving the poorest students. The picture this map paints matches the privatization data and map above pretty closely. The deepest and most consistent school funding gaps are in the Southeast and Southwest, with far smaller funding gaps in the Upper Midwest and Northeast.

These privatization and funding gap trends threaten to rob students in these particular places of their civic and economic futures. For instance, Raj Chetty and other researchers at Harvard performed a study of what you might call the American Dream—the extent to which lower-income children break the bonds of their families' poverty and enter the middle or upper class.[21] Looking at real-life outcomes for children, they found that upward mobility or the lack thereof was largely a function of each state's willingness to invest in its people through things like education, higher education, health, and welfare. Those investments, of course, were a function of tax revenues. The places where children had the smallest chance of upward mobility were heavily concentrated in the Southeast, particularly in North Carolina, South Carolina, Georgia, Alabama, and Mississippi. In fact, the only places in North Carolina, South Carolina, and Georgia where there was more than just the most minimal chance of upward mobility was in the mountain region (predominantly white) where those three states meet.

Outside the Southeast, the opportunity for upward mobility was far more prevalent, though not everywhere. In the far west in California, Nevada, and New Mexico, large zones of very low opportunity existed, but zones of more substantial opportunity could also be found. The Great Lakes states were similar to the far west states, with substantial pockets of low opportunity in urban centers but more opportunity outside of them. The very highest and most consistent levels of upward mobility, however, were in the so-called flyover states—from Wisconsin to Idaho and North Dakota to central Texas. Very few places of complete social immobility were found in these regions. In short, the study's measure of the American Dream, to no surprise, matches up with the earlier maps on privatization and public school funding gaps.

Yet these maps are not just a retelling of our old racial history, and the victims are not just minority students. The move against public education may have begun and be winning in the same old places, but this time the attack presents a danger that has the capacity to sweep more broadly. In prior eras, the racial dimensions of attacks on public education obscured any threat to public education. That is not to say it was all about race. Southern plantation owners, for instance, wanted to retain political power at the expense of both blacks and lower- and middle-class whites. But in the mid- and late 1800s, race was the primary ideological wedge for resisting public education. Similarly, during the civil rights movement, race was the political wedge that gave the anti-education crowd strength. There was no serious appetite for deconstructing public education itself.

Today, race remains a powerful undercurrent fueling the notion that government spends too much money on other kids' education. But today, that undercurrent is more fractured and complicated. The radical individualist-libertarian movement is stoking the dissatisfaction of a relatively diffuse and diverse group of individuals to push its own agenda. Some of the most dissatisfied families are upset for the same reasons they were decades ago: public schools expose them to diversity, equity, and culturally sensitive issues they would rather avoid. Yet a lot of other families are uncomfortable with public school because they sense, or are told, public schools are lacking in quality. That sense may be affected by subtle racial and other biases, but on the surface, it is articulated as a neutral question of academic quality. And dissatisfaction with the quality of education that families experience in public school—whether real or perceived—is a dissatisfaction not bound by race or socioeconomics. Many minority families are just as sympathetic to school choice as majority families are. Many poor families are just as sympathetic to school choice as wealthy ones.

The privatization movement promises all these families positive outcomes—liberty, freedom, and better education. Even if the promises are hollow, attacks on public education in prior eras could not muster a plausible positive justification. Prior attacks were more about maintaining the status quo than offering families something new or better. In this way, a direct, yet more positive, attack on public education is also more danger-ous. It draws on a larger constituency. It is not obviously mean-spirited. This allows it to masquerade with a high degree of legitimacy in a way it previously could not. This also means public education could go out with a whimper, not a bang. Only after the fact would many realize what had happened.

These fundamental challenges to public education force us to ask whether public education can survive once again, and if it does not, will democracy be irreparably damaged? No cliff hangers on this dire ques-tion. I do believe public education will survive, though that alone is no more comforting than education's survival would have been to African Americans living through the damage that Jim Crow did to their lives and society as a whole. Education's survival, then and now, can mean as little as the capacity for schools to exist and democracy to rise once again at a later date. Survival does not mean that education—or democracy—remains on solid ground in the interim. And to be clear, I am saying I believe education *will* survive, not that it already has.

The current trajectory of public education remains troubling. Edu-cation and political leaders at the very highest levels still aim to do pub-lic education harm. They still manage to pass major pieces of legislation that do just that. They still manage to ward off political movements that would repair public education. They, for the most part, still hold the keys to government power. Their tactics, in some instances, have grown harsher, more manipulative, and even vindictive toward those who de-fend public education. Yet this uglier side of the movement may also be an early sign of desperation or fear—desperation because they now sense their days of unfettered expansion are numbered and they should grab the remaining spoils of war as soon as possible. At the very least, they sense the future of their movement is more uncertain now than it was just a couple years ago. Feet in the streets made that much clear.

In 2018, teachers finally reached their breaking point and started talking about strikes and walkouts. Media attention then helped educate the general public on what had happened to public education funding and the teaching profession over the past decade. In that environment, public education advocates, who had long pointed out the damage privatization was doing, saw their concerns gain traction. Together, public education advocates and teachers organized massive statehouse protests and other public demonstrations across the country. And it happened in the most unlikely of places—in deep Republican country, in nonunion states, and in the South, not in bastions of liberalism or pro-labor sentiment. The education movement even dared dub itself RedforEd. It caught hold and grew into a national catchphrase.

The first teacher strike was in West Virginia in 2018. The state went nearly 70 percent Republican in the presidential election a year and a half earlier.[22] The second teacher walkout was in Kentucky. Kentucky voted 62.5 percent Republican (and only 32.7 percent Democrat) in the prior election.[23] After that, the protests and walkouts jumped westward to Oklahoma and Arizona. Republicans took twenty-four of twenty-five seats in the Oklahoma State Senate[24] and held solid control in Arizona. From there, major protests seemed to pop up every month in every place imaginable over the next year: Colorado, California, South Carolina, North Carolina, Georgia, Virginia, Oregon, and Washington.[25] Smaller-scale protests and threats to strike popped up in even more places.

The Southeast, however, was on fire with activism in one form or another. The only Southern states east of the Mississippi where teachers didn't mount or threaten a major protest were Tennessee and Alabama. South Carolina, for instance, had not seen significant teacher organizing or advocacy since the 1970s. In 2019, teachers produced a protest unprecedented in scope. South Carolina's 1970s protests typically involved a few hundred teachers at the state capital. In 2019, the crowd was estimated at 10,000, spilling into the streets and blocking downtown traffic. So many teachers used personal leave days to participate that some school districts completely closed. In 2018 in North Carolina, a crowd twice that size marched down the road leading to the state capital and did it again in 2019.

As the moniker RedforEd suggests, the pro–public education and teacher movement also defies conventional politics. In 2019, 84 percent of public school parents indicated that they would support teachers who went on strike over school funding issues.[26] On a number of issues, public school parents were more aggressive than teachers. Parents supported strikes 20 to 25 percent more often than teachers.[27] The general public beyond those directly connected to schools has also been steadfast in its support for public education and teachers. Two-thirds or more of the public indicated support for teachers when they went on strike.[28] On the more specific issue of teacher salaries, "nearly 90 percent of Democrats, 78 percent of independents, and 66 percent of Republicans think teachers don't get paid enough."[29]

Stepping away from teacher-specific issues, support for public education is so overwhelming and bipartisan that party affiliation does not tell you much—not even in the South. In 2018, a group of nonprofit organizations surveyed a demographically representative group of registered Southern voters. The group they surveyed skewed conservative, white, and male. But you would not have known it from the results: 74 percent of voters "saw differences in the quality of education for students across each of their states"; 85 percent said "states should fix differences in education"; and 85 percent said "states should adjust funding to address differences" in the quality of education across their states.[30] A majority even supported raising taxes if necessary.[31] On almost every single question, no more than two or three percentage points separated Democrats from Republicans.

These numbers and teacher protests scared those levying attacks on public education. They may, in fact, have pressed their advantage too far for too long. Their messaging succeeded for the better part of a decade, but their messaging could not hide underlying reality. And it apparently had not changed people's general fundamental belief about public education. This rude awakening for the individualistic-libertarian movement also helps explain their harsher tactics since the protests.

In West Virginia, for instance, after more than a year of teacher vigilance and pressure (including two strikes), the legislature took steps to quell their opposition. West Virginia's 2019 omnibus education budget tied the passage of teachers' raises to other measures designed to punish teachers for future strikes or walkouts. The legislation prohibited teachers from using personal leave to participate in a strike and docked teachers' pay if schools closed as a result of a strike. That same bill also welcomed charter schools into the state for the first time (which makes almost no sense given the state's geography and demography). Arizona and Oklahoma lawmakers introduced similar bills to dock teachers' pay during strikes, but they went even further, aiming to fine any person in the state of Arizona who aids or abets in closing schools when they are supposed to be open—i.e., during strikes—up to $5,000.[32] An Oklahoma bill would revoke the certification of teachers participating in future walkouts.[33]

Just as Richard Nixon sought to camouflage desegregation resistance with a veneer of enforcing law and order, those introducing these anti-teacher bills claim that they want to ensure schools run in an orderly manner and that students do not miss important learning time. But the real effect would be to further shield the state from demands that they meet their constitutional duty in public education. The demand that states honor the constitutional obligations grew so loud over the past two years that the only way privatization can weather the political pressure is to make a substantial source of that pressure illegal. Regardless of whether these proposed bills pass anytime soon, they send clear messages to teachers.

My sense, however, is that it is too late for that to work. In states like Florida, where it was already illegal for teachers to strike, the state has been able to persist in its agenda. But in other states, the cat, so to speak, appears to be out of the bag. Now, far more than teachers are involved in the fight to save public education. Look back at the streets of Phoenix, Arizona. The 50,000 people who flooded those streets included more than just teachers. Those honking their car horns in support and those cheering in front of their televisions were not teachers, either. And when teachers flooded Kentucky's capital, students made it a point to protest, too. In other words, the sleeping tiger supporting public education awoke. As long as its eyes remain wide open, it won't miss the fight. That much, I hope, is relatively obvious and certain. But widespread bipartisan support

for public education may teach us something else new and more important in this modern era.

Looking at our country more broadly, a number of democratic, constitutional, and civil norms are seemingly under attack: separation of
powers, checks and balances, a limited executive branch, an independent judiciary, and the basic way legislators interact with each other
when they disagree. Once so confident in liberal democracy, the rule of
law, and the idea that we are a nation governed by laws not men, scholars
now recoil at the routine abandonment of the rule of law and democratic
norms. "Might" seems to make "right" too often. A growing and disturb-
ingly large slice of the public is sympathetic toward more authoritarian
ways of running government. Liberal democracy, scholars admit, is not
as stable and robust as the world once thought. They have seen it broken
several times abroad recently, just like any other form of government,
when the economy did not live up to popular expectations.

But if this book is anything, I hope it is a pleasant reminder of the
presence of silver linings—silver linings that, when added together,
could reveal enduring truths. While it is hard to forecast in the middle
of storms, I see one potential enduring truth in the unraveling of American norms: public education, for whatever reason, is less fragile than our
other democratic norms. It has been under assault just as much as any
of our norms, maybe more. It has suffered just as many blows, maybe
more. But average Americans won't let go of public education. Public
education, due to its unique status in our democracy, may be an exception to the country's overall political trends.

In *The People vs. Democracy*, Yascha Mounk details the populist
uprising sweeping the United States and other countries.[34] The populist majority insists that democratic principles entitle it to set its own
rules, even rules that conflict with historical and constitutional norms.
If the popular majority favors the autocrat or dislikes the results that
democratic norms and constitutional rights require, the popular majority should win. We've never done it that way before, but current events
often reflect a new reality—and public education tracked that reality for
the better part of a decade.

Over the past decade, newly elected politicians denigrated and undermined public education. They regularly failed to ensure constitutionally adequate and equal education and, sometimes, even breached more explicit and straightforward constitutional commands. As new political majorities took or consolidated power at the state level, they felt empowered to redefine public education as they saw fit. Many political leaders thought voters' desire for educational improvement was a desire or sympathy for abandoning public education. Other political leaders thought the loudest voices for tax cuts and school choice represented the voices of the people. The education resistance is now showing that those leaders were mistaken all along. Public education is at least one institution the populist revolt has no desire to tear down. That fact suggests that public education may very well be both the practical and ideological foundation upon which our democracy still rests, even as the rest of democracy sometimes looks like it is crumbling. Does that then mean that the public education resistance portends something else positive for democracy?

The answer to that calls for more than I am willing to speculate, but as I neared the end of writing this book, a wise friend asked a hard question—a come-to-Jesus moment, so to speak. After I had summarized this book, my friend asked if African Americans, and America more broadly, made a mistake in placing so much hope in education during Reconstruction and the civil rights movement. With all the challenges that kids and families face outside school and new studies showing schools are failing to close life opportunity gaps, would African Americans have been better off today had they insisted on economic justice?

My mind raced. I was slow to respond. My first thought was that a decent job and housing for everyone would fix a lot of problems. Then, schools would not be tasked with the impossible job of fixing all of society's ills. But then I thought of the enduring truths in this book, took a deep breath, and said that African Americans and America had been right. The reason is relatively simple: public education has always represented the idea of America, not its reality. No doubt, we want reality to match the education idea. An idea, if that is all it ever becomes, is not worth a hill of beans. And the idea of public education has been about creating tangible benefits for everyday people—even if it has not ended inequality. But the power of public education owes just as much, if not more, to the idea it represents.

Public education represents a commitment to a nation in which a day laborer's son can go to college, own a business, maybe even become president. It represents a nation in which every person has a stake in setting the rules by which society will govern itself, where the waitress's children learn alongside of and break bread with the senator's and CEO's children. Public education represents a nation where people from many different countries, religions, and ethnic backgrounds come together as one for a common purpose around common values.

We know that the idea has never been fully true in our schools, but we need to believe in that idea. That idea is part of what makes us America. The pursuit of that idea, both in fact and in mind, has long set us apart from the world, as early as the first half of the 1800s when only one other country in the world could rival our educational access (and it had a big head start on us). Pursuing that idea still captures the American imagination today. It involves 10,000 school districts serving 50 million students for the lion's share of their waking lives between the ages of five and eighteen. Those schools fail as often as not to live up to the American idea, but they connect parents, families, teachers, students, and the general public to public education in ways that are not just about historical pomp, circumstance, and rhetoric. These experiences and the ideas behind them are not nearly as easy to break as the economy, political process, or other norms.

CHAPTER 11

FINAL THOUGHTS

THE RESILIENCE OF THE IDEA OF PUBLIC EDUCATION AND OUR personal connections to school do not, unfortunately, mean that public education will be in a better place five years from now. Recent events may tell us Americans' tolerance for the attack on public education is limited and they will actively resist at some point. But that response does not mean the public knows how to build or rebuild a better public education system. Equally important, the incursion into public education happened for a reason. It was not just about bad people doing bad things. It was also about good people watching bad things happen. As much as Americans support public education, they have a real and palpable dissatisfaction with it, too. That dissatisfaction won't go away just by squelching privatization measures. So long as widespread dissatisfaction remains, so, too, will privatization calls.

What is the solution to the discontent in public education? What does a better education system look like? A full answer would require another full book, but a few general points are in order. First, we need to begin having serious conversations about what our schools should be doing. They have, in very important respects, lost their way in recent decades. On the one hand, they are asked to do far more than they ever have before—to compensate for all of society's economic, housing, technology, and health ills. On the other, they are asked to produce a far narrower result—better results on standardized tests of a relatively thin set of curricula. The laser-like focus on that narrow result has also made them less responsive to the whole child and to families' perspectives about their children.

These changes have drawn any and every critique you can imagine. But the most salient include the notion that schools are teaching the wrong things, not teaching them well, and, even worse, indoctrinating students. A growing segment of the public is disillusioned with the country (for a number of different reasons), and their experience with public schools crystallizes that disillusionment, making schools—as they have always been—the locus of social tension and conflict. Another segment, which increasingly includes solidly middle- and upper-class families, perceives their children's future higher education and work opportunities as uncertain. A good life is no longer guaranteed by simply following the rules. So they try to maximize every opportunity and work every angle they can for their kids.

An important part of responding to these families is to take seriously education's original mission to prepare students for citizenship and life. This does not mean indoctrinating students with a particular political view, but rather helping them think seriously about their own views and the world. Nor does citizenship preparation mean teaching to a test or making students workplace ready. Citizenship preparation won't come in the form of another set of standardized curricula and tests. It requires schools to take the time to help students engage issues and each other, learn to problem solve, and value compromise and common values. In a world where doing these things has always depended on vocabulary, thinking, and the written word, it means critical literacy, not rote memorization or bland reading. In short, schools must teach students the skills and knowledge that do not show up on standardized tests but which give their education deeper meaning. If schools do this in a conscious and impartial way, parents and children of all groups will find more satisfaction in public education.

Another solution to disillusionment (for all demographic groups) is relatively straightforward: fully fund public education and a steady stream of high-quality teachers and support staff. About half of the nation's schools are doing pretty well. They generally have the resources and staff they need to run their schools and the capacity to do more for their kids when needed. But the other half of public schools cannot provide an adequate education with the resources currently available to them, much less do everything else that is frequently demanded of them. Yet most politicians only talk about their low outputs and then use those low outputs to label them as failing. The failing label then justifies abandoning them for charters, vouchers, and reform.

Breaking this cycle requires states to make public education their foremost financial priority—and Congress should help them. State constitutions demand this. Much of the failure to do it revolves around the confusion—or misinformation—over the extent to which money matters. Fifty years ago, the effect of money on student outcomes was uncertain—largely due to data and analytical limits. Today it is not—at least not among scholars. If any debate lingers, it is only over the best uses of money in the schools: higher teacher salaries, smaller class sizes, pre-kindergarten expansion, more mental health counselors, more support services, or a little bit of all of the above? But money is absolutely necessary for all of these things, and increasingly sophisticated studies show things like a 20 percent increase in school funding, when maintained across time, can wipe out roughly half of the graduation gap between low- and middle-income students. Similarly, a 10 percent increase in funding correlates with a 5 percent jump in graduation rates in high-poverty districts. The state of Kansas's own study showed, with a 99 percent level of confidence, that "a 1 percent increase in student performance was associated with a .83 percent increase in spending."[1]

States do not need to experiment with public education; they need to fund it. Fair school funding can revitalize the teaching force, offer struggling students the support services they desperately need, and minimize the incentive for parents to opt out of the system. If states do this, they will not only improve outcomes for struggling students, they will improve the overall environment in their schools and, thus, the experience of all students and families.

Money alone, however, never has and never will be a complete solution. Racial and socioeconomic school segregation is dragging down public education and society as a whole. Separate and unequal public education perpetuates a system of winners and losers, incentivizing parents who can to simply protect their own interests, which makes matters even worse. In the end, public education settles for a few islands of opportunity rather than the common good of all. Yet the so-called winners come up short in important ways, too. They think the islands are offering the maximum chances for success when, in fact, those homogeneous islands are denying students the diverse learning environments that improve critical thinking, civic values, social cohesion, and the skills most valued in higher education and employment.

For many of these same reasons, our fractured political system is connected to our segregated and unequal school system. That fractured political system surely takes a toll on schools and drives segregation and inequality. But the same phenomenon works in reverse. Steps to reduce segregation and inequality will not only help address the various disadvantages that poor and minority students face, they will improve our education system and democracy. Our public education system, since its beginning, has aimed to bring disparate groups together. Public schools were to be the laboratory and proving grounds where society takes its first steps toward a working democracy that includes all. Lest we forget, racial equality and integration is not an idea of the 1950s and 1960s. It is an idea of the 1860s, embedded in state constitutions of that era. Lest we forget, a socioeconomically equal playing field is not an idea of the 1960s, either. It is an idea that drove the Massachusetts Constitution of 1780, the Northwest Ordinance of 1785 and various other state constitutions that followed.

In sum, the global solution to public discontent and building a better education system is about the framework we use to answer difficult education policy questions. The framework is the same as it has always been. The framework is one where we understand public education as a constitutional right. This means public education is the state's absolute and foremost duty. This means the state must help students, teachers, and districts overcome obstacles, not blame them when they don't. This means the state must fully fund schools and reform policies unrelated to money when they impede adequate and equal opportunity. This means the state cannot manipulate educational opportunity by geography, race, poverty, or anything else for that matter. This means the state cannot favor alternatives to public education over public education itself. This means the state must honor the constitution over its own ideologies and bias. This, finally, means that public education must be in service of our overall constitutional democracy.

Every education policy we face must be filtered through these principles. Some people will not like the answers these filters produce, particularly when they suggest rigid limits on charters and vouchers. For instance, states and the federal government should prohibit charter schools in places where they increase segregation. States should prohibit charter funding practices that have the effect of reducing funding for traditional public schools or increasing inequalities between schools. Likewise, states should prohibit all private school vouchers and tax credits unless they are willing to impose rules and regulations that ensure the programs do not counteract the democratic values that underlie public education. Absent rules that reinforce those values, government has no more interest in funding private education than it does in funding oversized vehicles with poor fuel efficiency for every family that wants one.

Constitutions, of course, can be changed. But states should never consider fundamental changes to the right to education (unless it is to strengthen it) or how education decisions are made. Our constitutions long ago knew that dangers would come. They created safeguards to help ensure that education decisions were more objective, more professional, and less partisan. Education policy fails when it is aimed toward short-term agendas. If public education is going to do more than just survive, if it is going to get to a better place, it must always remain true to the democratic and constitutional norms that got it this far.

These things, however, are easier said than done. In one way or another, someone else has said them many times before. Yet here we are. What gives me any hope that democracy and public education will emerge from this assault any better than they did after the fall of Reconstruction or the civil rights backlash? While the future is by no means certain, America's aspirations have followed a consistent trajectory. Two steps forward. One step back.

The current assault on public education has already taken it one step back. It wants to take the nation two, if not three, steps back. It's not going to happen—at least not with education. It never has before, and public sentiment finally says it won't this time, either. The question is whether America's public schools can take a few steps forward after immediately having been pulled back. That I don't know.

Right now, public education is in uncharted territory. Yet so was the movement to restore the right to education in state courts when integration was being dismantled in the federal courts. Constitutional protections for public education could have just as easily fallen apart without that state movement. Instead, advocates went on a multi-decade winning streak in a lot of states. And while assailed from every angle in the last decade, the state constitutional right to education is, in many respects, more firmly entrenched today than at any other time in history. Every day people talk about the right to education in a way they haven't for a long time. We have a stronger foundation to build on.

It seems to me that the real task is to understand what this current battle is about. To call out the opposition for what it is and help a wider audience understand. To recognize that we are within reaching distance of America's education aspirations, if we can muster the resolve to press forward rather than just survive the attack trying desperately to drag public education backward. The specific proposals above are a relatively easy lift if we can do that.

THIS BOOK HAS TAKEN THE LONG VIEW OF HISTORY. NO SINGLE event will change the truths our history teaches. Yet, going to press with this book without acknowledging the new world we entered shortly after I finished writing it would leave it incomplete. Education policy will be no more immune to the coronavirus than any person or sector. I imagine that the history of public education, like everything else, will divide into the world before and after the coronavirus. I hope the public health crisis will have subsided by the time you read this and immunity in the form of a vaccine will be soon on its way.

I have told the story of another immunity, the one our forefathers created for public education. They placed education in our state constitutions, not for the good times, but for the bad ones, hoping that constitutional commitments would force America to stay its educational course through unforeseen circumstances. Unfortunately, the nation's miserable response upholding its public education commitments following the last unforeseen circumstance, the financial crisis of 2008, gives me serious pause about the response to the current crisis.

Congress's coronavirus stimulus bill, the CARES Act, all but ignored the real possibility that history might repeat itself and education budgets slip into a freefall. As the financial effects of the new crisis began but before they were even fully felt, states were already looking to cut education. Three states immediately cut teacher salary increases for the coming year—increases that were intended to begin repairing the damage from the last recession. Other states were contemplating the same. These quick pivots on education could be the tip of the iceberg. New York City Schools, for instance, feared they would not receive their full aid from the state due to school closures. Early estimates projecting that the virus would cost New York $9 to $15 billion in tax revenues made those fears reasonable. California, similarly, faced the possibility that the coronavirus would eliminate the rainy day reserves it had been amassing.

Now is the time to learn from mistakes, not repeat them. What are the most poignant education lessons to remember as the nation makes its way through this new crisis? First, as the Supreme Court wrote in *Brown v. Board of Education*, public education is "the most important function of state and local governments." It serves as the "foundation of good citizenship" and "democratic society." Thus, we sacrifice it at a peril to ourselves and our democracy.

But on a much more basic level, lawmakers must acknowledge that schools are not roads. Huge new education cuts will have lasting negative effects well after the virus is gone and the economy has recovered. When states cut education last time, students paid the price. Studies showed that the 2008 cuts depressed achievement and current funding levels remain woefully inadequate. The 2008 cuts alone will have lifetime impacts on a generation of students and their communities. Students in the most marginalized schools cannot afford to suffer new harms on top of the last ones.

Another important lesson is that ideologues and interest groups with an axe to grind against education—or money to make—will use crisis to their advantage. Betsy DeVos quickly floated plans on how to use her executive discretion during the current pandemic to spur more voucher programs. Some charters were contemplating applying for coronavirus relief funds (even though no one had suggested their staff funds were in jeopardy) because, after all, they were businesses too. And online learning, out of absolute necessity, quickly became an everyday part of life.

Just as vouchers and charters established footholds during the 2008 recession that have proven nearly impossible to dislodge, online learning is in a position to do the same. It will offer a shiny panacea—an excuse to avoid making other needed investments in schools—even once the crisis passes. No doubt, states should invest in the infrastructure and expertise to provide seamless online learning in the event of similar emergencies in the future. Those investments might also allow for creative supplemental services during good times. But those expenditures should not be another obligation for schools to absorb within their existing budgets. Many schools simply will not be able to afford it without sacrificing other essential services.

No matter what, online learning cannot replace what happens in schoolhouses. Excessive screen time negatively impacts students in multiple ways, and many disability and support services simply cannot be delivered over the internet. Even if we somehow solved those problems, we can't replace the organic learning that happens between students. Plus, school teaches far more than just the three Rs. Group activities, music, drama, sports, playtime, negotiating conflict and the banter at the lunchroom table are all important parts of growing up, becoming well-adjusted adults, and fostering a sense of the collective common good that is central to our democratic project.

If states cut public education with the same reckless abandon this time as last, the harm will be untold. A teaching profession that spent the two years prior to 2020 protesting shamefully low salaries may simply break. The number quitting the profession altogether will further skyrocket. No one will take their place. The number of college students pursuing teaching degrees was already shockingly low. Class sizes will continue on their decade-long expansion. And the pre-kindergarten opportunities, mental health counselors, and other supports that disadvantaged students so desperately need—but which states wouldn't fund during good times—might as well be on permanent hold.

But if the current crisis teaches the nation anything, it is just how hard and important schools' jobs are. Parents quickly realized that kids cannot stare at a screen or book for seven hours a day, nor should they. Their employers, and hopefully lawmakers, painfully realized just how central school services are to everyone's lives and, thus, the basic operation of the economy. From meals, socialization, and physical activity to academics, aftercare, and specialized learning support programs, public schools literally form the foundation of daily life. It wasn't until they were closed that most could fully appreciate how much we need and miss them.

I do not know how many additional losses our schools can take on top of the last ones or how much online learning is appropriate, but I do know one thing. A century and a half ago citizens began approving state constitutions that made public education an absolute priority of every state—and the first priority in several states. They did it for a very good reason. They knew times like these would come. They knew the foundation of society had to be solid. If the coronavirus demands cuts to state services, so be it. But education has to be the last, not the first, place states look to make them. I trust that having finally come off the sidelines to challenge the war on public education in 2018 and 2019 education advocates will not remain idly by when they see the warning signs this time.

ACKNOWLEDGMENTS

My initial vision for this book lacked the historical depth and normative scope that now appear between its covers. It was not yet a "big book," as some call them. If I succeeded in writing a big book, I owe Matthew Carnicelli, my agent, for pushing me—sometimes outside my comfort zone—to make larger connections. His push wasn't just talk. He devoted time and effort to helping me develop my ideas. That is not the case with many agents. I feel lucky to have worked with him.

Sheryll Cashin and Erwin Chemerinsky shared their wisdom when I was waffling between the safer route of an academic press and the risk of a trade press. Sheryll offered two nuggets that stuck with me: first, if she was going to take the time to write a book, she would write one that people would actually want to read; second, law professors' lives are pretty secure. They have the liberty to take chances and controversial positions that other writers and scholars cannot—and just enough standing that someone might pay attention to them. Sheryll offered this as food for thought, not judgment, but my mind was made up by the time she'd finished talking.

Alex Roskell left his door open to me for the better part of a year. He regularly gave sage advice and basic directions—from finding and selecting an agent to conceptualizing the book and closing it out. Writing a book can be lonely; it was not so with Alex's company.

Inge Lewis helped with several technical parts of the book, but her most valuable contribution was as a first reader. Her reactions gave me confidence and important feedback. Just a couple of pages on African Americans' first exposure to schooling became a full chapter because her interest was piqued.

Vanessa McQuinn and Rachel Ford helped put the final touches on the manuscript, catching various errors that I would have otherwise missed. For any they might have overlooked, the responsibility is mine alone.

Bob Bockman either humored me or shared my fascination with the stories I recounted of the South Carolina freedmen. He is far too kind of a man to know the difference. Either way, his reactions helped me find deeper meaning and increased my excitement.

Jon Hale lent an education historian's eye to the manuscript. His suggestions prompted some important additions and warned me away from a pitfall.

Michelle Adams encouraged me to think more deeply about how my own experiences relate to the racial themes of the book.

I am exceedingly grateful to Charles Hamilton Houston's family for permission to use one of their treasured pictures. The text and pictures in this book represent distinct points. The text is my telling of the story, often just skimming the surface. For the thoughtful reader, the pictures reveal a deeper and clearer reality than my words can capture. It was a true privilege to collect and reproduce them for others to see.

Last, I want to thank my family—Claire for the unvarnished feedback I need and can only take from someone I fully trust; Rohan for listening and being interested or loving enough to give thoughtful responses; and Malina for a sunny disposition that makes me want to try things.

NOTES

INTRODUCTION

1. "Journals of Continental Congress," in *A Century of Lawmaking for a New Nation: U.S. Congressional Documents and Debates, 1774–1875*, ed. Worthington C. Ford et al. (Washington, DC: Library of Congress, 1904–37), 28:378, http://memory .loc.gov/cgi-bin/ampage?collId=lljc&fileName=028/lljc028.db&recNum=389 &itemLink=r?ammem/hlaw:@field(DATE+17850520)z:%230280388&linkText=1.

2. "Northwest Ordinance; July 13, 1787," *Avalon Project* (Washington, DC: US Government Printing Office, 1927), http://avalon.law.yale.edu/18th_century /nworder.asp.

3. "George Washington, Eighth Annual Message (December 7, 1796)," *Avalon Project* (New York: Bureau of National Literature, Inc., 1897), https://avalon.law.yale .edu/18th_century/washs08.asp.

4. John Adams, *The Works of John Adams, Vol. VI, Defence of the Constitutions*, ed. Charles Francis Adams (Boston: Little, Brown and Co., 1851), 168.

5. Ibid.

6. Wisconsin v. Yoder, 406 U.S. 205, 221 (1971) (summarizing Jefferson).

7. Sun Go and Peter Lindert, "The Uneven Rise of American Public Schools to 1850," *Journal of Economic History* 70, no. 1 (March 2010): 3.

8. James E. Yeatman, *A Report on the Condition of the Freedmen of the Mississippi* (St. Louis: Western Sanitary Commission, 1864), 2, https://archive.org/details /reportonconditio00yeat.

9. US House of Representatives, *Report on the Condition of Affairs in the Late Insurrectionary States*, in *Reports of Committees of the House of Representatives for the Second Session of the Forty-Second Congress*, vol. 1–2, vol. 267, 280

(1872); J. W. Alvord, *First Semi-Annual Report on Schools and Finances of Freedmen January 1, 1866* (Washington, DC: US Government Printing Office, 1868), 10.

10. *Debates of the Convention to Amend the Constitution of Pennsylvania*, vol. II (Harrisburg, PA: B. Singerly, 1873), 387.

11. Yeatman, *A Report on the Condition of the Freedmen of the Mississippi*, 388.

12. Marta Jewson, "New Orleans Becomes First Major American City without Traditional Schools," *Lens*, July 1, 2019, https://thelensnola.org/2019/07/01/new -orleans-becomes-first-major-american-city-without-traditional-schools.

13. James Hohmann, "The Daily 202: Koch Network Laying Groundwork to Fundamentally Transform America's Education System," *Washington Post*, January 30, 2018, www.washingtonpost.com/news/powerpost/paloma/daily-202/2018 /01/30/daily-202-koch-network-laying-groundwork-to-fundamentally-transform -america-s-education-system/5a6feb8530fb041c3c7d74db/?utm_term=.6fe 53f435e2c.

14. Ibid.

15. Kate Abbey-Lambertz, "Betsy DeVos Compares School Choice Critics to 'Flat-Earthers,'" *Huffington Post*, May 23, 2017, www.huffingtonpost.com/entry /betsy-devos-school-choice-flat-earthers_us_5924a9b7e4b0ec129d30556f [https:// perma/cc/6FD3-CYL8].

16. Gabby Morrongiello, "Trump: Dems Trap Students in 'Failing Government Schools,'" *Washington Examiner*, September 8, 2016, www.washingtonexaminer .com/trump-dems-trap-students-in-failing-government-schools.

17. David Nagel, "Charter School Support Is a Prerequisite for Race to the Top Funds," *Journal*, June 9, 2009, http://thejournal.com/articles/2009/06/09/charter -school-support-is-a-prerequisite-for-race-to-the-top-funds.aspx [http://perma.cc /TSA5-YR2K].

18. Michael Leachman, Kathleen Masterson, and Eric Figueroa, *A Punishing Decade for School Funding* (Washington, DC: Center on Budget and Policy Priorities, 2017), www.cbpp.org/research/state-budget-and-tax/a-punishing-decade-for-school -funding.

19. Phi Delta Kappan, *Frustration in the Schools: Teachers Speak Out on Pay, Funding, and Feeling Valued* (Arlington, VA: Phi Delta Kappan, September 2019), https://pdkpoll.org/assets/downloads/2019pdkpoll51.pdf.

20. Matt Barnum, "Internal Memo Offers Candid Postmortem of Charter Fight in Massachusetts," *Chalkbeat*, April 16, 2018, www.chalkbeat.org/posts/us/2018/04 /16/internal-memo-offers-candid-postmortem-of-charter-fight-in-massachusetts/; Kimberly Hefling, "Democrats Feud over Charter Schools in Massachusetts," *Politico*, November 7, 2016, www.politico.com/story/2016/11/democrats-divided -on-mass-charter-school-expansion-230888.

21. James Vaznis, "Poll Finds Hunger for More Charter Schools," *Boston Globe*, July 1, 2014, www.bostonglobe.com/metro/2014/06/30/poll-suggests-support -boston-for-more-charter-schools/1y4wXDVqPfBqjdcqGxfZsN/story.html; "Massa- chusetts Voters Back Marijuana Legalization, More Charter Schools," *Western New*

England University Polling Institute, April 14, 2016, www1.wne.edu/polling-institute /news/2016-spring-marijuana-charter-schools.cfm.

22. Amanda Terkel, "How Betsy DeVos Became the Most Hated Cabinet Secretary," *Huffington Post*, October 24, 2017, www.huffingtonpost.com/entry/betsy -devos-most-hated-secretary_us_59ee3d3be4b003385ac13c9b.

23. Ibid.

24. Derek Black, "Eighty Percent of Southern Voters Want Improvements in School Funding: Why Won't Their States Act?," *Education Law Professors Blog*, February 13, 2018, http://lawprofessors.typepad.com/education_law/2018/02/eighty -percent-of-southern-voters-want-improvements-in-school-funding-why-wont-their -states-act.html.

25. Phi Delta Kappan, *Teaching: Respect but Dwindling Appeal*, *PDK Poll* (Arlington, VA: Phi Delta Kappan, September 2018), http://pdkpoll.org/assets /downloads/pdkpoll50_2018.pdf.

26. Peter Greene, "DeVos: Leaving Students Behind And Launching National School Vouchers," Forbes, March 29, 2020, www.forbes.com/sites/petergreene/2020 /03/29/devos-leaving-students-behind-and-launching-national-school-vouchers /#3741050f6b4a.

27. Corbett Smith, "U.S. Secretary of Education to Striking Teachers in Oklahoma: 'Keep Adult Disagreements' out of Schools," *Dallas News*, April 6, 2018, www .dallasnews.com/news/education/2018/04/06/us-secretary-education-striking -teachers-oklahoma-keep-adult-disagreements-schools.

28. Rebecca Klein, "Nation's Top Teachers Confront Betsy DeVos in Private Meeting," *Huffington Post*, May 1, 2018, www.huffingtonpost.com/entry/betsy -devos-top-teachers_us_5ae79725e4b055fd7fcef147.

29. See, e.g., Yascha Mounk, *The People vs. Democracy: Why Our Freedom Is in Danger & How to Save It* (Cambridge, MA: Harvard University Press, 2018).

CHAPTER 1. THE CURRENT CRISIS

1. Bruce D. Baker, David G. Sciarra, and Danielle Farrie, *Is School Funding Fair? A National Report Card*, 3rd ed. (New Brunswick, NJ: Rutgers University; Philadelphia: Education Law Center, 2014), 12–13 tbl.2, https://drive.google .com/file/d/0BxtYmwryVI00cTJYU3ljd1BKLXM/view; Marguerite Roza, "Breaking Down School Budgets," *Education Next* 9 (Summer 2009), http://education next.org/breaking-down-school-budgets-2/ (specifying programing costs in public schools).

2. Bruce D. Baker, David G. Sciarra, and Danielle Farrie, *Is School Funding Fair? A National Report Card*, 4th ed. (New Brunswick, NJ: Rutgers University; Philadelphia: Education Law Center, 2015), 8, https://drive.google.com/ file/d/0BxtYmwryVI00cVZueUhhYlBsdE0/view.

3. Michael Leachman, Kathleen Masterson, and Eric Figueroa, *A Punishing Decade for School Funding* (Washington, DC: Center on Budget and Policy

Priorities, 2017), www.cbpp.org/research/state-budget-and-tax/a-punishing-decade
-for-school-funding.

4. *Investing in Our Future: Returning Teachers to the Classroom* (Washington,
DC: Executive Office of the President, 2012), https://obamawhitehouse.archives
.gov/sites/default/files/Investing_in_Our_Future_Report.pdf.

5. Michael Leachman, "Timeline: 5 Years of Kansas' Tax-Cut Disaster," *Center
on Budget and Policy Priorities* (blog), May 24, 2017, www.cbpp.org/blog/timeline
-5-years-of-kansas-tax-cut-disaster.

6. Michael Leachman and Chris Mai, *Lessons for Other States from Kansas'
Massive Tax Cuts* (Washington, DC: Center on Budget and Policy Priorities, 2014),
www.cbpp.org/research/lessons-for-other-states-from-kansas-massive-tax-cuts.

7. Russell Berman, "Where Republicans Went Wrong in Kansas," *Atlantic*,
June 22, 2015, www.theatlantic.com/politics/archive/2015/06/where-republicans
-went-wrong-in-kansas/396398.

8. Grover Norquist, "What's Really the Matter with Kansas?," *OZY*, April 25,
2018, www.ozy.com/opinion/whats-really-the-matter-with-kansas/86269 (defending
the cuts and plan that Brownback had implemented).

9. Trymaine Lee, "Another Philadelphia Student Dies at a Public School with
No Nurse," MSNBC, May 22, 2014, www.msnbc.com/msnbc/another-student
-dies-school-no-nurse.

10. Joy Resmovits, "Tom Corbett Pressured by Civil Rights Groups on Philadelphia School Funding," *Huffington Post*, October 11, 2013, www.huffpost.com
/entry/tom-corbett-philadelphia-schools_n_4080350.

11. All but a few states have passed statutes governing the creation and operation of charter schools. Those statutes invite non-governmental entities to file
applications with the state, asking for authority and funding to run schools. In
many ways, charter schools are similar to public schools. They are publicly funded,
open to all, and free to attend. As a general matter, however, they operate outside
of states' normal bureaucratic structures, such as school boards and superintendents. Instead, they operate based on the charter or contract they sign with the
state. For a more detailed description of charter schools, see Derek W. Black,
"Charter Schools, Vouchers, and the Public Good," *Wake Forest Law Review* 48,
no. 2 (2013): 445.

12. *Highlights of the North Carolina Public School Budget* (Raleigh: North Carolina Department of Public Instruction, 2015), 30. Funding for charters went up
every year of the Recession and recovery except one.

13. "PA's Chester-Upland School District Reaches Settlement in School Funding Lawsuit," *SchoolFunding*, September 4, 2012, http://schoolfunding.info/news
/pas-chester-upland-school-district-reaches-settlement-in-school-funding-lawsuit.

14. Seyward Darby, "Education Wars," *New Republic*, December 5, 2008,
https://newrepublic.com/article/63704/education-wars.

15. Alyson Klein, David J. Hoff, and Catherine Gewertz, "Obama: Duncan
'Doesn't Blink' on Tough Decisions," *Education Week*, December 16, 2008, www
.edweek.org/ew/articles/2008/12/16/16duncan_ep.h28.html.

16. Jonas Persson, "New Documents Show How Taxpayer Money Is Wasted by Charter Schools—Stringent Controls Urgently Needed as Charter Funding Faces Huge Increase," *PRWatch*, May 8, 2015, www.prwatch.org/files/5-8-15_final_cmd _reporters_guide_on_charter_waste_and_lack_of_accountability.pdf.

17. Erica Frankenberg and Genevieve Siegel-Hawley, "Choosing Diversity: School Choice and Racial Integration in the Age of Obama," *Stanford Journal of Civil Rights and Civil Liberties* 6, no. 2 (October 2010): 244 (discussing specific federal budget increases for charter schools and their comparison to other programs).

18. Persson, "New Documents," app. 1 (from $175 million in 2008 to $208 million in 2013).

19. Melissa Korn and Caroline Porter, "Obama's Proposed Budget Seeks More for Education," *Wall Street Journal*, February 2, 2015, www.wsj.com/articles /obamas-proposed-budget-seeks-more-for-education-1422898651.

20. David Nagel, "Charter School Support Is a Prerequisite for Race to the Top Funds," *Journal*, June 9, 2009, http://thejournal.com/articles/2009/06/09/charter school-support-is-a-prerequisite-for-race-to-the-top-funds.aspx.

21. Erik W. Robelen, "State Picture on Charter Caps Still Mixed," *Education Week*, August 3, 2009, www.edweek.org/ew/articles/2009/08/03/37charter.h28.html; Derek W. Black, "Civil Rights, Charter Schools, and Lessons to Be Learned," *Florida Law Review* 64, no. 6 (December 2012).

22. "Number and Enrollment of Public Elementary and Secondary Schools, by School Level, Type, and Charter and Magnet Status: Selected Years, 1990-91 through 2012-13," *National Center for Education Statistics*, January 2015, tbl. 216.20, https://nces.ed.gov/programs/digest/d14/tables/dt14_216.20.asp (growing from 4,388 charter schools to more than 6,000).

23. Ibid. (from 1.27 million charter school students to 2.26 million).

24. Ibid.

25. Marge Pitrof, "Milwaukee Voucher Program Turns 25: The History," WUWM 89.7, November 17, 2014, www.wuwm.com/post/milwaukee-voucher-program -turns-25-history#stream/0.

26. See, e.g., Zelman v. Simmons-Harris, 536 U.S. 639, 646 (2002); Jackson v. Benson, 578 N.W.2d 602, 617 (Wis. 1998).

27. See, e.g., Derek Black, "Voucher Movement Finally Coming Clean? New Push Is All about Middle Income Students," *Education Law Professors Blog*, July 31, 2015, https://lawprofessors.typepad.com/education_law/2015/07/voucher-movement -finally-coming-clean-new-push-is-all-about-middle-income-students.html [https:// perma.cc/UBN7-9BML].

28. *Corporate Tax Credit Scholarship Program: June Quarterly Report* (Tallahassee: Florida Department of Education, 2009), www.stepupforstudents.org/wp -content/uploads/2015/09/ctc-stats-09-06.pdf.

29. *Florida Tax Credit Scholarship Program* (Tallahassee: Florida Department of Education, 2015), www.fldoe.org/core/fileparse.php/7558/urlt/FTC_Nov_2015.pdf.

30. Ibid.

31. Geoff Fox, "House Passes Family Empowerment Scholarship," *rede-finED*, April 30, 2019, www.redefineonline.org/2019/04/house-passes-family -empowerment-scholarship.

32. Curt Anderson, "Florida Governor Signs Bill for New Private School Vouchers," *Crux*, May 9, 2019, https://cruxnow.com/church-in-the-usa/2019/05/09 /florida-governor-signs-bill-for-new-private-school-vouchers.

33. Indiana, for instance, allows families with incomes of up to $193,000 to participate. "School Voucher Qualifications," *Institute for Quality Education*, n.d., www.i4qed.org/calculator/voucher-qualification.

34. Bruce Baker, Danielle Farrie, Theresa Luhm, and David G. Sciarra, *Is School Funding Fair? A National Report Card* (New Brunswick, NJ: Rutgers University; Philadelphia: Education Law Center, March 2016), 8, https://drive.google .com/file/d/0BxtYmwryVI00WGExT3EtVGhDclE/view. Earlier 2014 and 2015.

35. Michelle Ye Hee Lee, "Mike Pence's Claim that Indiana Has the Largest School Voucher Program," *Washington Post*, August 12, 2016, www.washingtonpost .com/news/fact-checker/wp/2016/08/12/mike-pences-claim-that-indiana-has-the -largest-school-voucher-program.

36. *Choice Scholarship Program Annual Report: Participation and Payment Data* (Indianapolis: Indiana Department of Education, February 2015, rev. June 2015), 6, 22.

37. Schwartz v. Lopez, 382 P.3d 886, 892 (Nev. 2016).

38. Valerie Strauss, "Betsy DeVos and Her Allies Are Trying to Redefine 'Public Education.' Critics Call It 'Absurd,'" *Washington Post*, February 28, 2019, www.washingtonpost.com/education/2019/02/28/betsy-devos-her-allies-are-trying -redefine-public-education-critics-call-it-absurd.

39. See, e.g., Madison Teachers Inc. v. Walker, 851 N.W.2d 337 (Wis. 2014) (litigation over legislative changes to collective bargaining rights); *The Recession's Impact on Teacher Salaries* (Washington DC: National Council on Teacher Quality, 2013), 1, www.nctq.org/dmsView/The_Recessions_Impact_On_Teacher_Salaries _NCTQ_Report (finding 80 percent of districts enacted "a total pay freeze or pay cut in at least one of the school years between 2008-09 and 2011-12" and 95 percent froze or cut previously automatic cost of living and experience based raises); Deborah R. Gerhardt, "Pay Our Teachers or Lose Your Job," *Slate*, January 5, 2014, www.slate.com/articles/life/education/2014/01/north_carolina_s_assault_on _teachers_has_to_stop.html.

40. David Madland and Alex Rowell, "Attacks on Public-Sector Unions Harm States: How Act 10 Has Affected Education in Wisconsin," *Center for American Progress Action Fund*, November 15, 2017, www.americanprogressaction.org /issues/economy/reports/2017/11/15/169146/attacks-public-sector-unions-harm -states-act-10-affected-education-wisconsin.

41. Eric Lipton, "Billionaire Brothers' Money Plays Role in Wisconsin Dispute," *New York Times*, February 21, 2011, www.nytimes.com/2011/02/22/us/22koch.html.

42. Ibid.

43. Molly Beck, "Gov. Tony Evers Seeks to Freeze Enrollment in Private Voucher Schools, Suspend Charter School Expansion," *Milwaukee Journal Sentinel*,

February 25, 2019, www.jsonline.com/story/news/politics/2019/02/25/tony-evers
-seeks-freeze-vouchers-suspend-charter-expansion/2971998002.

44. Valerie Strauss, "Yes, Scott Walker Really Did Link Terrorists with Protesting Teachers and Other Unionists," *Washington Post*, February 27, 2015, www
.washingtonpost.com/news/answer-sheet/wp/2015/02/27/yes-scott-walker-really
-did-link-terrorists-with-protesting-teachers-and-other-unionists.

45. Lyndsey Layton, "Chris Christie to Teachers Union: You Deserve a Punch
in the Face," *Washington Post*, August 3, 2015, www.washingtonpost.com/local
/education/chris-christie-to-teachers-union-you-deserve-a-punch-in-the-face/2015
/08/03/86358c2c-39de-11e5-8e98-115a3cf7d7ae_story.html?utm_term=.ba
96a6487860.

46. Richard D. Kahlenberg, "Tenure: How Due Process Protects Teachers and
Students," *American Educator* (Summer 2015), www.aft.org/sites/default/files/ae
_summer2015_kahlenberg.pdf.

47. See, e.g., Sean P. Corcoran, *Can Teachers Be Evaluated by Their Students'
Test Scores? Should They Be? The Use of Value-Added Measures of Teacher Effectiveness in Policy and Practice* (Annenberg Institute for School Reform at Brown
University, 2010), 13; Moshe Adler, *Review of Measuring the Impacts of Teachers*
7 (Providence, RI: National Education Policy Center, April 2014), 7, http://nepc
.colorado.edu/files/ttr-chetty-teachimpacts_0.pdf (discussing research demonstrating that different tests can produce different results).

48. Valerie Strauss, "Arne Duncan Issues New Statement with the 'Right Lessons' from Vergara Trial," *Washington Post*, June 15, 2014, www.washingtonpost
.com/news/answer-sheet/wp/2014/06/15/arne-duncan-issues-new-statement-with
-the-right-lessons-from-vergara-trial/?utm_term=.5805726557a1.

49. Barbara Martinez, "Teacher Seniority Rules Challenged," *Wall Street Journal*, February 19, 2010, www.wsj.com/articles/SB100014240527487033150045750
73561669221720 (indicating 60,000 were laid off in 2009 alone); Travis Wal-
dron, "Local Governments Have Cut 130,000 Teaching Jobs in the Last Year,"
Think Progress, July 6, 2012, thinkprogress.org/chart-local-governments-have
-cut-130-000-teaching-jobs-in-the-last-year-eb5c1e67f8c3#.b4x01rent; *Investing in
Our Future*.

50. Noelle M. Ellerson, *A Cliff Hanger: How America's Public Schools Continue to Feel the Impact of the Economic Downturn* (Arlington, VA: American Association of School Administrators, 2010), 14, www.aasa.org/uploadedFiles/Policy_and
_Advocacy/files/CliffHangerFINAL(1).pdf.

51. "Data Tools," *Title II Higher Education Act*, https://title2.ed.gov/Public
/DataTools/Tables.aspx; Marjorie A. Suckow and Roxann L. Purdue, *Teacher Supply
in California: A Report to the Legislature Annual Report 2013-2014* (Sacramento:
California Commission on Teacher Credentialing, April 2015), 17, www.ctc.ca.gov
/reports/TS-2013-2014-AnnualRpt.pdf (finding a 55 percent drop over five years in
the number of persons pursuing and completing education degrees in California,
from 44,692 in 2008 to 19,933 in 2012).

52. "Data Tools," *Title II Higher Education Act*.

53. Andrea Eger and Nour Habib, "Crisis Hits Oklahoma Classrooms with Teacher Shortage, Quality Concerns," *Tulsa World*, August 16, 2015, www.tulsaworld .com/news/education/crisis-hits-oklahoma-classrooms-with-teacher-shortage-quality -concerns/article_54627559-bcc0-5ae5-b654-9b7eec46ab3c.html (in a month and a half, the Oklahoma Department of Education received 526 requests for teacher certification exemptions); Rebecca Klein, "Kansas Underfunded Education and Cut Tenure. Now It Can't Find Enough Teachers to Fill Classrooms," *Huffington Post*, July 31, 2015, www.huffingtonpost.com/entry/kansas-teacher-shortage_us _55b913ebe4b0074ba5a729d5 (reporting school district started year with uncertified teachers and had to use substitutes).

54. See, e.g., Kristen A. Graham, "Looking for a Few Thousand Substitute Teachers," *Philadelphia Inquirer*, August 31, 2015, http://articles.philly.com/2015-09 -01/news/66074823_1_retired-teachers-subs-philadelphia-teachers; Klein, *Kansas Underfunded Education*.

55. Eger and Habib, *Crisis Hits Oklahoma Classrooms*; Coburn Palmer, "New Kansas Education Law Opens Classrooms to Unlicensed Teachers, State Faces Major Teacher Shortage," *Inquisitr*, July 17, 2015, www.inquisitr.com/2261038 /new-kansas-education-law-opens-classrooms-to-unlicensed-teachers-state-faces -major-teacher-shortage/ (granting six districts an exemption).

56. *District Intern Credentials* (Sacramento: State of California Commission on Teacher Credentialing, 2015), 3 (permitting interns to teach after 120 hours of training or six credit hours of course work).

57. Charles Clotfelter, Helen F. Ladd, and Jacob Vigdor, "Who Teaches Whom?: Race and the Distribution of Novice Teachers," *Economics of Education Review* 24, no. 4 (2005); Erica Frankenberg, *The Segregation of American Teachers* (Cambridge, MA: The Civil Rights Project at Harvard University, 2006), 25–26, www.racialequitytools.org/resourcefiles/frankenberg.pdf.

58. Brandon L. Wright, "President Donald Trump Quotes about Education," *Fordham Institute*, November 23, 2016, https://fordhaminstitute.org/national /commentary/president-donald-trump-quotes-about-education.

59. Donald Trump (@realDonaldTrump), "We need to fix our broken education system!," Twitter, February 27, 2016, 7:02 PM, https://twitter.com/realDonald Trump/status/703777173296046080.

CHAPTER 2. A NATION FOUNDED ON EDUCATION

1. Lawrence A. Cremin, *The American Common School: An Historic Conception* (New York: Bureau of Publications Columbia University, 1951), 29.

2. James Madison to W. T. Barry, August 4, 1822. See also Cremin, *The American Common School*, 30.

3. John Adams, *A Dissertation on the Canon and Feudal Law* no. 3, ed. Robert J. Taylor (Cambridge, MA: Harvard University Press, September 30, 1765), 120.

4. Adams, *A Dissertation on the Canon and Feudal Law*.

5. Ibid.

6. Carl F. Kaestle, *Pillars of the Republic: Common Schools and American Society, 1780–1860* (New York: Hill and Wang, 1983), 6 (quoting Noah Webster, *On the Education of Youth in America* (Boston: I. Thomas and E.T. Andrews, 1790)).

7. Benjamin Rush, "Of the Mode of Education Proper in a Republic, 1798," Selected Writings, 87–89, 92, 94–96, Vol. 1 *The Founders' Constitution*, eds. Philip B. Kurland and Ralph Lerner (Chicago: University of Chicago Press, 2000), chapter 18, document 30, http://press-pubs.uchicago.edu/founders/documents/v1ch18s30.html.

8. John Andrew Wimpey, "Pioneer Concepts of American Public Education," *Peabody Journal of Education* 35, no. 2 (September 1957): 83 (quoting Adams, *The Works of John Adams VI*, 168).

9. Wimpey, "Pioneer Concepts," 83 (quoting "Thoughts on Government," in *The Works of John Adams IV*, 199).

10. John Adams to Mathew Robinson Jr., March 23, 1786, https://rotunda.upress.virginia.edu/founders/FOEA-03-01-02-0563.

11. "President Thomas Jefferson, 6th Annual Message to Congress, December 2, 1806," *Avalon Project* (Washington, DC: US Government Printing Office, 1927), https://avalon.law.yale.edu/19th_century/jeffmes6.asp.

12. Cremin, *The American Common School*, 110–11.

13. Thomas Jefferson, Preamble, Bill 79, "A Bill for the More General Diffusion of Knowledge."

14. Ibid.

15. Thomas Jefferson to John Adams, October 28, 1813.

16. From Thomas Jefferson to George Washington, January 4, 1785, Founders Online, https://founders.archives.gov/documents/Jefferson/01-09-02-0135.

17. Ibid.

18. John Adams to Mathew Robinson Jr., March 23, 1786, *Rotunda*, https://rotunda.upress.virginia.edu/founders/FOEA-03-01-02-0563.

19. To George Washington from Thomas Jefferson, January 4, 1786, *Founders Online*, https://founders.archives.gov/documents/Washington/04-03-02-0419.

20. From Thomas Jefferson to George Wythe, August 13, 1786, *Founders Online*, https://founders.archives.gov/documents/Jefferson/01-10-02-0162.

21. From Thomas Jefferson to James Madison, December 20, 1787, Founders Online, https://founders.archives.gov/documents/Jefferson/01-12-02-0454.

22. Michael J. Klarman, *The Framers' Coup: The Making of the United States Constitution* (New York: Oxford University Press, 2016), 296.

23. Jonathan Hughes, "The Great Land Ordinances," in *Essays on the Economy of the Old Northwest*, ed. David C. Klingaman (Athens: Ohio University Press, 1987), 2, http://minnesotalegalhistoryproject.org/assets/hughes.pdf.

24. "George Washington, Eighth Annual Message to Congress, December 7, 1796," *American History from Revolution to Reconstruction and beyond*, www.let.rug.nl/usa/presidents/george-washington/annual-message-1796-12-07.php.

25. Thomas Condit Miller and Hu Maxwell, *West Virginia and Its People*, vols. 2–3, *Family and Personal History* (New York: Lewis Historical Publishing Co., 1913), 559.

26. "From James Madison to William T. Barry, August 4, 1822," *Founders Online*, https://founders.archives.gov/documents/Madison/04-02-02-0480.

27. *Education in the 50 States: A Deskbook of the History of State Constitutions and Laws about Education* (Washington, DC: Institute for Education Equity and Opportunity, 2008), 29.

28. James Jesse Burns, *Educational History of Ohio: A History of Its Progress since the Formation* (Columbus, OH: Historical Publishing Co., 1905), 46.

29. Madison to Barry, 30.

30. Doris Kearns Goodwin, *Team of Rivals: The Political Genius of Abraham Lincoln* (New York: Simon and Schuster, 2006), 207.

31. "Abraham Lincoln: Lewiston, IL, August 17, 1858," *A Guide to Ethics St. Olaf College*, https://pages.stolaf.edu/ein/christian-ethics/christian-ethics/abraham -lincoln-lewiston-il-august-17-1858.

CHAPTER 3. EDUCATION AS FREEDOM

1. This idea owes its genesis to "The war . . . put down the insurrection of barbarism against civilization, and opened the way for education which is the real liberation. The sword may make the freedman, but only the truth makes the freeman." "Education of the Freedmen," *Nationalist*, March 19, 1866. *Nationalist* was a paper or magazine in Mobile, Alabama in the post–Civil War period. This quote can be found in Hilary Green, *Educational Reconstruction: African American Schools in the Urban South, 1865–1890* (New York: Fordham University Press, 2016), 44.

2. Edward L. Pierce, "The Contrabands at Fortress Monroe," *Atlantic Monthly* 8 (November 1861): 626–40.

3. James E. Yeatman, *A Report on the Condition of the Freedmen of the Mississippi* (St. Louis: Western Sanitary Commission, 1863), 3.

4. Heather Andrea Williams, *Self-Taught: African American Education in Slavery and Freedom* (Chapel Hill: University of North Carolina Press, 2005), 35–36.

5. Yeatman, *Condition of the Freedmen of the Mississippi*, 3.

6. Walter Lynwood Fleming, *Civil War and Reconstruction in Alabama* (London: Macmillan & Co., Ltd., 1905), 458.

7. James D. Anderson, *The Education of Blacks in the South 1860-1935* (Chapel Hill: University of North Carolina Press, 1988), 5.

8. "Letter from W.C. Gannett," *Freedmen's Record*, April 28, 1865, 91.

9. Rep. Moulton, Cong. Globe, 39th Cong., 1st Sess. 3044 (1866), https://memory.loc.gov/cgi-bin/ampage?collId=llcg&fileName=073/llcg073.db&recNum =165.

10. Christopher M. Span, *From Cotton Field to Schoolhouse: African American Education in Mississippi* (Chapel Hill: University of North Carolina Press, 2012), 43.

11. Green, *Educational Reconstruction*, 2, 3.

12. Span, *From Cotton Field to Schoolhouse*, 43.

13. Anderson, *The Education of Blacks*, 18.

14. Williams, *Self-Taught*, 138.

15. Anderson, *The Education of Blacks*, 10.

16. Williams, *Self-Taught*, 70.

17. Ibid.

18. Anderson, *The Education of Blacks*, 5.

19. J. W. Alvord, *Fourth Semi-Annual Report on Schools for Freedmen, July 1, 1867* (Washington, DC: US Government Printing Office, 1867), 93.

20. Booker T. Washington, *Up from Slavery: An Autobiography* (Garden City, NY: Doubleday & Co., 1901), 4.

21. Ibid., 5.

22. J. W. Alvord, *Fifth Semi-Annual Report on Schools for Freedmen, January 1, 1868* (Washington, DC: US Government Printing Office, 1868), 4.

23. "A Timeline of Our History," *Penn Center*, n.d., www.penncenter.com /explore-penn-centers-history. In various forms, its education work would continue well into the middle of the next century, before morphing into a social organization and cultural heritage center. Ibid. Luana M. Graves Sellars, "PennCenter and the Port Royal Experiment," *Hilton Head Monthly*, January 30, 2017, www.hilton headmonthly.com/living/4078-penn-center-the-port-royal-experiment;"Reconstruction Era National Monument," *Penn Center*, January 19, 2017, www.penncenter.com /news/reconstructioneranationalmonument.

24. Robert C. Morris, *Reading, 'Riting, and Reconstruction: The Education of Freedmen in the South 1861–1870* (Chicago: University of Chicago Press, 1976), 7.

25. Maxine D. Jones, "The American Missionary Association and the Beaufort, North Carolina School Controversy, 1866-67," 48 *Phylon* 48, no. 2 (Summer 1987): 103–11, www.jstor.org/stable/274774?seq=1#metadata_info_tab_contents.

26. Peter Kolchin, *First Freedom: The Responses of Alabama's Blacks to Emancipation and Reconstruction* (Tuscaloosa: University of Alabama Press, 2008), 84.

27. See "Letter from Abraham Lincoln to Nathaniel Banks, August 5, 1863," in *Works of Abraham Lincoln*, Vol. 6 (New Brunswick, NJ: Rutgers University Press, 1953), 365.

28. "Journal of the House of Representatives of the United States, 1861–1862, Monday, June 2, 1862," *A Century of Lawmaking for a New Nation: U.S. Congressional Documents and Debates 1774–1875*, https://memory.loc.gov/cgi-bin/query /r?ammem/hlaw:@field(DOCID+@lit(hj059126)).

29. Robert N. Scott, *The War of the Rebellion: A Compilation of the Official Records of the Union and Confederate Armies* vol. 34, no. 2, ser. 1 (Washington, DC: US Government Printing Office, 1891), 228–29, https://babel.hathitrust.org/cgi/pt ?id=uc1.c035412926;view=1up;seq=234.

30. "General Orders No. 38 (March 22, 1864)," in Elihu Root, *The War of the Rebellion: A Compilation of the Official Records of the Union and Confederate Armies* vol. 4, ser. 3 (Washington, DC: US Government Printing Office, 1900), 193–94, https://babel.hathitrust.org/cgi/pt?id=hvd.hwsk39;view=1up;seq=209.

31. "Lincoln's Visit to Richmond," National Park Service, n.d., www.nps.gov/rich /learn/historyculture/lincvisit.htm

32. "Lucy Chase Letter," *The Freedmen's Record*, April 18, 1865, 95.

33. As of the last census before the Civil War.

34. Kolchin, *First Freedom*, 86.

35. Williams, *Self-Taught*, 142.

36. Ibid., 143.

37. Alvord, *Fourth Semi-Annual Report on Schools for Freedmen*, 6.

38. Williams, *Self-Taught*, 36.

39. J. W. Alvord, *Third Semi-Annual Report on Schools for Freedmen, January 1, 1867* (Washington, DC: US Government Printing Office, 1867), 5.

40. Span, *From Cotton Field to Schoolhouse*, 43–44.

41. Kolchin, *First Freedom*, 85.

42. "Lucy Chase Letter," *The Freedmen's Record*, April 18, 1865, 96.

43. Frederick Douglass, *Life of an American Slave* (Boston: Anti-Slavery Office, 1845), 36, http://utc.iath.virginia.edu/abolitn/abaufda8t.html.

44. Williams, *Self-Taught*, 13 (look at actual law).

45. Ibid., 14 (look at actual law).

46. Ibid., 7.

47. Ibid.

48. Douglass, *Life of an American Slave*, 37.

49. Ibid., 19.

50. Ibid., 20.

51. Ibid., 41.

52. Ibid., 25.

53. "The Board of Education," *The Freedmen's Record*, (1865), 144–45.

54. Alvord, *First Semi-Annual Report*.

55. Ibid.

56. J. W. Alvord, *Second Semi-Annual Report on Schools and Finances of Freedmen, July 1, 1866* (Washington, DC: US Government Printing Office, 1868), 12.

57. Alvord, *Fifth Semi-Annual Report*, 8.

58. Alvord, *First Semi-Annual Report*, 5.

59. H. Exec. Doc. No. 70, 39th Cong., 1st Sess., 334 (1866).

60. Eric Foner, *Forever Free: The Story of Emancipation and Reconstruction* (New York: Vintage Books 2005), 89.

61. Alvord, *First Semi-Annual Report*.

62. Alvord, *Second Semi-Annual Report*, 14.

63. Williams, *Self-Taught*, 42.

64. Ibid., 43 ("Testimony of Harry McMillan before the American Freedmen's Inquiry Commission, June 1863," *Wartime Genesis of Free Labor: The Lower South*, ed. Ira Berlin, Thavolia Glymph, and Steven F. Miller (Cambridge, MA: Cambridge University Press, 2012), 250–54.

65. Ibid., 138 (Freedman, Trent Camp, North Carolina).

66. Ibid., 67.

67. Ibid., 68.

68. Alvord, *Second Semi-Annual Report*, 13.

69. Lawrence A. Cremin, *The American Common School: An Historic Conception* (New York: Bureau of Publications Columbia University, 1951), 149. By comparison, Cremin points out that Michigan "moved early and decisively to establish a comprehensive public system extending from the elementary school through the state university." Ibid.

CHAPTER 4. RECONSTRUCTION: A NATIONAL RECOMMITMENT TO EDUCATION AND DEMOCRACY

1. Cong. Globe, 40th Cong., 1st Sess. 167 (1867), https://memory.loc.gov/cgi-bin/ampage?collId=llcg&fileName=078/llcg078.db&recNum=302.

2. Cong. Globe, 40th Cong., 1st Sess. 168 (1867), https://memory.loc.gov/cgi-bin/ampage?collId=llcg&fileName=078/llcg078.db&recNum=303.

3. "Law Creating the Freedmen's Bureau," *Freedmen & Southern Society Project*, updated August 26, 2019, www.freedmen.umd.edu/fbact.htm.

4. Ibid.

5. "War Department, Bureau of Refugees, Freedmen, and Abandoned Lands," *Freedmen's Record*, October 9, 1865, 177.

6. "Negro Affairs in North Carolina," *The Freedmen's Record*, vol. 1 (Boston, MA), September 1865.

7. Oliver Otis Howard, *Autobiography of Oliver Otis Howard Major General US Army*, vol. 2 (New York: Baker & Taylor Company, 1907), 368.

8. Eric Schnapper, "Affirmative Action and the Legislative History of the Fourteenth Amendment," *Virginia Law Review* 71, no. 4 (1985): 753, 780–81.

9. Alan Brinkley, *American History: Connecting with the Past*, vol. 2, 15th ed. (New York: McGraw-Hill Education, 2014), 409.

10. Alvord, *Fifth Semi-Annual Report*, 6.

11. Span, *From Cotton Field to Schoolhouse*, 29.

12. Ibid.

13. Green, *Educational Reconstruction*, 49.

14. "Proceedings of the Colored People's Convention of the State of South Carolina" (Charleston: South Carolina Leader Office, 1865), 9–10, https://docs.google.com/viewerng/viewer?url=http://coloredconventions.org/files/original/fb7ce2e02cc45786fb4530926135de24.pdf.

15. Ibid., 30.

16. "A Century of Lawmaking for a New Nation: U.S. Congressional Documents and Debates, 1774–1875," *Journal of the House of Representatives of the United States* 63 (December 14, 1865): 69, https://memory.loc.gov/cgi-bin/ampage?collId=llhj&fileName=063/llhj063.db&recNum=68&itemLink=D?hlaw:1:./temp/~ammem_m2Dr:%230630069&linkText=1.

17. Cong. Globe, 39th Cong, 1st Sess. 3044 (1866), https://memory.loc.gov/cgi-bin/ampage?collId=llcg&fileName=073/llcg073.db&recNum=165.

18. Ibid.

19. Ibid.

20. Ibid., 3045.

21. Ibid.

22. Ibid.

23. Act of March 2, 1867, ch. 158, 14 Stat. 434.

24. The Department was reduced to an "Office of Education" and then to a "Bureau of Education" within the Department of the Interior. See Cong. Globe, 40th Cong., 2nd Sess. app., 521 (1868).

25. Reconstruction Act of 1867, ch. 153, 14 Stat. 428, 428 (1867).

26.Cong. Globe, 40th Cong., 1st Sess. 581 (1867). Sumner explained that the amendment was a simple "safeguard for the future" and a natural corollary to universal suffrage, which Congress was already requiring. Ibid., 166–67 (statement of Sen. Sumner).

27. Cong. Globe, 40th Cong., 1st Sess. 167 (1867).

28. Ibid.

29. Ibid.

30. Ibid., 168.

31. Ibid., 168.

32. Ibid., 169.

33. Ibid., 170.

34. Reconstruction Act of 1867, ch. 153, § 5, 14 Stat. 428, 429.

35. See Derek W. Black, "The Constitutional Compromise to Guarantee Education," *Stanford Law Review* 70 (2018): 735, 781–83 (summarizing Congress's acts and intentions).

36. Isaac Wheeler Avery, *The History of the State of Georgia from 1850 to 1881: Embracing the Three Important Epochs: The Decade before the War of 1861–5; The War; The Period of Reconstruction* (New York: Brown & Derby, 1881), 391.

37. See An Act to Admit the State of Mississippi to Representation in the Congress of the United States, ch. 19, 16 Stat. 67, 68 (1870); An Act to Admit the State of Texas to Representation in the Congress of the United States, ch. 39, 16 Stat. 80, 81 (1870); An Act to Admit the State of Virginia to Representation in the Congress of the United States, ch. 10, 16 Stat. 62, 63 (1870).

CHAPTER 5. A CONSTITUTIONAL CHORUS FOR THE RIGHT TO EDUCATION

1. See, e.g., Cynthia E. Browne, *State Constitutional Conventions: From Independence to the Completion of the Present Union, 1776–1959: A Bibliography* (Westport, CT: Greenwood Press, 1973), 5, 39, 46, 80, 112, 167, 234.

2. *Proceedings of the Constitutional Convention of South Carolina Held in Charleston, S.C. Beginning January 14th and Ending March 17th, 1868* (Charleston: Denny & Perry, 1868), 10 (noting that purpose of convention is "to frame a new Constitution" so as "to secure a Republican form of Government"), https://archive

.org/details/proceedingsofcon00sout/page/n1; ibid., 628–807 (referencing a re-publican form of government more than fifty times over seven days: February 29, March 2, March 3, March 4, March 5, March 6, and March 7).

3. Ibid., 10.

4. Ibid., 642–822 (reprints of 1868 convention debates on February 29, March 3, March 4, March 5, March 6, and March 7).

5. Ibid., 264.

6. Ibid., 704.

7. Ibid., 173.

8. Ibid., 873.

9. Ibid., 711.

10. Ibid., 873.

11. Pierce v. Soc'y of Sisters, 268 U.S. 510 (1925). The Court in *Pierce v. Society of Sisters* recognized an equally important wrinkle, however. The state can mandate education, but it cannot mandate that students attend public school. Parents have a right to control the upbringing of their children and this entitles them to send their children to private schools if they prefer (although the state retains the power to regulate those schools in the interest of ensuring they are providing students with the necessary basic skills).

12. *Constitutional Convention of SC 1868*, 688.

13. Ibid., 696.

14. Ibid., 696–98 (I reordered the last paragraph, which actually preceded the others).

15. Thomas J. Kirkland and Robert M. Kennedy, *Historic Camden, Part Two: Nineteenth Century* (Columbia, SC: State Company, 1926), 200, https://babel .hathitrust.org/cgi/pt?id=coo.31924052629742;view=1up;seq=228.

16. *Constitutional Convention of SC 1868*, 692.

17. Ibid., 695.

18. Ibid., 695.

19. Ibid., 702.

20. Ibid.

21. Ibid., 703.

22. The specific yeas and nays for compulsory education were not counted, as it passed as part of the overall education provisions. The convention held a separate vote as to whether to included affirmative language indicating that all schools would be "free and open to all the children and youth of the State, without regard to race or color." S.C. Const. of 1868, art. 10, § 10. This even more controversial measure still passed with 80 percent voting in favor. James Lowell Underwood and W. Lewis Burke, *At Freedom's Door: African American Founding Fathers and Lawyers in Reconstruction South Carolina* (Columbia: University of South Carolina Press, 2000), 15.

23. Seventy-three percent of African Americans supported the poll tax, whereas only 62 percent of whites supported it. Ibid., 10. The language, however, included

a proviso that no one would be disqualified from voting for failure to pay the tax. Ibid., 9–10.

24. *Constitutional Convention of SC 1868*, 925.

25. See generally Robert F. Williams, *The Law of American State Constitutions* (New York: Oxford University Press, 2009), 91 (indicating that "these conventions produced 'progressive documents'" that "established free public schools (attendance was compulsory in some states)," but noting that "there was disagreement, however, about integrated schools"). In addition to integration concerns, the cost of a new education system and how to fund it was a concern. See, e.g., *Official Journal of the Proceedings of the Convention, for Framing a Constitution for the State of Louisiana* (New Orleans: J. B. Roudanez & Co., 1867–1868), 277, https://archive.org/details /officialjournalo01loui_0/page/n5.

26. See, e.g., *Constitutional Convention of SC 1868*, 692, 696 (discussing the challenges of supporting education, but emphasizing its necessity in a republican form of government); Williams, *The Law*, 91 (indicating that "these conventions produced 'progressive documents'" that "established free public schools (attendance was compulsory in some states)" (quoting Foner, *Forever Free*, 143–44)).

27. *Journal of the Proceedings of the Constitutional Convention of the People of Georgia* (Augusta, GA: E. H. Pughe, 1868), 482–83 (offering an amendment to strengthen rather than weaken education clause by ensuring one or more schools in every district as soon as possible); *Louisiana Convention of 1868*, 60–61, 200–01 (including majority and minority reports, both of which agreed on the same core aspects of delivering education to all the youth).

28. See, e.g., Ala. Const. of 1868, art. XI, § 10 (providing that proceeds from all new and old state lands "shall be inviolably appropriated to educational purposes"); ibid. art. XI, § 11 (requiring that one-fifth of general annual state revenues "be devoted exclusively to the maintenance of public schools"); Fla. Const. of 1868, art. VIII, §§ 4, 7 (devoting resources to an education fund and requiring per-capita distribution among counties); see also John Mathiason Matzen, *State Constitutional Provisions for Education: Fundamental Attitude of the American People Regarding Education as Revealed by State Constitutional Provisions, 1776–1929* (New York: Teachers College, 1931), 129–39 (tracking the new common school funds in state constitutions).

29. Ga. Const. of 1868, art. VI., § 3; James Lowell Underwood, "African American Founding Fathers: The Making of the South Carolina Constitution of 1868," in *At Freedom's Door: African American Founding Fathers and Lawyers in Reconstruction South Carolina* (Columbia: University of South Carolina Press, 2000), 1, 9–10.

30. *Georgia Convention of 1868*, 482–83 (offering an amendment to strengthen rather than weaken education clause by ensuring one or more schools in every district as soon as possible); *Louisiana Convention of 1868*, 60–61 (majority and minority reports on how best to deliver education, but both agreeing on the same core aspects of delivering education to "all the youth in the state").

31. See, e.g., *Debates and Proceedings of the Convention Which Assembled at Little Rock, January 7th, 1868 to Form a Constitution for the State of Arkansas* (Little

Rock, AR: J.G. Price, 1868), 441–42, 626–27; *Louisiana Convention of 1868*, 292. Ironically, even some of the racism, however, was grounded in notions of the necessities of a republican government.

32. See, e.g., *Journal of the Constitutional Convention of the State of North Carolina* (1868), 235–36, https://babel.hathitrust.org/cgi/pt?id=nc01.ark:/13960 /t43r1s371&view=1up&seq=7.

33. See, e.g., Ala. Const. of 1867, art. XI, § 6 ("It shall be the duty of the board to establish, throughout the State, in each township or other school-district which it may have created, one or more schools. . . ."); Ark. Const. of 1868, art. IX, § 1 ("A general diffusion of knowledge and intelligence among all classes being essential to the preservation of the rights and liberties of the people, the General Assembly shall establish and maintain a system of free schools. . . ."); Fla. Const. of 1868, art. IX, § 1 ("It is the paramount duty of the State to make ample provision for the education of all the children residing within its borders. . . ."); Ga. Const. of 1868, art. VI, § 1 ("The general assembly . . . shall provide a thorough system of general education. . . ."); La. Const. of 1868, tit. VII, art. 135 ("The general assembly shall establish at least one free public school in every parish throughout the State, and shall provide for its support by taxation or otherwise."); Miss. Const. of 1868, art. VIII, § 1 ("As the stability of a republican form of government depends mainly upon the intelligence and virtue of the people, it shall be the duty of the legislature to . . . establish[] a uniform system of free public schools. . . ."); N.C. Const. of 1868, art. IX, § 2 ("The general assembly . . . shall provide, by taxation and otherwise, for a general and uniform system of public schools. . . ."); S.C. Const. of 1868, art. X, § 3 ("The General Assembly shall . . . provide for a liberal and uniform system of free public schools throughout the State."); Tex. Const. of 1868, art. X, § 7 ("It shall be the duty of the legislature of this State to make suitable provisions for the support and maintenance of a system of public free schools. . . ."); ibid. § 4, 310 ("The legislature shall establish a uniform system of public free schools throughout the State.").

34. Both state constitutions mandated that the state maintain a common education fund, but Tennessee's constitution oddly only indicated that the state shall "cherish literature and science" and "encourage" schools. Ky. Const. of 1850, art. XI, § 1; Tenn. Const. of 1834, art. XI, § 10. One could certainly read this as a constitutional mandate. Steven G. Calabresi and Michael W. Perl, "Originalism and *Brown v. Board of Education*," *Michigan State Law Review* (2014): 429, 455–56.

35. Ala. Const. of 1867, art. XI, § 6; Ark. Const. of 1868, art. IX, § 1; Fla. Const. of 1868, art. IX, § 1; Ga. Const. of 1868, art. VI, § 1; La. Const. of 1868, tit. VII, art. 135; Miss. Const. of 1868, art. VIII, § 1; N.C. Const. of 1868, art. IX, § 2; S.C. Const. of 1868, art. X, § 3; Tex. Const. of 1868, art. X, § 7.

36. Ga. Const. of 1868, art. VI, § 1 ("The general assembly . . . shall provide a thorough system of general education. . . ."). Miss. Const. of 1868, art. VIII, § 1 ("As the stability of a republican form of government depends mainly upon the intelligence and virtue of the people, it shall be the duty of the legislature to . . . establish[] a uniform system of free public schools. . . ."); N.C. Const. of 1868, art.

IX, § 2 ("The general assembly . . . shall provide, by taxation and otherwise, for a general and uniform system of public schools. . . ."); S.C. Const. of 1868, art. X, § 3 ("The General Assembly shall . . . provide for a liberal and uniform system of free public schools throughout the State.").

37. *Report of the Debates and Proceedings of the Convention for the Revision of the Constitution of the State of Ohio*, vol. 2 (Columbus, OH: S. Medary, 1851), 698.

38. Ala. Const. of 1867, art. XI, § 6 ("It shall be the duty of the board to establish, throughout the State, in each township or other school-district which it may have created, one or more schools. . . .").

39. Fla. Const. of 1868, art. IX, § 1 ("It is the paramount duty of the State to make ample provision for the education of all the children residing within its borders. . . .").

40. La. Const. of 1868, Title VII, art. 135 ("The general assembly shall establish at least one free public school in every parish throughout the State, and shall provide for its support by taxation or otherwise.").

41. An Act for the Admission of Kansas into the Union, ch. 20, § 1, 12 Stat. 126 (1861); An Act to Enable the People of Nevada to Form a Constitution and State Government, and for the Admission of Such State into the Union on an Equal Footing with the Original States, ch. 36, 13 Stat. 30 (1864); An Act to Enable the People of Nebraska to Form a Constitution and State Government, and for the Admission of Such State into the Union on an Equal Footing with the Original States, ch. 59, 13 Stat. 47 (1864); An Act for the Admission of the State of Nebraska into the Union, ch. 36, 15 Stat. 391 (1867); Virginia v. West Virginia, 78 U.S. (11 Wall.) 39, 43–44 (1870) (quoting An Act for the Admission of the State of "West Virginia" into the Union, and for Other Purposes, ch. 6, 12 Stat. 633 (1862)).

42. Kan. Const. of 1859, art. VI, § 2; Neb. Const. of 1866, art. I, § 16; Nev. Const. of 1864, art. XI, § 2; W. Va. Const. of 1863, art. X, § 2.

43. Prior to Missouri's, only New Jersey's and Wisconsin's statutes had included this language, but Illinois, Pennsylvania, Nebraska, and Colorado followed Missouri's lead. John C. Eastman, "When Did Education Become a Civil Right? An Assessment of State Constitutional Provisions for Education, 1776–1900," *American Journal of Legal History* 42, no. 1 (1998): 1, 23.

44. *Journal of the Missouri State Convention* (St. Louis: Missouri Democrat, 1865), 196.

45. Ibid.

46. Those states included Michigan, Indiana, Ohio, Minnesota, and Oregon. Ind. Const. of 1851, art. VIII, § 1; Mich. Const. of 1850, art. XIII, § 4; Minn. Const. of 1857, art. VIII, § 1; Ohio Const. of 1851, art. VI, § 2; Or. Const. of 1857, art. VIII, § 3.

47. See *Education in the 50 States: A Deskbook for the History of State Constitutions and Laws about Education* (Philadelphia: Institute for Educational Equity and Opportunity, 2008), 29.

48. *Debates of the Convention to Amend the Constitution of Pennsylvania*, vol. 1–9 (Harrisburg, PA: Benjamin Singerly, 1873), https://catalog.hathitrust.org/Record

/001143867; *Pennsylvania Convention of 1873*, vol. 2 (Harrisburg, PA: Benjamin Singerly, 1873), 241, https://babel.hathitrust.org/cgi/pt?id=mdp.39015025026132 &view=1up&seq=245. Delegate Carter similarly announced that "the most import-ant interest requiring attention in our State is unquestionably that of education." Ibid., vol. 2, 389. This notion was echoed on several occasions without objection. See, e.g., Del. Mann, *Pennsylvania Convention of 1873*, vol. 2, 678 ("most im-portant of all the interests of the State."); Del. Mann, ibid., vol. 2, 436 ("most important" section of the constitution); Del. Darlington, ibid., vol. 7, 691–92 (ed-ucation is "more incumbent upon the whole people of this Commonwealth than any other."); Del. Curtin, ibid., vol. 7, 686–87 (nothing "more beneficial . . . than our system of common school education").

49. *Pennsylvania Convention of 1873*, vol. 1, 444.

50. *Pennsylvania Convention of 1873*, vol. 2, 387.

51. Ibid., vol. 2, 385–91.

52. Ibid., 388.

53. Pa. Const. of 1873, art. IV, § 8; Ibid., art. VI, § 4.

54. See, e.g., *Pennsylvania Convention of 1873*, vol. 2, 386. They only relented at the end of the convention when the Committee on Revisions suggested moving it as a matter of basic symmetry and structure.

55. Pa. Const. of 1873, art. III, § 15.

56. Ibid.

57. *Pennsylvania Convention of 1873*, vol. 2, 436.

58. Ibid., vol. 2, 426–62.

59. Calabresi and Perl, *Originalism*, 458 n132 (explaining that in 1875, New Jer-sey adopted its education clause, leaving Connecticut as the only state without one).

CHAPTER 6. THE FALL

1. James Lowell Underwood, *The Constitution of South Carolina*, vol. 2, *The Journey toward Local Self-Government* (Columbia: University of South Carolina Press, 1988), 68.

2. Underwood, vol. 2, 68.

3. Anderson, *The Education of Blacks*, 81.

4. Ibid.

5. Michael J. Klarman, *Unfinished Business: Racial Equality in American His-tory* (New York: Oxford University Press, 2007), 44.

6. Ibid.

7. Anderson, *The Education of Blacks*, 96.

8. James K. Vardaman, "Negro Education," *Commonwealth* (*Greenwood, MS*), June 30, 1899, 4, https://chroniclingamerica.loc.gov/lccn/sn89065008/1899-06-30 /ed-1/seq-4.pdf. (4th column, 4 paras from bottom).

9. Dorothy Overstreet Pratt, *Sowing the Wind: The Mississippi Constitutional Convention of 1890* (Jackson: University Press of Mississippi, 2018), 55.

10. Ibid., 24.

11. Anderson, *The Education of Blacks*, 101.

12. Neil R. McMillen, *Dark Journey: Black Mississippians in the Age of Jim Crow* (Champaign: University of Illinois Press, 1989), 41.

13. "Mississippi Constitutional Convention: Promptly Organized and Ready to Go to Work," *Pascagoula Democrat Star*, August 15, 1890, http://chroniclingamerica.loc.gov/lccn/sn87065532/1890-08-15/ed-1/seq-2.

14. Wythe Holt, *Virginia's Constitutional Convention of 1901–1902* (New York: Garland Publishing, Inc., 1990), 152.

15. *Constitutional Convention of SC 1868*, 10.

16. Ibid., 925.

17. *Journal of the Constitutional Convention of the State of South Carolina* (Columbia, SC: Charles A. Calvo Jr., 1895), 10.

18. Albert D. Kirwan, *Revolt of the Rednecks: Mississippi Politics* (Lexington: University of Kentucky Press, 1951), 1876–1925 69–70.

19. James Lowell Underwood, *The Constitution of South Carolina: The Struggle for Political Equality*, vol. 4 (Columbia, University of South Carolina Press, 1994), 134–35.

20. John Hope Franklin, *From Slavery to Freedom: A History of African Americans*, 3rd ed. (New York: Alfred A. Knopf, 1967), 339.

21. Robert Luckett Jr., "The Southern Manifesto as Education Policy in Mississippi," *Journal of School Choice* 10 (2016): 462–78.

22. No doubt due to the effects of Black disfranchisement. U.S. Bureau of the Census, "Chapter Y, Government: Elections and Politics," *Bicentennial Edition: Historical Statistics of the United States, Colonial Times to 1970* (Washington, DC: US Government Printing Office, 1975), 1071–72, www2.census.gov/library/publications/1975/compendia/hist_stats_colonial-1970/hist_stats_colonial-1970p2-chY.pdf; "United States Historical Election Returns, 1824 to 1968," (Ann Arbor, MI: Interuniversity Consortium for Political and Social Research, 1999), www.icpsr.umich.edu/icpsrweb/ICPSR/studies/1; US Census Bureau, *Bicentennial Edition: Historical Statistics of the United States, Colonial Times to 1970* (Washington, DC: US Government Printing Office, 1975), 1071–1072, www.census.gov/library/publications/1975/compendia/hist_stats_colonial-1970.html.

23. Klarman, *Unfinished Business*, 32.

24. Ibid.

25. Ibid.

26. Pratt, *Sowing the Wind*, 117.

27. Ibid.

28. Anderson, *The Education of Blacks*, 95.

29. Miss. Const. of 1890, art. VIII, § 207.

30. S.C. Const. of 1895, art. XI, § 7.

31. Ala. Const. of 1901, art. XIV, § 256 ("separate schools shall be provided for white and colored children").

32. Pratt, *Sowing the Wind*, 114.

33. Puitt v. Gaston Cty. Comm'rs, 94 N.C. 709, 714–19 (1886).

34. Claybrook v. City of Owensboro, 16 F. 297, 302 (D. Ky. 1883).

35. Ibid.

36. Pratt, *Sowing the Wind*, 117.

37. *Constitutional Convention of SC 1895*, 91; Paul E. Herron, *Framing the Solid South: The State Constitutional Conventions of Secession, Reconstruction, and Redemption, 1860–1902* (Lawrence: University Press of Kansas, 2017), 206.

38. Herron, *Framing the Solid South*, 206.

39. Klarman, *Unfinished Business*, 43.

40. Franklin, *From Slavery*, 387.

41. Klarman, *Unfinished Business*, 45.

42. Franklin, *From Slavery*, 87.

43. Charles C. Bolton, *The Hardest Deal of All: The Battle over School Integration in Mississippi, 1870–1980* (Jackson: University Press of Mississippi, 2005).

44. Ibid.

45. Ibid. (By 1950, white teachers made on average $1,806 per year while their black counterparts collected 39 percent of that total, or roughly $711 per year).

46. Klarman, *Unfinished Business*, 46–47.

47. Mississippi State Department of Education, "Manner of Apportioning the Common School Fund (by Ex-Superintendent of Education, A. A. Kincannon)," in *Biennial Report of the State Superintendent of Public Education to the Legislature of Mississippi* (Jacksonville, FL: Vance Printing Co., 1900).

48. Richard Kluger, *Simple Justice: The History of* Brown v. Board of Education *and Black America's Struggle for Equality* (New York: Vintage Books, 2004), 170.

49. Ibid., 171.

50. United States v. Reese, 92 U.S. 214 (1876).

51. Plessy v. Ferguson, 163 U.S. 537 (1896).

52. Ibid.

53. 175 U.S. 528 (1899).

54. *Cumming*, 175 U.S. at 544.

55. Charles William Dabney, *Universal Education in the South: From the Beginning to 1900*, vol. 1 (Chapel Hill: University of North Carolina Press, 1935), 175–76.

56. Ibid., 173–75.

57. Ibid., 176–77.

58. Ibid., 180.

59. Thomas J. Jarvis, ["inaugural address, Raleigh, North Carolina"] January 18, 1881, p 12.

60. Pratt, *Sowing the Wind*, 115.

61. Ibid., 118.

62. Ibid., 172.

63. Eric Etheridge, "A Confederate Veteran Speaks: What the Monuments Mean," *Breach of Peace*, August 21, 2017, https://breachofpeace.com/blog/?p=760.

64. Miss. Const. of 1890, art. XII, § 243.

65. Ibid.

66. Pratt, *Sowing the Wind*, 175.

67. Ratliff v. Beale 74 Miss. 247, 20 So. 865, 869 (Miss. 1896).

68. Anderson, *The Education of Blacks*, 25–26.

69. Ibid., 27.

70. Ibid., 19.

CHAPTER 7. THE SECOND RECONSTRUCTION

1. Richard Kluger, *Simple Justice: The History of* Brown v. Board of Education *and Black America's Struggle for Equality* (New York: Vintage Books, 2004), 132.

2. Nathan R. Margold, Preliminary Report to the Joint Committee Supervising the Expenditure of the 1930 Appropriation by the American Fund for Public Service, 1931, NAACP Records, Manuscript Division, 070.00.06, Library of Congress.

3. Kluger, *Simple Justice*, 133.

4. Jay Clay Smith Jr., *Emancipation: The Making of the Black Lawyer, 1844–1944* (Philadelphia: University of Pennsylvania Press, 1995), 132.

5. Kluger, *Simple Justice*, 134 (quoting Margold Report).

6. Ibid., 165.

7. *Encyclopedia of African American Education*, vol. 1, ed. Kofi Lomotey (Thousand Oaks, CA: SAGE Publications, 2010), 649.

8. Pearson v. Murray, 182 A. 590, 592 (1936) (quoting Clark v. Maryland Inst., 87 Md. 643 (1898)).

9. *Pearson*, 182 A. at 594.

10. State of Missouri *ex rel*. Gaines v. Canada, 305 U.S. 337, 345 (1938).

11. Ibid., 349–50.

12. Ibid.

13. Kluger, *Simple Justice*, 256.

14. Ibid., 257.

15. Ibid., 258.

16. 332 U.S. 814 (1947).

17. Sweatt v. Painter, 339 U.S. 629, 632 (1950).

18. McLaurin v. Okla. State Regents for Higher Ed., 339 U.S. 637, 640 (1950).

19. Ibid.

20. Kluger, *Simple Justice*, 268.

21. Brief for Petitioner, Sweatt v. Painter, 339 U.S. 629 (1950), 1950 WL 78681 (U.S.), at *12.

22. Ibid., *13.

23. Ibid., *18 (quoting Sidney Post Simpson, "The Function of a University Law School," *Harvard Law Review* 49 (1936): 1069).

24. Ibid., *18–20.

25. Ibid.

26. Sweatt v. Painter, 339 U.S. 629, 633–35 (1950).

27. Ibid.

28. Ibid.

29. Ibid.

30. Ibid.

31. McLaurin v. Okla. State Regents for Higher Ed., 339 U.S. 637, 641–42 (1950).

32. Kluger, *Simple Justice*, 295.

33. Ibid., 303.

34. Brief for Appellants, Brown v. Bd. of Educ. of Topeka, 1952 WL 82046 (U.S.), at *9.

35. Ibid.

36. Ibid.

37. Brief for Appellants, Brown v. Bd. of Educ. of Topeka, 1953 WL 78288 U.S., at *15–16.

38. Ibid., *28.

39. Brown v. Bd. of Ed. of Topeka, Shawnee Cty., Kan., 347 U.S. 483, 489, (1954), *supplemented sub nom.* Brown v. Bd. of Educ. of Topeka, Kan., 349 U.S. 294, (1955).

40. *Brown*, 347 U.S. at 493.

41. Ibid., 495.

42. Bolling v. Sharpe, 347 U.S. 497, 500 (1954).

43. Also deleted were references to prior education liberty cases and the rationale upon which the Court could have treated education as a fundamental right. Those cases and references can still be found in NAACP's brief in *Bolling*.

44. Green v. Cty. Sch. Bd. of New Kent Cty., Va., 391 U.S. 430, 437–38 (1968).

45. Ibid., 438–39.

CHAPTER 8. THE CIVIL RIGHTS BACKLASH

1. "Southern Manifesto on Integration," Supreme Court History, Educational Broadcasting Corporation, last modified December 2006, www.thirteen.org/wnet /supremecourt/rights/sources_document2.html.

2. Cooper v. Aaron, 358 U.S. 1, 8–9 (1958).

3. Ibid.

4. Ibid., 9–13.

5. Ibid., 18 (internal citations omitted).

6. Griffin v. Cty. Sch. Bd. of Prince Edward Cty., 377 U.S. 218, 221–22 (1964).

7. Ibid.

8. Ibid.

9. See Wilbur B. Brookover, "Education in Prince Edward County, Virginia, 1953–1993," *Journal of Negro Education* 62, no. 2 (1993):149, 151 ("With support from then-President John F. Kennedy and his brother, Attorney General Robert F. Kennedy, and with private funds from various sources, The Prince Edward County

Free Schools operated for one year from fall 1963 to spring 1964. The public school facilities were made available to the Free Schools, which were open to all students in Prince Edward County. However, only a few (one or two perhaps) White students attended.").

10. Griffin v. Cty. Sch. Bd. of Prince Edward Cty., 377 U.S. 218, 229–30 (1964) (summarizing the Virginia Supreme Court's opinion).

11. Cty. Sch. Bd. of Prince Edward Cty. v. Griffin, 204 Va. 650, 671 (1963).

12. James E. Ryan, *Five Miles Away, a World Apart: One City, Two Schools, and the Story of Educational Opportunity in Modern America* (New York: Oxford University Press, 2010), 61.

13. Ibid.

14. Gareth Davies, "Richard Nixon and the Desegregation of Southern Schools," 19 *Journal of Policy History* 19, no. 4 (2007): 367, 369.

15. Ibid.

16. Ibid.

17. Stephen E. Ambrose, *Nixon*, vol. 2, *The Triumph of a Politician 1962–1972* (New York: Simon & Schuster, 1989), 408.

18. William Rehnquist, "A Random Thought on the Segregation Cases" 1952, www.govinfo.gov/content/pkg/GPO-CHRG-REHNQUIST/pdf/GPO-CHRG -REHNQUIST-4-16-6.pdf.

19. *Nominations of William H. Rehnquist and Lewis F. Powell, Jr.: Hearing Before the Committee on the Judiciary, United States Senate*, 92nd Cong. 381 (1971), www.govinfo.gov/content/pkg/GPO-CHRG-REHNQUIST-POWELL/pdf/GPO -CHRG-REHNQUIST-POWELL-1-1.pdf.

20. *Nominations*, at 384.

21. Brief for the Commonwealth of Virginia, Amicus Curie, Swann v. Charlotte-Mecklenburg Bd. of Educ., 402 U.S. 1 (1971) (No. 281), 1970 WL 122664, at *17 (arguing against the "disruption" of busing and seeking racial balance "as an end in itself" and for giving school administrators "reasonable discretion . . . in assigning pupils").

22. Ibid.

23. Meyer v. Nebraska, 262 U.S. 390, 400 (1923).

24. San Antonio Indep. Sch. Dist. v. Rodriguez, 411 U.S. 1, 29 (1973).

25. Ibid.

26. Ibid., 36.

27. Ibid., 70.

28. Ibid., 99.

29. Ibid., 102–03.

30. Ibid., 111.

31. Ibid., 113.

32. Ibid., 114.

33. Ibid., 84.

34. Milliken v. Bradley, 418 U.S. 717, 782 (1974).

35. *Milliken*, 418 U.S. at 781–83.

36. B. Lynn Winmill, *"Brown v. Board of Education*: The Legacy and the Promise," *Advocate (Idaho State Bar)* 47, no. 5 (2004): 23, 25.

37. Message: From the President of the United States Relative to Busing and Equality of Educational Opportunity, and Transmitting a Draft of Proposed Legislation to Impose a Moratorium on New and Additional Student Transportation, H.R. Doc. No. 92-195, 92d Cong., 2d Sess. (1972)], 15. For more discussion, see Note, "The Nixon Busing Bills and Congressional Power," *Yale Law Journal* 81 (1972): 1542.

38. "The Nixon Busing Bills," 1542.

39. Ibid., 1545 (paraphrasing § 3(a) of the Moratorium Bill).

40. 20 U.S.C. § 1228.

41. 20 U.S.C. § 1702(a)(3), Pub. L. No. 93-380, 88 Stat. 484 (1974).

42. 20 U.S.C. § 1702(a)(4).

CHAPTER 9. REDISCOVERING THE CONSTITUTIONAL RIGHT TO EDUCATION

1. Serrano v. Priest, 5 Cal. 3d 584, 596 (Cal. 1971).

2. *Serrano*, 5 Cal. 3d at 618.

3. Ibid., 608.

4. Cal. Const. art. IX, §1.

5. *Serrano*, 5 Cal. 3d at 608.

6. Ibid., 608–09.

7. Serrano v. Priest, 18 Cal. 3d 728, 766–77 (Cal. 1976).

8. Ibid., 767–68.

9. 303 A.2d 273, 282.

10. *Robinson*, 62 N.J. at 490.

11. Ibid., 491.

12. Ibid., 491–92.

13. Ibid., 496.

14. Pauley v. Kelly, 162 W. Va. 672, 681–87 (1979) (incorporating Ohio's 1851 Convention discussions on the topic, which were background to West Virginia's).

15. *Pauley*, 162 W. Va. at 684 (quoting Ohio debates).

16. Rose v. Council for Better Educ., Inc., 790 S.W.2d 186, 198 (Ky. 1989).

17. Ibid.

18. Ibid.

19. Ibid., 189.

20. Ibid., 205.

21. Ibid.

22. Ibid.

23. Ibid., 206.

24. Ibid.

25. Ibid., 205–06.

26. Ibid., 189–90.

27. National Commission on Excellence in Education, *Nation at Risk: The Imperative for Education Reform* (Washington DC: US Government Printing Office,

1983), 5, https://babel.hathitrust.org/cgi/pt?id=mdp.39015004170224&view=2up &seq=2. See also Susan H. Bitensky, "Theoretical Foundations for a Right to Education under the U.S. Constitution: A Beginning to the End of the National Education Crisis," *Northwestern University Law Review* 86, no. 3 (1992): 550, 555–62.

28. Joetta L. Sack, "The End of an Education Presidency," *Education Week*, January 17, 2001.

29. *Rose*, at 212.

30. See, e.g., Alabama Opinion of the Justice, 624 So. 2d 107, 165–66 (Ala. 1993); Idaho Schs. for Equal Educ. Opportunity v. Evans, 850 P.2d 724, 734 (Idaho 1993); McDuffy v. Secretary, 615 N.E.2d 516, 554 (Mass. 1993); Claremont Sch. Dist. v. Governor, 703 A.2d 1353, 1359 (N.H. 1997); Leandro v. State, 488 S.E.2d 249, 255 (N.C. 1997); Abbeville Cty. Sch. Dist. v. State, 515 S.E.2d 535, 540 (S.C. 1999). Some courts established standards directly fashioned after those in *Rose*, while others looked at their own state's statutory and regulatory academic standards as a point of departure in determining the meaning of a constitutional education. See, e.g., *Evans*, 850 P.2d at 724; Abbott by Abbott v. Burke, 693 A.2d 417, 427 (N.J. 1997); Campaign for Fiscal Equity v. State, 719 N.Y.S.2d 475, 484 (Sup. Ct. 2001).

31. Michael A. Rebell, "Poverty, 'Meaningful' Educational Opportunity, and the Necessary Role of the Courts," *North Carolina Law Review* 85 (2007): 1467, 1483 n.73.

32. See generally Derek W. Black, "Averting Educational Crises," *Washington University Law Review* 94 (2017): 423.

33. See, e.g., Doe v. Superintendent of Schs., 653 N.E.2d 1088 (Mass. 1995) (expulsion); Sheff v. O'Neill, 678 A.2d 1267 (Conn. 1996) (segregation); Vergara v. State, 209 Cal. Rptr. 3d 532 (Cal. Ct. App. 2016) (teacher tenure); see also James E. Ryan, *Schools, Race, and Money*, 109 *Yale Law Journal* 249, 308–10 (1999) (noting that present education funding litigation revolves around the right to an adequate education).

34. Illinois, to its credit, finally made some important changes to its grossly inequitable funding formula in 2017. Sarea Burnett and Sophia Tareen, "Illinois Governor Signs Sweeping School Funding Changes," *AP News*, August 31, 2017.

35. Campaign for Fiscal Equity, Inc. v. State, 100 N.Y.2d 893, 906 (N.Y. 2003).

36. Ibid., 906–07.

37. Ibid., 908.

38. Michael A. Rebell, *Flunking Democracy: Schools, Court, and Civic Participation* (Chicago: University of Chicago Press, 2018), 5–6.

39. Fla. Const. art. IX, § 1 ("paramount duty of the state"); Ga. Const. art. VIII, § 1, para. I ("shall be a primary obligation of the State"); Seattle Sch. Dist. No. 1 v. State, 585 P.2d 71, 91 (Wash. 1978); Rose v. Council for Better Educ., Inc., 790 S.W.2d 186, 205 (Ky. 1989); Leandro v. State, 488 S.E.2d 249, 255 (N.C. 1997); Claremont Sch. Dist. v. Governor, 635 A.2d 1375, 1381 (N.H. 1993) (*Claremont I*) ("The right to an adequate education mandated by the constitution is not based on

the exclusive needs of a particular individual, but rather is a right held by the public to enforce the State's duty.").

40. *Rose*, 790 S.W.2d at 211.

41. *Claremont I*, 635 A.2d at 1376 ("We hold that part II, article 83 imposes a duty on the State to provide a constitutionally adequate education to every educable child."); Lake View Sch. Dist. No. 25 of Phillips Cty. v. Huckabee, 351 Ark. 31, 71 (Ark. 2002) ("We conclude that the clear language of Article 14 imposes upon the State an absolute constitutional duty to educate our children. . . .").

42. *Huckabee*, 351 Ark. at 74 (quoting Robinson v. Cahill, 62 N.J. 473 (1973)).

43. *Rose*, 790 S.W.2d at 213.

44. Abbott by Abbott v. Burke, 119 N.J. 287, 296 (N.J. 1990).

45. Claremont Sch. Dist. v. Governor, 794 A.2d 744, 754 (N.H. 2002).

46. *Abbott*, 119 N.J. at 377.

47. Fla. Const. art. IX, § 1 ("paramount duty of the state").

48. Ga. Const. art. VIII, § 1, para. I ("shall be a primary obligation of the State").

49. Seattle Sch. Dist. No. 1 v. State, 585 P.2d 71, 91 (Wash. 1978) ("a paramount duty to make ample provision for the education of all children residing within the State's borders, the constitution has created a 'duty' that is supreme, preeminent or dominant") (footnote omitted).

50. Nev. Const. art. XI, § 6 (requiring education to be funded before any other programs are funded).

51. "Address to the Nation on the National Education Strategy, April 18, 1991," in *Public Papers of the Presidents of the United States: George Bush, 1991* (Washington, DC: US Government Printing Office, 1992), 396.

52. "Cuomo Ready to Slash Spending," *WBFO Newsroom*, n.d., https://news.wbfo.org/post/cuomo-ready-slash-spending.

53. Kayla Lattimore, "DeVos Says More Money Won't Help Schools; Research Says Otherwise," *NPR Education*, June 9, 2017, www.npr.org/sections/ed/2017/06/09/531908094/devos-says-more-money-wont-help-schools-research-says-otherwise.

54. Maureen Downey, "Betsy DeVos Reignites Debate on Whether Class Size Matters," *Atlanta Journal-Constitution*, April 2, 2019, www.ajc.com/blog/get-schooled/betsy-devos-reignites-debate-whether-class-size-matters/VDHjWAD0HvkusJ666SJNxM.

55. Rebell, "Poverty," 1484–85.

56. Ibid., 1479.

57. Bruce D. Baker, *Does Money Matter in Education?*, 2nd ed. (Washington, DC: Albert Shanker Institute, 2016), i, www.shankerinstitute.org/sites/shanker/files/moneymatters_edition2.pdf.

58. Ibid.

59. Ibid.

60. Ibid., 19.

61. C. Kirabo Jackson et al., "The Effects of School Spending on Educational and Economic Outcomes: Evidence from School Finance Reforms," *Quarterly Journal of Economics* 131 (2016):157.

62. Ibid., 241.

63. Rose v. Council for Better Educ., 790 S.W.2d 186, 213 (Ky. 1989).

64. Abbott by Abbott v. Burke, 119 N.J. 287, 295–96 (N.J. 1990).

65. DeRolph v. Ohio, 677 N.E.2d 733, 746 (Ohio 1997).

66. Sheff v. O'Neill, 678 A.2d 1267 (Conn. 1996).

67. Ibid., 1280 (emphasis added).

68. Ibid., 1281.

69. Phillip Leon M. v. Greenbrier Cty. Bd. of Educ., 199 W. Va. 400, 407 (W. Va. 1996), *holding modified by* Cathe A. v. Doddridge Cty. Bd. of Educ., 200 W. Va. 521(W.Va. 1997).

70. Cong. Globe, 40th Cong., 1st Sess. 168 (Mar. 16, 1867) (statement of Sen. Morton).

71. See, e.g., Ala. Const. of 1868, art. XI, § 10 (proceeds from all new and old state lands "shall be inviolably appropriated to educational purposes. . . ."); ibid., art. XI, § 11 (requiring that one-fifth of general annual state revenues "be devoted exclusively to the maintenance of public schools").

72. Fla. Const. of 1868, art. IX, § 7 (requiring the distribution of funds among counties based on number of children residing in each county between four and twenty-one years old).

73. League of Women Voters v. State, 355 P.3d 1131, 1139–40 (Wash. 2015); Bush v. Holmes, 919 So.2d 392, 408–11 (Fla. 2006). But see Meredith v. Pence, 984 N.E.2d 1213, 1221–25 (Ind. 2013) (upholding vouchers against constitutional attack); Wilson v. State Bd. of Educ., 89 Cal. Rptr. 2d 745, 758–60 (Ct. App. 1999) (finding that California's constitutional requirements regarding public schools did not prevent the creation of charter schools).

74. Cruz-Guzman v. State, 916 N.W.2d 1, 9 (Minn. 2018).

75. Marbury v. Madison, 1 Cranch 137, 177 (1803).

76. Ibid., 163.

77. Rose v. Council for Better Educ., Inc., 790 S.W.2d 186, 209 (Ky. 1989).

78. Ibid.

79. Columbia Falls Elementary Sch. Dist. No. 6 v. State, 109 P.3d 257, 261 (Mont. 2005).

80. Lake View Sch. Dist. No. 25 v. Huckabee, 91 S.W.3d 472, 484 (Ark. 2002).

81. Hussein v. State, 973 N.E.2d 752, 754 (N.Y. 2012).

82. Gannon v. State, 319 P.3d 1196, 1230 (2014).

CHAPTER 10. THROUGH HISTORY'S EYES

1. Joe Sonka, "A Day After Apologizing for Rhetoric, Bevins Calls out 'Thug Mentality' of Teachers Protesting Pension Bill," *Insider Louisville*, March 21, 2018, https://insiderlouisville.com/government/a-day-after-apologizing-for-rhetoric

-bevin-calls-out-thug-mentality-of-teachers-protesting-pension-bill/; Joe Sonka, "Gov. Bevin Rails Against 'Selfish' and 'Uninformed' Teachers Protesting His Stalled Pension Bill," *Insider Louisville*, March 14, 2018, https://insiderlouisville.com /government/gov-bevin-rails-against-selfish-and-uninformed-teachers-protesting -his-stalled-pension-bill.

2. Gabby Morrongiello, "Trump: Dems Trap Students in 'Failing Government Schools,'" *Washington Examiner*, September 8, 2016, www.washingtonexaminer .com/trump-dems-trap-students-in-failing-government-schools.

3. Louis Freedberg, "Trump Frames 'School Choice' Agenda as Civil Rights Initiative," *EdSource*, March 8, 2017, https://edsource.org/2017/trump-frames-school -choice-agenda-as-civil-rights-initiative/578092.

4. Kevin Wheatley, "Gov. Bevin Says Strike by Ky. Teachers Would Be 'Irresponsible' and 'Illegal,'" *WDRB*, April 9, 2018, www.wdrb.com/news/education/gov -bevin-says-strike-by-ky-teachers-would-be-irresponsible/article_102a9960-7f69 -5ebc-ae91-2962899b7c66.html.

5. "NC Governor Vetoes Bill that Could Have Paved Way for Charter Schools," *WSOCTV*, December 22, 2018, www.wsoctv.com/news/local/nc-governor -vetoes-bill-that-could-have-paved-way-for-charter-schools/892863806.

6. Seth Cline, "Unchartered Territory," *US News*, June 4, 2018, www.usnews .com/news/education-news/articles/2018-06-04/how-charlottes-suburbs-could -change-the-charter-school-movement.

7. Rob O'Dell, "Voters Confused by Prop. 305 School Voucher Measure, Republic Poll Shows," *AZCentral*, October 4, 2018, www.azcentral.com/story/news /politics/elections/2018/10/04/arizonans-confused-prop-305-school-voucher-measure -nov-ballot/1500081002.

8. Kara Finnigan et al., *Evaluation of the Public Charter Schools Program: Final Report* (Washington DC: US Department of Education, Policy and Program Studies Service, 2004), www2.ed.gov/rschstat/eval/choice/pcsp-final/finalreport.pdf.

9. CREDO, *Charter School Performance in Ohio* (Washington DC: Thomas B. Fordham Institute, 2014), https://fordhaminstitute.org/ohio/research/charter -school-performance-ohio.

10. Ann Webber et al., *Evaluation of the DC Opportunity Scholarship Program: Impacts Three Years after Students Applied* (Washington DC: US Department of Education, National Center for Education Evaluation and Regional Assistance, Institute of Education Sciences, 2019), https://ies.ed.gov/ncee/pubs /20194006/pdf/20194006.pdf; Jonathan N. Mills and Patrick J. Wolf, "The Effects of the Louisiana Scholarship Program on Student Achievement after Four Years" (EDRE Working Paper 2019-10, University of Arkansas, April 23, 2019), www .uaedreform.org/wp-content/uploads/Mills-Wolf-LSP-Achievement-After-4-Years -final.pdf.

11. Nancy MacClean, *Democracy in Chains: The Deep History of the Radical Right's Stealth Plan for America* (New York: Penguin Random House, 2017).

12. Lynn Parramore, "Meet the Economist behind the One Percent's Stealth Takeover of America," *Institute for New Economic Thinking*, May 30, 2018,

www.ineteconomics.org/perspectives/blog/meet-the-economist-behind-the-one
-percents-stealth-takeover-of-america.

13. James Hohmann, "The Daily 202: Koch Network Laying Groundwork to
Fundamentally Transform America's Education System," *PowerPost*, January 30,
2018, www.washingtonpost.com/news/powerpost/paloma/daily-202/2018/01/30
/daily-202-koch-network-laying-groundwork-to-fundamentally-transform-america
-s-education-system/5a6feb8530fb041c3c7d74db/?utm_term=.50ffebed7fa1.

14. Ibid. (quoting Stacy Hock).

15. Patrick Gibbons, "Florida's New School Voucher Law Will Revive 20-Year-
Old Legal Battle," *EducationNext*, May 9, 2019, www.educationnext.org/floridas
-new-school-voucher-law-will-revive-20-year-old-legal-battle-family-empowerment
-scholarship.

16. News Service of Florida, "DeSantis Pursues New School Voucher Program," *LRN*, February 15, 2019, www.wlrn.org/post/desantis-pursues-new-school
-voucher-program.

17. Jeffrey S. Solochek and Josh Solomon, "Gov. Ron DeSantis Signs Bill
Allowing Private School Vouchers," *Tampa Bay Times*, May 9, 2019, www
.tampabay.com/blogs/gradebook/2019/05/09/ron-desantis-touts-florida-vouchers
-ahead-of-planned-billsigning/?utm_email=4474B4C195A6D4B96434953F39
&utm_source=listrak&utm_medium=email&utm_term=https%3A%2F%2Fwww
.tampabay.com%2Fblogs%2Fgradebook%2F2019%2F05%2F09%2Fron-desantis
-touts-florida-vouchers-ahead-of-planned-bill-signing%2F&utm_campaign=times
-news-at-noon.

18. Orlando Sentinel Editorial Board, "New Voucher Program Isn't about
Choice, It's about Sabotaging Public Schools," *Orlando Sentinel*, May 1, 2019, www
.orlandosentinel.com/opinion/editorials/os-op-florida-vouchers-private-schools-bill
-20190501-story.html.

19. Tanya Clay House et al., *Grading the States: A Report Card on Our Nation's
Commitment to Public Schools* 8 (New York: Network for Public Education; Quincy,
MA: Schott Foundation for Public Education, 2018), http://schottfoundation.org
/report/grading-the-states.

20. Bruce D. Baker et al., *The Real Shame of the Nation: The Causes and Consequences of Interstate Inequity in Public School Investments* (New Brunswick, NJ:
Rutgers University; Philadelphia: Education Law Center, 2018), https://drive.google
.com/file/d/1cm6Jkm6ktUT3SQplzDFjJIy3G3iLWOtJ/view.

21. Raj Chetty et al., "The Economic Impact of Tax Expenditures: Evidence from
Spatial Variation across the U.S.," IRS (2015), www.irs.gov/pub/irs-soi/14rptax
expenditures.pdf; Raj Chetty et al., "Where Is the Land of Opportunity? The Geography of Intergenerational Mobility in the U.S. States," *Quarterly Journal of Economics*
129 no. 4 (2014): 1553, 1591 (map printed in gray scale). Lighter colors = more absolute upward mobility, www.nber.org/papers/w19843.pdf (contains the colored map).

22. "West Virginia Results," *New York Times*, November 8, 2016, www.nytimes
.com/elections/2016/results/west-virginia.

23. "Kentucky Results," *New York Times*, November 8, 2016, www.nytimes .com/elections/2016/results/kentucky.

24. "Oklahoma Results," *New York Times*, November 8, 2016, www.nytimes .com/elections/2016/results/oklahoma.

25. See, e.g., Brittany Shoot, "In 2018, Labor Strikes Had the Largest Increase of the Last Three Decades. Here's Why," *Fortune*, February 14, 2019, https://fortune .com/2019/02/14/strike-teacher-salary-pay-general-strike-union-labor-walkout/. Abigail Abrams, "The Number of U.S. Workers Involved in a Strike in 2018 Was the Highest Since 1986," *Time*, February 8, 2019, https://time.com/5525512 /american-workers-strikes-bureau-labor-statistics.

26. Tim Walker, "Poll: Parents Continue to Stand Beside Educators in Fight for Funding," *National Education Association (NEA) Today*, August 5, 2019, http:// neatoday.org/2019/08/05/2019-pdk-poll-results.

27. PDK Poll, *Frustration in the Schools: Teachers Speak out on Pay, Funding, and Feeling Valued* (Arlington, VA: Phi Delta Kappa Poll, 2019), https://pdkpoll.org /results.

28. Chris Jackson and Mallory Newall, "Most Americans Believe Teachers Have a Big Impact, but Are Paid Unfairly," *Ipsos Public Affairs*, September 12, 2018, www.ipsos.com/en-us/news-polls/Views-on-American-Teachers; Alexia Fernández Campbell, "Most Republicans and Democrats Agree that American Teachers Need a Raise," *Vox*, April 24, 2018, www.vox.com/policy-and-politics/2018/4/24/17274808 /teacher-strikes-public-opinion-poll.

29. Campbell, "Most Republicans and Democrats Agree."

30. "The Education Poll of the South," *Public Opinion Strategies*, October 2017, www.gpee.org/wpcontent/uploads/2018/02/Education_Poll_of_the_South _Fact_Sheet_R2.pdf.

31. Karen DeVivo, ed., *Accelerating the Pace: The Future of Education in the American South* (Atlanta: Standard Press, 2018), ii, https://files.eric.ed.gov/fulltext /ED584846.pdf.

32. H.B. 2017, 54th Leg., 1st Sess. (Ariz. 2018), www.azleg.gov/legtext /54leg/1R/bills/HB2017P.pdf.

33. Holly Yan, "Across the US, More Cities Ditch Columbus Day to Honor Those Who Really Discovered America," CNN, October 8, 2018, www.cnn .com/2018/10/08/us/columbus-day-vs-indigenous-peoples-day/index.html.

34. Yascha Mounk, *The People vs. Democracy: Why Our Freedom Is in Danger & How to Save It* (Cambridge, MA: Harvard University Press, 2018).

CHAPTER 11. FINAL THOUGHTS

1. *Cost Study Analysis: Elementary and Secondary Education in Kansas: Estimating the Costs of K-12 Education Using Two Approaches* (Topeka: Legislative Division of Post Audit, State of Kansas, January 2006), Iihtltp://www.kslegresearch.org/KLRD -web/Publications/Education/Education_Cost_Study/Cost_Study_Report.pdf.

INDEX

DEREK W. BLACK holds the Ernest F. Hollings Chair in Constitutional Law at the University of South Carolina Law School. His areas of expertise include education law and policy, constitutional law, civil rights, and voting. The focus of his current research is the intersection of constitutional law and public education, particularly as it pertains to educational equality and fairness for disadvantaged students. Professor Black has published thirty scholarly law review articles, including in journals such as the *Yale Law Journal, Stanford Law Review, NYU Law Review, California Law Review, Cornell Law Review, Northwestern University Law Review*, and *Vanderbilt Law Review*. His work has been cited and relied upon several times in the federal courts, including the US Supreme Court. He provides regular commentary for national print, radio, and television media and has served as an expert witness in federal and state education cases.

Professor Black is the author of *Ending Zero Tolerance: The Crisis of Absolute School Discipline* and *Education Law: Equality, Fairness and Reform*, a textbook used in numerous law schools.